EDUCATION &
PHILOSOPHY
AN INTRODUCTION

Sara Miller McCune founded SAGE Publishing in 1965 to support the dissemination of usable knowledge and educate a global community. SAGE publishes more than 1000 journals and over 800 new books each year, spanning a wide range of subject areas. Our growing selection of library products includes archives, data, case studies and video. SAGE remains majority owned by our founder and after her lifetime will become owned by a charitable trust that secures the company's continued independence.

Los Angeles | London | New Delhi | Singapore | Washington DC | Melbourne

EDUCATION & PHILOSOPHY

AN INTRODUCTION

ANSGAR ALLEN & ROY GODDARD

Los Angeles | London | New Delhi
Singapore | Washington DC | Melbourne

Los Angeles | London | New Delhi
Singapore | Washington DC | Melbourne

SAGE Publications Ltd
1 Oliver's Yard
55 City Road
London EC1Y 1SP

SAGE Publications Inc.
2455 Teller Road
Thousand Oaks, California 91320

SAGE Publications India Pvt Ltd
B 1/I 1 Mohan Cooperative Industrial Area
Mathura Road
New Delhi 110 044

SAGE Publications Asia-Pacific Pte Ltd
3 Church Street
#10-04 Samsung Hub
Singapore 049483

Editor: James Clark
Assistant editor: Rob Patterson
Production editor: Tom Bedford
Copyeditor: Christine Bitten
Indexer: Cathy Heath
Marketing manager: Dilhara Attygalle
Cover design: Sheila Tong
Typeset by: C&M Digitals (P) Ltd, Chennai, India
Printed by CPI Group (UK) Ltd, Croydon, CR0 4YY

© Ansgar Allen and Roy Goddard 2017

First published 2017

Library of Congress Control Number: 2016956223

British Library Cataloguing in Publication data

A catalogue record for this book is available from
the British Library

ISBN 978-1-4462-7315-9
ISBN 978-1-4462-7316-6 (pbk)

At SAGE we take sustainability seriously. Most of our products are printed in the UK using FSC papers and boards.
When we print overseas we ensure sustainable papers are used as measured by the PREPS grading system.
We undertake an annual audit to monitor our sustainability.

Contents

About the Authors

Ansgar Allen is a Lecturer in Education at the University of Sheffield. He teaches in the areas of educational philosophy, history and theory, and is the author of *Benign Violence: Education In and Beyond the Age of Reason* (Palgrave Macmillan, 2014) and *The Cynical Educator* (Mayfly, 2017).

Roy Goddard worked for most of his career as a teacher in comprehensive schools before joining the education department at Sheffield University, teaching in Initial Teacher Education and then working on courses for teachers in middle management roles and with overseas Masters students. He has published on governmentality and education, the idea of mastery in education and on the relation between recent developments in nihilist thought and education.

Acknowledgments

The authors would like to thank Wilfred Carr who was involved in the shaping of the project at an early stage, and James Clark at SAGE for inviting us to write the book and for everything he has done in seeing it through to publication along with his team – Robert Patterson, Rachael Plant, Monira Begum and Christine Bitten. SAGE and the authors would like to thank the following reviewers for their comments on the original proposal:

Carrie Winstanley, Roehampton University
Darren Garside, Bath Spa University
David Lewin, University of Strathclyde
Heather Brunskell-Evans, University of Leicester

1

Introduction

Why we wrote this book

In this book we explore how philosophical thought has construed the aims and the nature of education, how it has been brought to bear on matters of educational organisation, conduct and practice. In doing this we will consider thought which has directly addressed itself to educational matters, and also philosophical enquiry which has not directly dealt with education, but which, in our view, has significance for thinking and practising in the field of education. We believe that engagement with philosophical thinking can be useful to the practice of education, that it offers understandings which might enhance the professional lives of teachers and researchers at every level of the education system. However, this book is not intended to make its readers 'smarter' – more fluent and supple in managing and moving through the systems they operate within. We will not be offering ways of sprucing up teaching by way of the application of a few philosophical ideas or algorithms. In fact, we would not be unhappy if we made our readers more uncomfortable, more uncertain about their place within the structures of education. We hope to disturb what has been called the common sense of education, to encourage a questioning, even sceptical stance towards existing pieties concerning this vast national and international enterprise. We believe that such doubt and uncertainty are a necessary prelude to becoming more aware – aware of the histories and currents of thought that have shaped and continue to shape the social sphere of education and aware of the limitations that bear down upon practice and the possibilities available for change. It is our conviction that such informed understanding can illuminate and guide the choices about practice and commitments that present themselves to educational professionals. We think this is preferable to – comfortably, obligingly – not thinking too hard about such choices. Our over-riding concern is to persuade that such engagement might illuminate understanding of the policies and practices of education in relation to our present period, the era of mass compulsory schooling. However, to do this we consider the long history of educational thought and practice that has, for good or ill, shaped our current understandings of what education is for and how it should be organised.

We argue that philosophy, or the activity of reflective, deliberative thought, has mirrored and at times influenced the ways in which human beings have understood and sought to order their existence and that it continues to do so. We can come to a fuller understanding of the world we live in and the place we occupy within it, if we become aware of how it has been investigated and configured by philosophy. Whether we think of the practice of education as what it might once have been, a process of moral and intellectual cultivation conducted in a relationship between a master and a pupil, or as the latter day project of mass schooling aimed at shaping the kinds of individuals required by a modern society, it has, more than most spheres of social existence, been caught up in, buffeted and contoured by the currents and eddies of competing schools of thought. As a result, education, as idea and practice, has become – perhaps always was – a field of contestation and no little confusion. In this book we will attempt to bring some clarity to the varied purposes education has come to serve in modernity by examining how thinking about education, under pressure from social change and the elevation of the idea of the economy to the chief concern of government, has developed since the collapse of the medieval order.

Why philosophy?

Why, though, bother about philosophy and its relation to education? No one else does, except, of course, philosophers of education. The machinery of education trundles on without a moment's thought being given to philosophy. The great majority of teachers in schools associate philosophising about education – along with all that other peripheral noise that surrounds teaching and learning in schools, the abstract theory and scholarship churned out by academia – as remote, obscure and irrelevant. In this view philosophy is laughably, pathetically, removed from the actualities of the school and of no usefulness to educators in their professional lives. In the university department of education, philosophy exists as a marginal presence, accommodated more for the cultural prestige it still just about retains and confers; it would perhaps seem a little philistine to jettison this last link with an old idea of education as having a civilising mission, with having something to do with moral enquiry. Students, or as government would have it, trainees, on the rapidly disappearing university teacher training courses or those in-school trainings which are becoming the main provider of initial teacher education, need have no contact with philosophical thinking, and little at all in the way of a theoretical perspective on their labours. You can, it appears, lead a life in education without having to bother about philosophy and what it might say about education. Education, as a system for equipping the population with the knowledges, the skills and the inclinations required for them to prosper and to contribute to the social good, carries on and will continue to do so without its workforce ever having to be troubled by a philosophical proposition or question. So, again, why bother?

Our answer to this question is one that rests squarely on personal experience. One of us, a comparatively new arrival in academia, has been struck by just how susceptible it is to the economic and political forces which are redefining the entire landscape of intellectual enquiry, turning academics into witting and unwitting accomplices of a system they may at times deplore, but nonetheless uphold. In this context, an engagement with philosophy has given him the opportunity to make some sense of the environment in which he works and consider ways of living differently within it. The other of us worked for many years in secondary education as a classroom teacher. During that time he would have found it impossible to continue in his role without constantly asking himself and discussing with others questions that seemed to bear vitally on what he was doing – questions such as these:

- What is education for?
- What values should it, or I, serve?
- What is the relationship between the teacher's idea of how they should operate in the classroom and official recommendations and requirements?
- What, if any, relation does schooling have to educational change?
- How can education's claim to develop critical thinking and to make people free be squared with its role in forming a responsible, morally observant citizenry?
- What should a teacher think (or do) about participating in systems of assessment and public examination that help structure inequality in society?

Many, perhaps most, teachers think in one way or another about questions of this sort at times in their careers. We argue here that such thinking can be extended and rendered more constructive in terms of the teacher's work through contact with – which is to say, reading and critically responding to – philosophical thought. We believe that the same applies for students of education who seek not only to pass their exams and improve their career chances, but also to reflect carefully on the systems within which they are constrained to work and study. For both of us, reading philosophy has helped us get through the fraught experience of working in education in a period of rapid and disconcerting change. By 'getting through' we mean that our engagement with philosophy and theory has helped us explore how educational relations might be better negotiated.

It is widely accepted by observers of every political stripe that education is in crisis. The central question, as we see it, is whether education, as something that exists somewhere within the system of mass schooling, can be returned to – or newly grounded upon – principles that serve the ends of a democratic society. If we are to seriously ask this question, we must remain open to the possibility that education could be, essentially and inescapably, in the core of its being, a system that serves and seeks to perfect governmental control, a system that owes nothing to dreams of enlightenment and social justice and everything to the goals of the bureaucratic management of populations.

Disclaimers

This book is not about to offer a stout and vigorous defence of the philosophy of education or, indeed, of the ways in which philosophy has in the past interacted with systems of teaching and learning. For a start, its writers are – happily – not qualified to stage such a defence. Neither of us is what might be called a trained philosopher, in that neither of us pursued qualifications as philosophers at university. One of us has a higher education background in the sciences, the other in literature and cultural studies. We write as teachers and researchers who have come to see philosophical or theoretical thought as indispensable to our understanding of what we do as educators. It will be apparent that we do not come to bury philosophy, although we will be critical of many of the ways in which it has presented itself to (and in) education. We see these backgrounds as providing us with what is referred to as, in an idiom that will not feature prominently in the book, a unique selling point. We have never been inducted into the community of philosophers that occupies academia, and have not as a result acquired the kind of professional identity, or – less charitably – defensiveness, that feels obliged to persuade the unenlightened of the uniquely informative perspectives and insights afforded by the discipline. We are outsiders, two teachers who, as we have already said, have been attracted to philosophical thought because this has helped us understand more clearly our roles as educational practitioners and the possibilities available within those roles.

We are conscious that what we propose – educators finding time to reflect philosophically on their practice, and students of education engaging with philosophical ideas that extend far beyond their core curricula – may readily be seen as an unlikely prospect in the pressured, highly regulated context of present-day schooling and university life. What we propose is also at odds with the conditions of an Anglo-Saxon intellectual culture that has always prized practice and pragmatism above what it sees as 'mere theory'. Ours is an intellectual culture that has for a long time been – there is no way of putting this politely – anti-intellectual.

We do not wish to suggest that without reading Plato and Nietzsche educational practitioners must inevitably become the dupes of a malign system. Clearly, educators, at every level or stage of education, are capable of thinking and speaking for themselves and will conduct their professional lives in accordance with values and understandings that they have developed during their time in education. We do, however, argue that the teacher, the researcher and the student will gain a fuller understanding of those roles and thus a surer command of the technical and moral practices that shape and constrain their activities, if they undertake the informed reflection we advocate. Of course, this is to make a big claim for a certain kind of thinking, and yet, we suggest, without such thinking educators and educated alike are more vulnerable to manipulation and recruitment to purposes and practices that they would not wish to support.

It will be clear that what we offer here is not a dispassionate account of the different schools of thought and social ideologies that have fed into the practice of education. We have sought to provide accurate accounts of philosophical (and non-philosophical) ideas that have, at various times, been recruited to consider the purposes and the practice of education, but as will become evident we present a particular view – our view – of their value.

Politics

It will probably already be clear that thinking philosophically is, for us, an urgently political activity, in that it requires us to address questions about the moral dimension and the social consequences of educational practice. Whether they actively choose to do so or not, those working and studying in education place themselves on a spectrum that indicates how they see themselves within the power relations that structure the domain. They may occupy positions in relation to authority that range from compliance, through degrees of adaptation, evasion, resistance and criticality, to more or less open revolt.

Compliant educators work at labours set for them by those in authority. They may adopt this stance because they see no reason to question, at a fundamental level, the ways in which power structures education or because they see no alternatives to compliance which would not be career-threatening. Educational compliance involves resigning oneself to authority's definitions of one's role and how it should be carried out, in accordance with whatever designs, objectives and justifications such authority might have determined. Such educational careers are possible and not, perhaps, unusual. They can, indeed, be carried out with dedicated industry and imagination. But another position is available towards the other end of the spectrum. The teacher or student may decide that she cannot in all conscience accept without much questioning the directions of authority, that she needs to understand and justify to herself what her role and practice might be, that she needs to explore the history of the institution in which she works and the moral resources that its traditions make available to her, and that if she is to have any sense of control and ease of mind about the practice of her craft, she needs to access the body of thought that has grown around the social domain she has entered. She will, typically, be concerned about the relationship between her professional ethic as a teacher, an ethic which will have been shaped and guided by the professional formation she has undergone at graduate and postgraduate levels and in her years as a practitioner, and the demands of those authorities who seek to order and control, to orientate and set limits to the ways in which she can work, within her workplace and beyond.

The latter individual – as teacher, as researcher, as student – may, of course, end up in a state of discontent, frustrated at the limitations imposed on what she now sees as the proper practice of education. She may well find herself coming into conflict with more senior figures within the educational hierarchy and with its wider bureaucratic machinery. This conflict may be conducted in a polite and civilised manner; it may not. However, at the very least her recognition of the difference between her actual role and the role she might fulfil – ought to fulfil, according to her best judgement – opens her to a more comprehensive awareness of the nature of the position she occupies, and therefore to a more faithful exercise of her educational practice. This is to say she may teach and study in a way that serves the educational values she has identified rather than working according to imported priorities which are intended to serve, let us say, bureaucratic or economic ends.

Impure thoughts

Thus, a life lived in education is essentially a life in which it is impossible to escape political engagement. To borrow (and slightly amend) something that Michel Foucault wrote, an educational politics may be seen as the art of not being governed so much or, we would add, not submitting to government in ways that contradict one's professional ethic. Education is political in that it is intimately involved with the values and interests that government serves and the social ends it pursues. Indeed, as we will see in Chapter 11, mass or popular education has been characterised as in itself a form of government, an enterprise that seeks to influence the conduct of the individuals who are subject to it in order to produce the productive and morally responsible citizenry required by a complex modern society. For now, for the purposes of this introduction, we would simply wish to register the fact that education is a social domain which has historical, political and cultural dimensions, that it is, in the real world, an essentially impure, untidy, often improvised undertaking which, if we are able to gain any grasp of its nature and meanings, will require more than a purely philosophical analysis. It is also a domain, or field of enquiry and practice, which is subject to incessant and diverse social and political pressures. Education is a site of struggle between competing interests and ideologies, an unstable and always changing construct. It is clear, therefore, that any consideration of the systems and practices of education has to draw upon perspectives, upon configurations of the field that must strain and transgress the tightly drawn boundaries of any one discipline, including those of philosophy. Therefore, although our focus will be on thinkers who would pass inspection by the gate-keepers of professional philosophy, we will also touch upon the ideas of academics and non-academics whose conceptualisations of the education realm fall outside the canons of philosophy.

Outline of the book

In Chapter 2 we begin our critical survey of philosophy and education by investigating definitions of Western philosophy through the contrasting approaches of modern academic philosophy and ancient Greek practical philosophy. Each philosophical tradition entails its own conception of and relationship to education. Such an investigation into the joint histories of education and philosophy provides opportunities for thinking differently about how education and philosophy might be related. In Chapter 3 we investigate two distinct and ancient conceptions of education (as paideia and as praxis) that have been resurrected in modernity as offering potential 'solutions' to current educational problems. As we do so, we argue against a straightforward adoption of past educational traditions, noting that any adoption, or attempted resurrection, is always a deformation of what it seeks to reproduce. In Chapter 4 we explore what happened in the western European tradition after the decline of the philosophical schools of antiquity and the rise of medieval Christian thought. We investigate how Christian institutions revised and extended the educational project of ancient philosophy, while also seeking to contain or render more palatable to Christian thinking the more disruptive aspects of the Graeco-Roman inheritance. Chapter 5 deals with the extraordinary cultural efflorescence that gathered speed during the period of the High Middle Ages and achieved full expression during the Renaissance. The keynote, perhaps, of this period was the sense of man (and these philosophies were addressed to men) as an individual who could, to an extent, govern his own destiny, a growing sense of man's moral and intellectual capacities and a tentative sense of his abilities to order his world. This nascent individualism strengthened and deepened the humanism that was at work in the medieval period and laid the foundations of what was to become modern liberal humanism. In this chapter we examine some of the contradictions surrounding the idea of humanism and what it bequeathed to modernity.

In Chapters 6 and 7 we consider some of the developments in thought which built on the Renaissance's preoccupation with the human self. We enter here the period that is referred to as the Age of Enlightenment, with science and philosophy buoyed not only by a confidence in man's capacities to understand how the world, the universe, was ordered, but also by a belief in the possibility that humanity could act upon and bring Nature into conformity with human purpose. Chapter 6 examines the ideas of René Descartes who is often seen as the thinker who first gave full expression to the idea that man could fully comprehend the universe in which he found himself, and the philosophy of John Locke who took a decidedly more cautious view of the extent of man's powers, but had faith, nevertheless, that he was capable of acting in and upon the world for the betterment of humankind. Chapter 7 contrasts the philosophies of David Hume and Immanuel Kant. Hume, like Locke, cast doubt on the idea that human reason was up to the job of forming a true and accurate picture of the cosmos. He did this with such thoroughness that Kant disclosed that he was for many years unable to respond to Hume's sceptical arguments until he had thoroughly thought them through. What resulted from this period of reflection was a body of philosophy that has been described as an accommodation between British empiricism and Continental rationalism, a system of thought that might be seen as setting the agenda for all subsequent philosophy. These chapters bring into relief ideas about the powers of human reason and the nature of knowledge that have profound implications for the practice of education. If the Enlightenment ushered us into modernity and the world that we recognise today, with all its technological, scientific and social achievements and benefits, it also presented subsequent philosophy with a range of problems that are debated to this day. Moreover, many thinkers have argued that modernity's scientific innovations, the technological transformations it has introduced and its destruction of, and failure to replace, the overarching moral order that existed in the Middle Ages, have produced ills and dangers that threaten humanity and its world.

Chapter 8 examines some of the critiques that have been mounted against the ambiguous inheritance of modernity. Chapter 9 focuses on the educational effects of a uniquely modern humanism, which replaces 'God' with the figure of 'man' as the source of meaning and purpose. This attempted substitution was always to be a difficult task, and education has ever since been marked by the uncertainty it generated. In the period of modernity, just as the point and purpose and the very ordering of society were called into question, so the purposes of education became uncertain. Kant effectively equated enlightenment with critique and Chapter 10 considers the origins and varied forms and purposes of what is sometimes seen as a distinctively Western mode of thought. It also engages with what are described as critiques of critique, of which there are, perhaps surprisingly, many. It goes on to introduce some of the educational pedagogies that have been developed under the banner of critique before considering what a critique might look like that was fit for the challenges of the present period.

In Chapter 11 we consider the idea of education as a process of moral formation, taking in the elite practices of a nineteenth-century liberal education and the influential German tradition of Bildung, both of which may be seen as geared towards developing the government of the self in line with high cultural values. It is suggested that they are also preparations for the government of others. The chapter concludes with an account of the exercise in moral management that took place with the introduction in the later nineteenth century of compulsory mass (or popular) education, when techniques derived from the Christian pastoral tradition and the burgeoning human sciences were deployed for the 'gentling' of the children of the urban poor. These techniques, it is argued, are in play in today's schools, although their origins in a programme of manipulative moral transformation go largely unrecognised and unacknowledged.

Chapter 12 reflects on the fate of two distinctively twentieth-century educational phenomena – progressive education and the modern research university. It explores the influence of the ideas of the American philosopher John Dewey on education as a preparation for life in a democracy. The chapter notes the commonalities existing between Deweyan progressivism and the education provided in the nineteenth-century moral school. It concludes with an account of the rise and gradual demise of the modern research university and its supersession by the entrepreneurial university.

The book's Epilogue begins with a critical account of the political philosopher Michael Oakeshott's defence of the idea of the university. It goes on to read the diminishing significance and educational role of the always somewhat quixotic figure of the professor of education as an apt measure of the erosion of educational values that besets the university. We conclude the book by returning to the predicament faced by the professional educator who seeks to engage critically with her practice, and we reflect on a version of professionalism that would place what the French philosopher Michel Foucault called practical insubordination at the core of educational conduct. The researcher, the teacher, and the student too, would here commit to a troubling of education, to a relationship of habitual, measured and reasoned confrontation with the authorities which aim to direct the conduct of the educator. Such a practical engagement would reveal the limits within which we operate and prompt exploration of opportunities for going beyond them.

2

Philosophical Schools

Marginal philosophy

As we have suggested, the philosophy of education does not loom large in the thinking of those who practise education or those who make decisions about the structuring of education systems. A distinguished philosopher of education of our acquaintance put the matter in the following way. Teachers in schools and colleges think that the philosophy of education is ivory-tower theorising that is disconnected from classroom realities; policy-makers think that it is too abstract and that it is incapable of producing constructive, practical solutions to educational problems; 'real' philosophers regard the philosophy of education with contempt as a career niche for those whose philosophical formation has not equipped them to contribute to 'real' philosophy; and philosophers of education cannot manage agreement as to the concerns, objectives and methods proper to their field of enquiry. As a result, the philosophy of education is effectively ignored at every level of the education system.

This book will not be entering into a defence or an attack upon the philosophy of education. It is useful, nevertheless, to explore the formation of this academic field in order to understand its traditional limitations and appreciate the benefits of broadening our scope of enquiry. In this chapter we briefly review the history of this subfield of philosophy and its various political commitments, before offering a critical introduction to academic philosophy in general. We then broaden our definition of Western philosophy by considering it in its aboriginal, ancient Greek forms. It becomes apparent that ancient philosophy barely resembles its modern self. Ancient philosophies were not studied in the abstract; they were adopted as a way of life. Each philosophy had its own associated moral and social comportment, which entailed a transformation in the philosopher's being.

The philosophy of education

When the philosophy of education was established in the 1960s as a distinct area of enquiry, it went energetically about the business of setting up all the appurtenances and distinguishing features of any academic field – such as university positions, accredited courses and modules, annual conferences, academic societies, research journals and canonical texts. Great efforts were made to carefully outline and limit its scope. It was felt that in order to establish the philosophy of education as a legitimate area of study, it would have to be clearly defined and defended as a form of enquiry distinct from other practices of research, such as those applying the methods of historical study, psychology and sociology to educational matters. The philosophy of education, like any other field, was built on systems of exclusion that determined what authentic educational–philosophical statements would look like, and consequently, what would count as educational philosophy. In producing this book, we are acutely aware of this history and its constraints. We want to make it clear that although we provide an introduction to aspects of the field (with its canonical texts and established ideas), our aim is to open philosophical and educational questions to an examination that will extend beyond the horizons of those seeking, first and foremost, to establish and defend a field of study.

In the 1960s, Richard Peters and Paul Hirst produced a series of texts that became foundational to the philosophy of education.[1] Both belonged to the tradition of 'analytic philosophy', which came to academic dominance in English-speaking countries during the twentieth century. The originators of analytic philosophy thought that philosophy should adopt the methods of mathematics and the natural sciences and thus bring a new rigour and clarity to the discipline. The current heirs of this tradition have, on the whole, rejected such scientific pretensions, but retain a respect for the methods of logical enquiry and a cautious narrowness of investigative focus, a concern for precision which often involves a commitment to the use of straightforward, 'plain' English. Philosophy of this kind aimed to break apart problems into more digestible units and address only those questions it believed it had the power to answer. All other versions of philosophy were excluded as insufficiently rigorous, and hence, insufficiently philosophical. The so-called big questions of philosophy – those that could never be broken down and tested – were ignored. (We will see that there have been exceptions to the analytical consensus concerning the practice of philosophy – essentially, philosophers within that tradition who have thought historically.)

It was under this influence that the philosophy of education was reduced from the outset to a '"second order" activity restricted to exposing and eradicating the incoherences and confusions inherent in the language through which our knowledge and understanding are embedded'.[2] The philosopher's role as the likes of Peters and Hirst understood it was to tidy up what were viewed rather condescendingly as the conceptual confusions of those working in education. As a conceptual clearing house, the philosophy of education fostered the illusion that it was separate from, perhaps above, all political and moral disagreement. It offered itself as a neutral arbiter, ensuring that any debate concerning educational matters was able to proceed with rationally agreed, value-free definitions of educational concepts. But as Wilfred Carr, an educational philosopher and critic of the field argued,

> this should not be allowed to obscure how, by the mid-1970s, the works of Peters and Hirst had somehow managed to provide the philosophical basis for a value-laden, 'first-order' account of the purpose and content of education of precisely the kind that the methodological principles of analytical philosophy explicitly proscribed.[3]

The form of education favoured here was precisely that type of education which most closely suited, in their view, the society in which they found themselves.

Though the academic field of education has since become more inclusive and diverse, its practitioners remain concerned that the philosophy of education is losing ground to other forms of intellectual enquiry. The philosophy of education no longer enjoys the status it once did. In schools and university education departments it is no longer widely presumed that the study of education necessarily begins with the study of its philosophy. Facing the possibility of its own near extinction, the philosophy of education currently enjoys a curious, if precarious, twilight life which thrives in journals and conferences but which has little or no vital connection to educational policy-making or practice.

Modern academic philosophy

It will become apparent that philosophy is, and always has been, overwhelmingly dominated by men. This does not mean it can be ignored or simply invalidated as a patriarchal discourse. Rather, that that discourse remains an enduring problem for philosophy. We should not underestimate just how uncomfortable and fraught with difficulty a woman's engagement with philosophy might be, given that philosophy has been riven with gendered assumptions for more than two and a half millennia.[4] Throughout this book, we make no effort to disguise the exclusivity of philosophy, and its overwhelming concern with that gendered epithet 'man', so common in philosophical discourse until relatively recently. Indeed, it is important to remain aware of that exclusivity, and its continued effects.

In the West philosophy is now a specialist subject, largely confined to the university. In its current form it has been separated from most practical day-to-day activities and is carried out by a select few. Unlike the philosophy of education, academic philosophy continues to enjoy high status, although its survival, depending as it does on intellectual prestige and distinction rather than any measurable effectivity, cannot be entirely secure. While its academic practitioners generally support and uphold its elite status, presumably in the belief that its position of detachment above the fray is what enables its uniquely privileged perspective, a few so-called 'popular philosophers' do exist, seeking to draw in the lay reader with the promise that philosophy can be relevant to, indeed can improve, the quality of everyday life. Almost invariably they operate within the boundaries of a philosophy that accepts the current ordering of our world as, more or less, a given – an ordering whose workings need the monitoring, the reprimands and the enhancements that philosophy can offer, but an ordering that does not need, and indeed should not be subject to, fundamental questioning. Here philosophy is presented as a means of reasoning about life more sensibly and thus improving its quality, at both personal and social levels.

While philosophical activity has the potential to confront and upset common-place assumptions, it largely avoids this task. In its contemporary rather sedate form, philosophy has become a cultural emblem, signifying the intellectual and moral seriousness of a society rather than performing any active role as a source of uncomfortable questions about the priorities and the values that shape life as we live it. The marginalisation of philosophy in this form has resulted from changes in the field of knowledge as a whole, a reconfiguration that has had consequences for intellectual enquiry in general. The modern sub-division of knowledge into specialist areas – each discipline adopting its own limited subject matter, methods of enquiry and discursive conventions – separated these specialist areas from the broader philosophical discussions in which they were once based. Pre-modern definitions of philosophy were far more inclusive, encompassing questions that ranged from what we would now describe as scientific, to psychological and sociological concerns.

In his critique of academic specialisation, the philosopher Alasdair MacIntyre explains why this could be dangerous. He takes the example of moral philosophy. Following academic specialisation, MacIntyre argues, 'psychological evaluations of personality traits and studies of political order' are separated from moral philosophy. The consequence of separation is that psychology and politics are now investigated as distinct disciplines 'in a way that presupposes that these are not essentially moral enterprises'.[5] His overall argument is this: when the scope of moral philosophy was diminished, the scope of moral questioning was also reduced.

The same argument applies to educational questions, which have been similarly reduced in scope. In its pre-modern context, education was not isolated from other social, political or theological concerns; such concerns were articulated within a common discourse. Educational questions were at the same time questions about the nature of existence and the nature of belief. As a vital aspect of intellectual activity, education brought into play questions about the ordering of society and the cosmos, debate about the universe given to humanity by God. Along with scientific, judicial and medical reasoning, it was located and had to account for its conclusions within a clearly recognised moral and theological order. In this context, the study and practice of education was a philosophical activity in the most extensive sense.

Philosophies and their contexts

When studying any particular philosophy, it helps to understand the context within which that philosophy was developed. It is mistaken to treat past philosophers and their doctrines as if they were contemporaries, and ask, for example, what Plato or Rousseau would have to say about this or that twenty-first century development in education. Such an approach would merely insert ideas formed in the social, political and cultural particularities of one historical moment into a very different present, into a society ordered to radically changed priorities.

Examining past philosophies from the perspective of our present also has the effect of limiting what can be included as genuine philosophy. There is a tendency, in other words, to accept only those ideas and arguments that are judged 'philosophical' by current standards as to what constitutes philosophy. Even the works of individuals identified in retrospect as the great philosophers of the past are sometimes divided like this, into those sections of their work that are taken to be worth reading as philosophy, and those parts that are viewed as too spiritual, poetic, speculative or insufficiently rigorous according to contemporary standards. This kind of approach, which defends philosophy against pseudo-philosophy, imposes arbitrary divisions on past work and cherry-picks it for ideas that fit with contemporary notions. Considerable violence is thus done to the complex intellectual and social integrity of the original work.

As Richard Rorty argues, philosophers have not been labouring over the same questions in the same terms throughout the ages.[6] There are no essential questions, and there are no essential ways of going about answering those questions that are essentially philosophical. Those who pretend that these timeless questions exist are claiming for themselves the dubious right to rule over our intellectual histories. Those who tell a history of philosophy must, then, be open about the fact that theirs is a partial account. Martin Heidegger makes a similar point, arguing that every historical investigation 'usurps a currently dominant mode of thought and makes it the guiding principle according to which the past is examined and rediscovered'.[7] Histories are always, consciously or otherwise, designed according to the needs and confines of the present. An account of the history of philosophy will unavoidably construct a 'dramatic narrative', as Rorty put it, tied to the drama of our times.[8]

Attention given to the history of philosophy is nevertheless important in that it provides accounts of very different conceptions of the world. These radically different conceptions cannot be accommodated easily to modern perspectives, but they do offer a glimpse into other ways of framing the world, reminding us of the constructedness, the provisionality of what we take to be the inescapable, natural, way of viewing and understanding our own. Another way of putting this is to say that history is essential to the study of philosophy because of the human tendency, so useful to the powerful, to forget. One might say that forgetting allows what are in fact arbitrary orderings of thought to assume the appearance of universal and unquestionable truths. These become the organising principles 'for a wide range of the practices in which we think and act and deal with the world'.[9] To engage with philosophy historically is to take aim at the common-places, conventional wisdoms and unquestioned background assumptions that organise our present. Confrontations such as these, driven by alternative conceptions of education, will not release us instantly from our current ingrained ways of thinking. We will remain attached to the many conventions of contemporary thought that continue to define how we think about education. An awareness of the provisionality of the present, and a history of alternative modes of thought, is insufficient on its own to release us from our conceptual confinement. If we want to see that our way of understanding things is just one option among others, it is necessary also to retrieve and understand the history of the conventions that currently constrain us.

Ancient philosophies and philosophical schools

In confronting the contingent, historically specific and limiting nature of present day education and philosophy, the meaning of philosophy itself must be brought into question. Here we concur with the French philosopher and historian Pierre Hadot, who argues that if we are to understand past philosophies, it is necessary to 'eliminate the preconceptions the word *philosophy* may evoke in the modern mind'.[10]

In the Western tradition of philosophy it is conventional to locate the origins of philosophy in ancient Greece. Like all so-called origins, this beginning is an arbitrary one. It does, though, reflect the profound influence of Greek culture on surrounding regions and subsequent history. Like other influential ways of thinking about the world, the success of Greek thought is not solely to be attributed to its intellectual potency. It was spread on the back of a very different kind of power, by way of the conquests of Alexander the Great, Aristotle's pupil. Alexander's exploits seeded Greek thought in Asia and were important to its survival and subsequent passing back to the West via Islam, but it was precisely its originality and power that appealed to Rome – that is, it survived on its own merits even after military defeat. Through imperial conquests ranging as far afield as India, a vast though short-lived empire was established, throughout which the influence of Greek culture extended. The subsequent Hellenistic period, from the fourth to the first century BCE, established the enduring and widespread influence of Greek philosophy in the Western and Middle Eastern world. Remarkable in its capacity to absorb the most diverse mythical and conceptual themes, classical Greek culture became the intellectual foundation stone of Western civilisation. All cultures of the Mediterranean world as it existed then would eventually express themselves through it. This process of amalgamation did distort the content of all the traditions involved, including the content of Greek culture itself.

But in doing so it established remarkable cultural continuities that still permeate and to a significant extent structure thought and life in the West today.

This unifying process ensured continuity at the heart of philosophical and literary traditions, where various philosophical schools managed to endure throughout the Hellenistic period. These ranged from Plato's Academy and Aristotle's Lyceum, which were run along institutional lines, to the movements and spiritual traditions of Scepticism and Cynicism that adopted more informal arrangements. In the centuries that followed, these schools gradually collapsed and amalgamated. Platonism had the strongest legacy at first, giving rise to Neoplatonism. Loosely deriving from its originating thinker, Neoplatonism strongly influenced philosophical and theological systems, maintaining a division between tangible things which are considered imperfect, and an ideal realm of intangible abstract entities. These intangible entities are considered only available to the philosopher, and include the idea of an overarching, abstract Good. This unifying phenomenon would dominate thought throughout the medieval period, with a Christian God becoming associated with this notion of an abstract Good (see Chapter 4).

While philosophy undoubtedly prospered during the Hellenistic period, having widespread influence, we should not be deceived into overestimating the role of the philosopher in this context. Though a philosophical tradition of sorts appears to have been established across kingdoms and empires, achieving a degree of permanence and influencing thought, culture and politics to the present day, the activities of everyday philosophers were often carried out in isolation from the communities in which they lived. In this period, to think philosophically was to adopt the conventions of an applied mode of reflection. Each philosophy referred to a way of life that was embedded in a particular discourse and set of practices. In some cases, these practices were sustained and passed on by a philosophical school, within which the way of life associated with a philosophy could be taught and learned. Here, to be a philosopher was to live the particular way of life developed and cultivated within that school of philosophical thought. As Hadot argues, this often 'implied a rupture' with one's surroundings, a 'rupture between the philosopher and the conduct of everyday life'. This break with daily life was 'strongly felt by non-philosophers' and 'in the works of comic and satiric authors, philosophers were portrayed as bizarre, if not dangerous characters'.[11]

The deliberate isolation of the philosopher did not necessarily signify the philosopher's personal or moral rejection of the world. It was not the result of a social critique through which the philosopher hoped to demonstrate by experiment and through example that another form of social life was possible. Characteristically, the philosopher's isolation was based on the philosopher's love of wisdom, a love that was combined with the conviction that wisdom is not a thing of this world. It was the love of wisdom that made the philosopher a stranger in society.

Each philosophical school preached its own form of life that would presumably allow its members to reach the elevated state of having achieved access to wisdom. To achieve wisdom, in other words, the philosopher or sage would learn to live in the world differently and relate to it differently in order to see it differently. From the philosopher's perspective, daily life as lived by those in the surrounding community must necessarily appear abnormal. This resulted in a perpetual conflict between the philosopher's view of the world, and the conventional, or common-sense, view of those who did not share the philosopher's vision. Strategies varied, ranging from those adopted by philosophers who refused the world of social convention seeking a total break from society, to those who tried to live within social convention, but in a more 'philosophical' manner. As we outline below, these strategies involved various practical exercises in self-control and contemplation. Ancient philosophy was not pursued then, as an abstracted, intellectual exercise. Both the theoretical and practical dimensions of ancient philosophy were closely interrelated. The pursuit of wisdom entailed something more profound and far reaching than the production of knowledge (where the latter is a distinctly modern preoccupation). The pursuit of wisdom took the form of a series of practical, personal adjustments in how the philosopher would relate to the world.

The Hellenistic schools

The way of life practised by each Hellenistic school, along with its accompanying conception of philosophy, varied widely. Of the four schools founded in Athens, by far the most influential, as we have indicated above, was Plato's Academy. As an institution it lasted several hundred years, and as a philosophy it continues to influence us even now. Hence Whitehead's famous description of the European philosophical tradition as 'a series of footnotes to Plato'.[12]

The Academy was originally conceived as an intellectual and spiritual community in which its members would learn to reorient themselves towards what is 'good'. This would involve the transformation of all involved. While members of Plato's Academy were intended to play a role in political affairs, it was believed that they must first learn to govern themselves in ideal conditions (that is, in isolation from the city state, the political unit of ancient Greek society), before taking on political responsibilities. Disciples were trained in part through a debating technique known as dialectics, where one interlocutor would defend a thesis such as "Can virtue be taught?" from attack by an interrogator. This was not simply a form of intellectual combat. It was a regulated activity, requiring that the interlocutors both agreed upon and submitted themselves to rules of conduct and argument. The point of dialogue was not to achieve a definitive conclusion, but to teach the interlocutors to live philosophically, establishing connections between their own thoughts and external conduct.

By contrast, members of the Lyceum associated with Aristotle were engaged in a more theoretical mode of enquiry. This was not geared towards the preparation of citizens expected to play an active role in political affairs, but was devoted to a form of life that was intended to liberate the mind from all worldly distraction.

Available to a select few, the philosophical life could be realised 'only in leisure and in detachment from material worries'.[13] Even under these conditions, pure contemplation was expected to be a rare achievement. Hence most of the philosopher's activity was geared towards attaining it, subordinating everything to the pursuit of knowledge and its contemplation. Again, this was an activity involving dialogue, where the discussion of problems was more important than any solution that might be arrived at, since the process of enquiry itself developed those habits that were deemed essential to the formation of the philosopher.

The Stoic and Epicurean schools were more dogmatic, in that they were based around a number of fixed doctrines and sayings that members were expected to learn, meditate upon and defend. Again, these traditions were intended to produce an effect on the philosopher which brought each disciple into alignment with the way of life practised by members of that school. Epicureanism claimed to be able to deliver its members from suffering so that they might be able to experience pleasure. Genuine pleasure was considered difficult to come by since we are distracted from it in life by a range of false pleasures that are, by definition, incapable of ever satisfying the desire for pleasurable experience. Epicurean pleasure was hence defined as the absence of hunger, thirst and cold, and as such, is a condition we must learn to appreciate under the guidance of Epicurean philosophy. It can only be enjoyed once we have limited our appetites, 'suppressing desires which are neither natural nor necessary, and limiting as much as possible those which are natural but not necessary' since the latter 'may result in violent and excessive passions'.[14] Unsurprisingly, the Epicurean school reserved the right to define which desires are acceptable, and which are to be avoided.

Stoicism operated rather differently, working not towards the pursuit of pleasure, but towards one's alignment with what is 'good'. Viewing the universe as largely indifferent to the plight of human beings, Stoics sought to develop a practical attitude that allowed the philosopher to happily consent to things beyond one's control, to all the accidents and setbacks that life throws up. It sought instead to focus on the one thing considered within one's control, which was the purity and consistency of one's intentions. This philosophical school taught a form of self-inspection designed to align everything one did or thought with this moral mission.

The philosophical schools of Scepticism and Cynicism had no formal organisation or philosophical dogmas, but were defined by their attitudes to life. The Sceptics argued that all human judgements are in error one way or another, and that we must suspend judgement in order to achieve peace of mind. They used philosophy as a way of purging themselves of all systems of judgement, including those associated with philosophy. Presumably, this would enable Sceptics to live a simple, calm and composed existence, since they would be unable to judge any single event in one's life to be better than any other. This was a philosophical way of life that enabled Sceptics to face all events, both happy ones and sad ones, with equanimity.

The Cynics were equally radical in their aspiration to reject what they considered doubtful. Theirs was a more rebellious (and to the modern mind, entertaining) existence however, since they focused instead on the arbitrary nature of all social constraints and conventions. Cynics opposed the world in which they found themselves, not through argument, but through an embodied, militant philosophy that subverted social norms. Diogenes, their most famous representative, is best known for disgracing his fellow Athenians by performing in public acts which most would prefer to keep private, namely masturbation and defecation. He lived on the street, begging and then berating any would-be benefactors. He was ungrateful, confrontational and shameless. Like the Sceptics, the Cynics operated without fixed institutions and were defined more than any other philosophical tendency by their distinct attitude to life and divergence from civilised existence. Cynics would ridicule social niceties and traditions by ignoring them, thereby demonstrating the arbitrary nature of those traditions and the possibility of living differently.

The strangeness of ancient philosophy

Ancient philosophies took on the rather exacting task of creating an entire way of life. They were far more ambitious in this sense than most modern academic forms of philosophy. To achieve this aim they were highly restrictive, where the dogmas and principles of each school were generally not open to debate. To adopt a philosophy, as Hadot put it, was to 'choose a school, convert to its way of life, and accept its dogmas'.[15] Discussion mostly occurred at a secondary level, leaving the central doctrines and practices of each philosophical school relatively untouched. That a philosopher would willingly adopt dogmas and forms of conduct that were to remain unquestioned looks peculiar to the modern eye. In many other respects, the traditions of ancient philosophy are very alien to us now. For this reason, Hadot argues, the philosophical works of antiquity 'almost always perplex the contemporary reader' who criticises them 'for their bad writing, contradictions, and lack of rigor and coherence'.[16] These modern reproaches are often, however, the product of a basic misunderstanding concerning the functions these philosophical works served.

In antiquity written philosophical texts performed a function that was subservient to oral instruction, where they were no substitute for direct engagement with an accomplished philosopher. They were intended, moreover, to be read aloud and so retained 'the starts and stops, the hesitations, and the repetitions of spoken discourse'. Indeed, how a text sounded was just as important as its philosophical rigour. These texts were designed to complement a philosophical education that was chiefly oral, where writing was 'only an aid to memory, a last resort' that would 'never replace the living word'. The literary productions of philosophers were sometimes little more than an 'extension or echo of their spoken lessons'.[17]

Here they reflected the various teaching methods adopted by the philosophical school in which the lessons took place. They could, for example, take the form of a dialogue in which a question is posed and then answered with reference to various general principles adopted by the school. For this reason, as Hadot argues, 'different works written by the same author' are not 'necessarily coherent on all points because the details of the argument in each work will be a function of the question asked'.[18] Another textual approach would be to discuss the meaning of a previous text through lengthy commentaries on it. The practice of textual interrogation could be seen as a model, later taken up and transformed by medieval scholasticism to which we return in Chapter 4. Crucially, these works were not intended for a general audience. They were designed to shape into a way of life the members of the particular philosophical school. These texts were written not so much to inform the reader but to form him.

These approaches to writing may appear strikingly odd when viewed across the long historical distance that separates us from the ancient world. But the literary traditions of recent philosophy are perhaps just as peculiar. The dominant literary form of contemporary philosophy – the academic paper contributed to a professional journal – has indeed been described as the 'most eccentric latecomer of all philosophical genre forms'.[19] That philosophical thought has willingly confined itself to single slabs of writing, the academic paper, with all its structural, stylistic, topical and hence intellectual constraints, is indeed one of the most remarkable and noteworthy of all the uncontested assumptions that make up contemporary academic discourse. It imposes its own restraints on what can be thought and done, but unlike ancient philosophy, the constraints of modern philosophy are rarely acknowledged.

In the next chapter we explore two traditions of ancient philosophy and education, paideia and praxis, which have appealed to modern thinkers. Here we investigate the continued attraction of ancient philosophy taken as a source of alternative ways of thinking and alternative practices. For this reason, we depart at points from the chronological sequence of this book and reflect on present-day educational problems and how they have been related and contrasted to previous ways of thinking and being. Switching in this way between present-day commentaries and ancient philosophies will exemplify how conceptions of the past are always invested by the concerns of the present.

3

Ancient 'Solutions'

Troubling education

The constraints heaped upon education in our period are, to an extent, openly lamented. Teachers, pupils, schools and universities are over-assessed and under-valued. This has become the typical and not unjustifiable complaint of our times. The charge sheet is lengthy and might be summarised in the following way. The practice of education is in danger of disappearing under the heavy machinery of examination and audit. Teachers at all levels are tied to relentless form filling and target setting, endless paperwork, incoming emails, and a whole raft of mush-rooming administrative tasks. Educators operate in perpetual response mode to fresh rounds of policy and institutional initiatives, regularly about-turning and desperately innovating in reaction to fluctuations in what may be justly described as customer satisfaction and consumer demand. They are required to keep a wary eye on changes in managerial style and shifts in institutional priority and to bear in mind matters of institutional reputation and prestige – the necessity of main-taining a strong outward facing profile or 'shopfront'. They do all this whilst often complaining about, and sometimes ridiculing, the system, but nonetheless find themselves having to take all this bureaucratic pressure seriously. The educational practitioner also has to keep a clear focus on her curriculum vitae, which needs to give constant attention to changes in the educational weather if she is to progress in her career or, worse, if she is to respond effectively to unexpected changes in her circumstances of employment. Suffering a highly reductive educational rational-ity that we designate, by way of shorthand, as so many forms of 'instrumentalism', the fear amongst some educators is that educational institutions have been so overburdened by various forms of examination, administration, inspection and audit that education in any sense that they understand it is becoming a marginal activity that has to be smuggled in somewhere as they otherwise perform according to the managerial and statutory requirement.

Many, including some educationalists, may view this sort of feeling as a slightly over-excited account of the state of education today, but it cannot be denied that academic and professional freedom is now subject to unprecedented levels of surveillance and interference from non-educational sources. Our universities and schools are so dominated by systems designed to manage performance that we have lost sight of the basic value and importance of education as an individual and social good, or so it is argued. Certainly, as a route to social justice, education is a manifest failure: though it claims to offer opportunity to all nothing could be further from the truth, with vast inequalities of opportunity, experience and outcome persisting, and showing every sign in recent years of widening. But many still insist that despite it all education could be redeemed or saved; if only the oppressive burdens weighing down upon it could be lifted, or eased, a more genuinely educational climate would return. Our schools and universities would begin a long process of recovery, they claim, one that would allow them to re-establish a more balanced approach, one in which examination, inspection and audit would have their place, but would no longer dominate. Alternatively, some argue, we would do better to look beyond our established institutions, and redeem education by pursuing it in other contexts as yet relatively untouched by instrumentalism.

There are other ways of construing education, we should add, that might suggest such dissatisfaction is naïve, that in its disappointment with the contemporary state of education it is far too optimistic in its understanding of what education can be. From this perspective, such expressions of disappointment remain interesting and significant, but for different reasons. Firstly, it is notable how much they insist that despite everything we must continue to believe in the intrinsic good of something called education. Secondly, they assume that if we remove its worst excesses and revive its neglected potential, education will be rescued from its current predicament. This draws a bottom line beyond which education cannot be brought into question. Subsequent attempts to 'heal' education of its afflictions do not then risk a radical questioning of education, and so leave many educational practices and assumptions unchallenged. Attempts to solve contemporary educational problems tend to underestimate just how entrenched these problems might be. It seems that few critics have the stomach for a more persistent questioning, one that would risk casting doubt on the educational enterprise in a more thoroughgoing sense. Such a questioning would not only critique its practices and excesses, it would also risk undermining the status education gives those of us who qualify as educated people. A more thoroughgoing critique of education would begin by recognising just how deeply implicated we are in contemporary educational practices, where to question education is to also question our educational achievements and so ourselves.

Criticisms of contemporary education, which are also at the same time attempts to redeem it, often draw resources from its past. In so doing they risk treating educational histories as a repository from which we might derive old or even ancient 'solutions' to contemporary educational problems. There is a tendency here to view the educational past as a history of advance in some areas and retreat in others, where the duty of the critic is to return education, where appropriate, to more wholesome versions of itself. The history of education is treated as offering a diverse heritage of techniques and understandings, some of which will present alternatives to present day practices. It is hoped that by returning to that heritage, contemporary education can be saved by once broader conceptions of education, ones that will allow us to escape our narrow confines.

In this chapter, we consider two ancient alternatives that have each in their own way been promoted as solutions to modern educational problems. Here we expand upon and develop the brief introduction to ancient philosophies offered in Chapter 2, extending the chronological narrative at some points whilst, at the same time, relating these ancient philosophies to our educational present. In so doing, we note that 'solutions' or alternatives are always defined in relation to how educational problems are themselves perceived and defined. Those advancing the alternative conceptions considered below would configure the problem of education, a problem to which they respond, in different terms.

First, we explore the tradition of Greek and Roman *paideia*, which is still viewed as offering a far broader and more holistic conception of education than is to be found in today's examination-obsessed, outcome-driven schools and universities. This educational tradition was concerned with the formation of civilised men. Its beneficiaries would be equipped to live a flourishing and productive life (rather than be prepared for an existence that was productive in the modern sense, that is, as a member of an obliging and flexible modern labour force). Second, we explore the practical philosophy of Aristotle, which has been revived for similar reasons, and is seen as offering an escape from more reduced, technocratic and instrumental ways of thinking and acting. This revival represents an attempt to replace our current obsession with outcomes with an interest in practices. A revived Aristotelianism such as this constitutes a radical effort to rethink how we orient ourselves towards education, as students and teachers.[1]

A return to beauty and goodness

In ancient Greece the aristocracy were raised on more than just philosophy. Indeed, philosophers often stood at the margins of a wider cultural training designed to form men, a training intended for those who were to become ideal members of their class. The Greek term *paideia* encompasses this educational tradition, describing a form of elite education or upbringing. Its purpose was to furnish the aristocracy with men who were considered both beautiful and good. This required a rounded education, one that integrated intellectual, moral and physical training. It demanded mastery of the so-called liberal arts (including rhetoric, grammar and philosophy) as well as physical prowess. The pursuit of refinement, perfection and excellence in these areas defined what it meant to become a man of worth in ancient society. The free man, the man who was not a slave, was expected to master these aristocratic virtues, for the ancient city-state was configured as an entity run by its best citizens (where *aristos* means 'best' and *-kratia* 'power'). Paideia was, therefore, that method by which the governing class groomed and perpetuated itself.

Paideia has been described by Peter Brown as 'a means of expressing social distance'. It required such sustained effort, such investment in one's education, that it convinced those emerging from it that they were, in the harshest terms, 'as superior to the uneducated as human beings were superior to mere cattle'.[2] But paideia had other effects too. It allowed an educated class to cohere around a sense of common culture and excellence. This tradition came into its own, arguably, when it was taken up by the Roman ruling class and extended across the vast territories of the Roman Empire, allowing educated people in positions of influence and power to communicate with one another through a shared language and set of social conventions.

Rhetoric operated here as the 'queen of subjects'[3] defining the conventions of the spoken word in antiquity, resulting in the highly 'formalized, elevated, reassuringly predictable, and invariably fulsome' (if not a little turgid) speech of high society.[4] Requiring considerable skill, it defined a highly restricted mode of address, demonstrating for all to see the high level of self-control achieved by the orator. To quote Brown at greater length:

> It carried with it a sense of quiet triumph over all that was slovenly, unformed, and rebellious in the human voice and so, by implication, in the human person. It was a fragile speck of order in a violent and discordant world.[5]

Auditors remained on the alert for those moments where poise gave way to unguarded language, thus reinforcing the sense of shame such moments would bring upon the speaker. The best orator would employ rhetoric in such a fashion that it would not give way to sudden shocks. The fact that this highly controlled discourse left 'little room for surprises', the fact that it 'was not designed to express sudden challenges and novel sentiments, and still less to indulge in unwelcome plain-speaking', suited its purpose perfectly, which was to maintain the polite, respectful discourse of a social group.[6] Its formalised structure both smoothed over difference within that social group, and protected it from interlopers who could not communicate in its terms. Those seeking an education in paideia would, then, have to first learn how to 'cleanse their tongues' in order to achieve the required grace and decorum.[7]

The high regard given to paideia was no mere conceit. Enthusiasts for this form of education sincerely hoped that the art of rhetoric could always get one out of a tight spot, swaying the will of the powerful by the force of personal eloquence. Indeed, the powerful might thereby be given an opportunity to display their learning and refinement by allowing themselves to be moved by the imposing presence of the orator, by displaying their ability to perceive the sonorous appeal of the educated supplicant. To give way in such a situation, with grace and decorum, could only heighten one's authority in this social sphere. The only people deaf to such appeals would be the uneducated themselves, who were unable by constitution to fully understand the beauty and refinements of those above them.

The influence of this conception of education and culture has been considerable, echoing down the centuries. Of particular interest is the period of late antiquity, spanning the second to the eighth centuries AD. This saw the decline of the Roman Empire and its passing over into the early medieval period. This was a time of flux and instability during which the Roman aristocracy would attempt to retain their influence, and would do so by appeal to paideia, that is, by appeal to a now ancient tradition that would, it was hoped, still be useful in justifying their pre-eminence as a group of notables.

The ancient Greek philosophical schools had by now largely dissipated. Their distinct teachings (those that had survived) were increasingly amalgamated as part of a wider cultural education, where knowledge of philosophy became another mark of refinement. Philosophers in the ancient sense still existed, but they remained largely at the margins. By the fourth century the pursuit of educated refinement or paideia survived against the backdrop of an empire that had become 'frankly authoritarian'. Viewed retrospectively, the continued influence of paideia as an educational tradition appears rather quaint, if not completely out of touch with the politics of a 'vast, despotic empire'.[8] Despotic rule would have, one presumes, little patience with the cultured refinements of educated persons. And so it seems odd at first sight that paideia was still championed, bringing with it the expectation of 'a benevolent, because cultivated, exercise of authority', where all members of the upper class benefit from common codes of courtesy and self-control.[9] Yet despotism over vast territories requires, Brown argues, extended networks of support in order to function, and within these frameworks paideia thrived, greasing the wheels of the imperial machinery by giving it the appearance of respectability.[10]

More than this, however, it expressed the morality of an increasingly weakened aristocracy, living in a world characterised, as Brown argues, 'by a chilling absence of legal restraints on violence in the exercise of power'.[11] A lurking fear of arbitrary violence caused elites fearful of maintaining their position to fall back on the advantages of their education. Educators could appeal, in turn, to a common fear of that 'tide of horror' which 'lapped close to the feet of all educated persons',[12] persons who were only exempt from corporal punishment because of their noble status. Educators could appeal to patrons (employers) who recognised the advantages of a culture of refinement in which anger is seen as a failure in decorum, and clemency (or mercy) is viewed as a manifestation of the dignity and poise of the powerful. It was sufficiently obvious to educated people of the day that ceremony and decorum 'did not simply exalt the powerful; it controlled them, by ritualizing their responses and bridling their raw nature through measured gestures'.[13]

The noble ideal of character formation was then a moral formation that became increasingly useful to a class of notables seeking to maintain its position. It assured that within the imperial system cultured individuals were still largely treated with respect. In contrast to those without such privilege, the educated person was protected from arbitrary violence, because he could appeal to a shared culture, and shared practice of refinement and propriety.

As an educational tradition paideia still influences us, though not without adjustment. It was revived in the nineteenth century to serve the purposes of a modern liberal education, an ailing aristocracy and a rising bourgeoisie (see Chapter 11). It still retains its appeal and is often evoked, though it has been shorn of its originating social context and transplanted to another very different social order. It holds a promise – that education can still elevate and protect those it touches. It achieves this effect through a cultivation of the self, a process involving the refinement of speech and diction, frequent appeal to shared culture and literary references, as well as to a system of good manners, respectable appearances and predictable conduct that soothe away any possible friction and conflict, rendering social relations polite and controlled. It continues to exist in the conventional figure of the educated person and cultivated individual who is reserved and measured, who conducts themselves with decorum, who observes social graces and etiquette, and places good form and demonstrable civility above all else. This is a culture of correct behaviour and due restraint that many still value, though it is also, arguably, a culture of concealment and denial. Principally, it is a denial of those relations of power and privilege that make its continued existence possible. So, if and when you agree to, defend and perhaps even enforce 'good manners' in an educational context, perhaps spare a thought for the social order these manners uphold.

A return to Aristotle

Some educational critics argue for a more ancient revival – a return to Aristotle. They seek to promote an Aristotelian version of *praxis* or practical reasoning, interpreted as a form of practical wisdom that can only be acquired (and manifested) in the enactment of a craft or profession. This changes our understanding of the nature of teaching, declaring that, as a form of praxis, it cannot be prescribed in advance or dictated externally. What is revived here is a conception of education which is designed to resist all forms of outside intervention and political meddling. The crucial argument is that, as a form of practical reasoning, praxis may only be developed via the day-to-day experiences of working in education. Praxis cannot be pre-defined, decided externally, or set down in writing, because as a type of 'informed action' it defines itself. As Wilfred Carr argues, praxis involves ongoing 'reflection on its character and consequences' that 'reflexively changes the "knowledge-base" which informs it'.[14] So praxis does not implement abstract knowledge nor does it produce it. Rather, praxis-based knowledge is situated, contingent and constantly changing. Equally, praxis does not involve a set of technical skills that can be taught or followed, because techniques are generally designed with pre-given ends in mind. Finally, the ends or aims of praxis are 'inseparable from, and intrinsic to, praxis and can only exist in praxis itself'.[15] Praxis involves a constant renegotiation of ends as well as means, a negotiation that can only take place in the contexts in which they occur.

Though the means, ends, and indeed norms of praxis are locally defined, it remains high-minded enough in its commitments. Its aim is to realise what is known as the 'good life', defined via Aristotle as 'a morally worthwhile form of human life'.[16] From this Aristotelian perspective the good life is never an end or object that might be dictated externally. It does not exist as something that can be theoretically specified in advance. The nature of the good life only becomes known through praxis. Outside the realm and rhythm of praxis, one cannot judge whether it has been reached, because the good life does not appear as an independent achievement. The good life is only ever manifested in action. In other words, it consists in how we respond to particular situations and scenarios, in all their temporal uniqueness. Clearly, this makes the schools inspectorate, or other agencies measuring and quantifying the 'goodness' or quality of education, entirely redundant. For the good life is understood as a form of morally worthwhile human existence that can only be achieved through praxis itself – praxis is both the means and end of a worthwhile life. From this perspective, certain activities allow us to realise the good inherent to human existence, others do not – highly technical activities would be in the latter category. Education is, or at least ought to be, in the former category.

Education, so the argument goes, can operate once more as a form of praxis and thereby save itself from the adverse effects of modernity, most notably, from the highly technicist ways in which education is now understood and evaluated. Educators can escape what we will later call 'instrumental rationality' (see Chapter 8) and orient themselves once more towards the good that is said to be inherent in their work. Indeed, it must be assumed that educational practice still has the capacity, in and of itself, to realise a morally worthwhile form of human life. For based on this assumption, and on the careful development of an associated educational mindset, it is quite possible, Carr argues, that educators will once again understand 'how the good internal to their practice may, in their own particular situation, be more appropriately pursued'.[17] They will once again realise that their primary objective is to discover the educational potential, the inherent goodness, of each unique educational moment through praxis. This pursuit will be based on the understanding that the ends and means of education must remain open to a deliberative process through which they are constantly negotiated. Under these conditions educators will set about practising, or hoping to practise, the good life that education promises.

According to this reading, praxis is driven by a desire for what is 'worthwhile', where that which is worthwhile can only be judged in action. It is 'guided by a moral disposition to act truly and justly', a quality the Greeks called *phronesis*.[18] Indeed, in a practical situation where thought and action, or theory and practice, are viewed as 'mutually constitutive' (i.e. forming one another), 'the only fixed element is *phronesis*, the disposition to act truly and rightly'.[19] Phronesis functions as a guiding virtue. We do not all have it, and like everything else, phronesis must be acquired in practice. Educational practice is concerned, then, not only with realising the inherent goodness of education, but also with cultivating the virtue, or disposition to do good, of the educational practitioner.

We should not underestimate the difficulty of a revival of praxis, should it be attempted, since it appeals to a pre-modern worldview, one that precedes modernity – an era we might describe, not to equivocate, as the age of measurement. Arguably our more scientific age has blinded us to the moral value inherent in practice. In an age of measurement, the quality of educational practice is evaluated very differently, that is through attempts to measure and objectify its success in achieving certain goals. Good teachers, in other words, are those who get good results. Once the basic characteristics of 'good teaching' have been codified in this way, efforts are made to reproduce good teaching in other contexts. The irony of this approach, from an Aristotelian perspective, is that it generates 'what can only be described as a bizarre and frightening reversal' of Aristotle's conception of phronesis. Attempts to codify a form of wisdom, to define rules of good conduct, exemplify 'just the kind of thinking that is the source of its wreckage'. Here, in these attempts to predict and predetermine good practice, we have 'an instance of the very cause of its loss'.[20] The point about phronesis, or practical wisdom, is that it cannot be codified since it is a form of situated judgement-making that is defined by its sensitivity to a particular context. Clearly, it requires a complete overhaul, if not reversal, of how we think and act.

Arguments for practice and against theory

As a proponent of the above ideas in education, the philosopher of education Wilfred Carr is alert to the magnitude of the task. Together with Stephen Kemmis, he nonetheless argues that a revival of educational praxis is possible. Indeed, for some critics, everything that is wrong with education today demands it be revived. This provides the impetus for a necessary revolution in education where educational practice is once again given the dignity and respect it deserves. The argument and impetus for a return to practice were produced, they claim, as a mid-twentieth century reaction to rising instrumentalism in education.[21] It was already feared by this point that educational thought and practice had become dominated by a calculation of means and ends, a trend that reflected the far broader 'technological domination of political and social systems'.[22] According to this newly risen technocratic rationality, educational curricula were now treated as 'products, appearing in the form of schemes of activities, teaching ideas, subject-matter content and textbooks'. This was replacing older liberal ideas (that had drawn from the different tradition of paideia), ideas that were at odds with technocratic reason, seeking as they once did to develop 'the cultivated person'.[23] In effect, a *new practicality* had come to the fore, an impoverished practicality, one governed by a 'technical view of education' that formed the basis of an expanding educational industry, both commercial and academic.[24] Reduced to the pursuit of measurable goals and outputs, to objectives that would be defined in advance and tested later, education had become increasingly amenable to commerce and outside manipulation.

The teaching profession had been betrayed in a different sense too, Carr argues. Teachers had also been de-professionalised as part of an ongoing separation of theory from practice, where educational theory remained the preserve of specialists, operating in a research environment at one remove from the daily grind of teaching. The university endeavour which produced that abstracted realm of educational theory was a product of the late nineteenth century.[25] As a theoretical pursuit educational research hoped to set education on a more rational footing, solving its difficulties, justifying its practices. What it achieved, however, was a basic and unbridgeable rift, where educational practice was henceforth viewed as the poor cousin of theory, against which it would always be judged deficient and in need of academic assistance.

Against these developments some, like Carr, drew inspiration from a revived Aristotelian philosophy, which claimed that educational practice must be more broadly conceived (as a form of praxis). The much-lamented gap between theory and practice is, in Carr's view, symptomatic of our recent malaise. This gap was 'firmly embedded', he argued, 'in the conceptual foundations on which the whole practice of educational theory has been built and will only be eliminated by eliminating some of the dubious assumptions in terms of which educational theory and its relationship to practice have always been understood'.[26] Considered dubious here, is the idea that educational practice should be expected to implement forms of knowledge developed elsewhere, in the academy for example. Indeed, placed in question is the idea that education should depend on the guidance of academic disciplines at all. By contrast, the idea of praxis conjures an activity that has the capacity to generate its own forms of knowledge, its own educational theories and principles, that are all contingent to the site of action. Praxis is so locally defined that its basic methodology, or practical procedures, cannot even be spoken of in advance. As such, a general methodology of praxis is unthinkable.[27] We are forever thrown back on the professional integrity and situated wisdom of the teacher.

As a practical endeavour, allowing educational ends as well as means to become problematic, praxis should encourage reflection on the wider social and political frameworks within which educational practice takes place. According to its proponents, this broader conception of practice would involve a day-to-day negotiation of those frameworks, both individually and through broader communities of praxis. These would be critical communities, but their version of critique would not follow a modern tendency for abstraction (something we return to in Chapter 10). These negotiations would recognise the complexity of lived experience, and avoid taking up a position above practice, a position which, by inevitable resort to idealisms and abstractions, would fail to understand those realities about which it speaks. Rather, these critical communities would, in principle, be able to subject all aspects of practice to an ongoing process of situated interrogation. The profession would become defined by its willingness and capacity to engage in a form of critical praxis that submitted all aspects of educational work to ongoing critique. This critique of education (a critique that is at the same time a practically oriented mode of improvement) would be guided, of course, by a shared moral disposition to do right by education, and by the communities the profession serves.

The overall objectives of educational praxis would remain a little obscure of course, since to define them once and for all would somewhat contradict the basic idea of an evolving community of praxis. The purpose of the educational endeavour might be vaguely gestured at (to facilitate 'a more rational and just society',[28] for instance) but the main educational and intellectual challenge is clearly located elsewhere. Namely, it is to radically overhaul the way in which we relate to educational work, and thereby rescue it from the narrow instrumentalism which currently infects it. The good intent of the educator, of the profession as a whole reconstituted in this way as a moral force guided by practical wisdom and phronesis, is assumed as a possibility and a necessity if education is to be delivered from the grasp of technocratic rationality.

The argument for education as praxis offers a powerful and persuasive critique of education as it is currently configured; its insistence on education as a practice that has its own distinctive and intrinsic purposes illuminates the barbarities imposed upon educational practice by an overweening governmental authority. If it has a weakness, considered as an enterprise for restoring education to its true vocation, it is one that it inherits from the moral theory of Alasdair MacIntyre.[29] MacIntyre proposed that the pursuit of virtue, of excellence in a particular practice, was a moral endeavour given meaning by a recognition and acceptance across society of a common moral system, of the kind that existed in the medieval world. Within this analysis, the practice of education, like any other practice in the Middle Ages, was conducted in the light of the Christian understanding of how the world was organised, and the ways in which the kingdom of God was to be established on earth. Each and every practice was aware of itself as contributing to this end, an end which gave them moral purpose. Power – government, authority – had no need to intervene in the conduct of particular modes of living and working because they were conducted according to a common moral system. As MacIntyre argues, modernity is characterised by a fragmentation of morality – there is, across post-Enlightenment societies, no general, agreed moral order. As a result, the moral meaning and integrity of a practice like education are lost, their essential purposes abandoned to the play of power. As we note in our concluding chapter this presents what appear to be insuperable problems for an idea of education based on its inviolable, its essentially moral and civilising purpose. There is no agreement as to what education is and what it is for. As a consequence, education becomes the means to ends prescribed by external authority and vested interest. Its essential purpose, as understood by the proponents of education as praxis, is violated and will continue to be violated and perverted by those who have the power to impose their will. MacIntyre's answer to the dire circumstances he describes is for the civilising impulses and traditions that exist in institutions like universities to hunker down and see out the storm, just as early medieval monks nourished and gave safe harbour to traditions of knowledge and an idea of moral order amidst the strife and disorder consequent upon the collapse of classical civilisation. This hope – it is hardly a strategy – would appear to founder on the brute fact that such a sequestering and preservation of knowledge and its moral purpose is, increasingly, made impossible, indeed illegitimate, by powers that fail to recognise that education has its own, intrinsic ends. MacIntyre said that it was not a matter of fending off the barbarians, that they already rule us – more thoroughly and intensively than he perhaps recognised.[30]

Doubting philosophy

Those who argue for a revival of Aristotelian praxis are clearly at the more radical end of those critics who seek to redeem contemporary education. They nonetheless retain a basic respect for philosophy, and the hope that through some kind of return to more ancient conceptions of philosophy education can be set upon a path that is true to its authentic, essential, nature. Undoubtedly, Aristotelian approaches to education do offer substantially different ways of thinking about education, as do the other traditions of ancient philosophy summarised above and in the previous chapter. They pose a challenge not only to how we think of contemporary education, but also to how we think of philosophy too. However there are good reasons to tread with caution when returning to older conceptions of philosophy, on the presumption that philosophy and education have somehow since become corrupted. The challenge we face may be greater than defeating the more recent reduction of education to instrumental ends and countering the reduction in scope and ambition and consequent specialisation of academic philosophy. Indeed, according to its most radical critic, Friedrich Nietzsche, we could be facing a problem with philosophy itself. Nietzsche's claim is that philosophy was derailed from its very beginning and is in fact a mere symptom of a collective human capitulation to a destructive negativity, a failure of spirit that resulted in a kind of debilitating mental exhaustion, rather than, as is so often presumed, an expression of intellectual vigour and nobility of spirit.[31] This is an argument he makes in his first book *The Birth of Tragedy*.

According to Nietzsche, the ancient Greeks (those existing before Socrates and Plato) accepted that the world in which they lived was full of mystery. They were, moreover, painfully aware that when it came to their survival and prosperity, the universe was profoundly indifferent to their suffering. In order to cope with this realisation, Nietzsche argues, the ancient Greeks attempted to rationalise existence, giving meaning to the world as a way of living within it, as a way of coping with its chaotic, unsympathetic nature. They invented Gods and myths (and eventually philosophy) so as to give the world some sort of illusory stability and purpose.

But the early Greeks knew what they were doing. Like the 'lucid dreamer' who is aware that he is dreaming, they knew this dream was a dream of their creation and decided to dream on. This determination to dream on gave rise to the creative tension found in the theatre of Greek tragedy, where myth was played out on stage, not to offer a comforting escape from reality but as a thematisation of the tragic nature of the human condition. Nietzsche claims that what was confronted in Greek theatre was the reality that the 'whole world of torment is necessary', a reality only made bearable by a heroic and knowing embrace of illusion.[32] Otherwise put, they could see with the assistance of tragic drama how the world of torment is bound to the quest for security by way of an embrace of illusion. They could perceive how it prompts us to find respite in dreaming.

The early Greeks realised, moreover, that it was ludicrous to hope to 'restore order to a chaotic world' once the dream of order had been dreamt. It made no sense to impose the idea of order, a product of illusion and fantasy, on a vast, indifferent universe, that was beyond their grasp and control. The challenge they faced was rather different; it was to learn to live with this realisation of the indifference of the universe, to accept the 'horror and absurdity of existence', to come to terms with the cruelty of nature, and openly confront the 'terrible destructions of world history', where the tragedy of human existence is located precisely in the fact that it is inevitable, unavoidable. Our existence is a product of forces that can never be fully explained or controlled. These forces can only be given representation, and thereby be confronted, in the weakened but nonetheless disturbing form of tragic art.[33] But the early Greeks would not allow themselves to become so lost in their retreat to cultured illusions that they forgot the forces these refined, dreamed ideas were in tension with.

This situation would not last – the tension established in tragic theatre between artistic representation and a recognisably hostile existence could not be maintained. Eventually, Nietzsche claims, the Greeks reached a point of exhaustion, and were no longer strong enough to maintain the tension they had once openly encountered. It was at this point that the illusions generated by human beings were mistaken for actualities. According to this rather provocative re-reading of ancient history, the beginning of philosophy, which for Nietzsche starts roughly with Socrates and Plato, announced this moment of fatigue. The philosopher, according to Nietzsche, represents precisely that person who retreats from a harsh reality into the realm of ideas. Philosophy henceforth forgets that it is merely generating diversions, that it is systematising existence in order to deny the indifference of the universe to the plight of human beings, clinging to a speck of earth, in the vastness of space.

Nietzsche's account of the origins of philosophy is controversial to say the least. But it raises profound suspicion concerning the role of early philosophy and its legacies. With Nietzsche one begins to wonder if the philosophical pursuit of wisdom and knowledge, which was to be so influential upon Western thought, was nothing more than a diversionary activity, a distraction from realities the philosopher was unable to bear. As we saw in Chapter 2, each philosophy promised its own diversion, claiming access to a reassuringly universal conception of reason. Each philosophy (barring perhaps Cynicism) endeavoured to give life meaning and purpose. This promise, the promise of philosophy, was nevertheless tied to a command: wisdom can only be approached if the person pursuing it learns to orient themselves to the world differently. Hence the security that philosophy claims to offer is conditional on one's trust in its ability to deliver that security. The reorientation demanded by each philosophical school could still be seen as productive, at least in its own terms. Each school offered points of view that might serve to subvert or at least call into question commonsense ways of seeing things and unquestioned social conventions. This was no mere intellectual exercise; it was not simply a matter of seeing things differently, of adopting different points of view. The point of ancient philosophy was to become different, to be transformed, or schooled, into becoming someone else. Each philosophy entailed exercises in self-denial to assist with that transition. The passions would have to be educated, for example, if the intellect was to roam. But if Nietzsche is correct, philosophy promised nothing more than servitude to a whole series of illusory goods. It helped educate the passions, but in so doing only perpetuated the myth of order and meaning that philosophy set out to create. In educational terms then, while education might offer great security, meaning and purpose, we should remain open to the possibility that the aims it serves are in some sense illusory. In this Nietzschean view, education could be nothing more than a distraction (a decidedly sophisticated distraction, admittedly) from the suffering and violence that surround us.

Lost in philosophy

It is worth remembering that ancient philosophy was first conceived as a practical, engaged and often-marginal activity. The philosophers of ancient Greece developed a culture of the self that was intended to transform the philosopher's relationship to the world. To adopt the regimen of a philosophical school, certain adjustments in personal habits were adopted. To adopt a philosophy was as much a matter of forming oneself, of disciplining the body, as it was a matter of intellectual transformation. By contrast, modern academic philosophy by and large seeks only to operate at the level of thought (or that kind of thought which philosophy thinks), where intellection is considered to occupy its own relatively distinct realm. At most, modern philosophy offers ways of seeing the world differently, but has relatively little to offer in terms of how to live differently (beyond a purely academic style of life, of course, which is not distinct to philosophy but characterises the modern research university as a whole, as we explore in Chapter 12). The ancient schools were far broader, then, in their conception of philosophy as a way of life, and so too in their conception of education. This suggests that philosophy and education might benefit from a closer look at their common history and thereby engage in a process that questions what they have become. And yet, although modern philosophy can appear somewhat lacking in rude vigour when set alongside ancient philosophy, we should not assume that ancient philosophy, or some version of it, could easily be revived. Similarly, we should not assume that education could be saved, by some kind of return to, or revival of, more ancient educational and philosophical traditions. Indeed, it is worth questioning this assumption, and the one that accompanies it, the idea that philosophy and education *should* be saved by returning to a more ancient conception of its duties. And here we might engage once more with Nietzsche's seminal critique, which suggested philosophy was, from the outset, little more than a diminished form of escapism. Its development allowed the philosopher to deny the harsh realities of the world and become lost in philosophy. In a similar way education served to deny and paper over the violence of empire. It gave the Roman aristocracy a medium for communication and social engagement that negotiated and appeased more brutal manifestations of power. Education and philosophy may be seen to appear, then, as questionable activities from the outset. These suspicions are worth retaining, as we work through the remainder of this book.

4

Education and God

Periodisation

In this chapter, we offer an account of medieval philosophy and education. The question of the time period covered by the term medieval has been much argued over, although there has been general agreement that the period of Roman hegemony ended at some time in the fifth century AD. The ensuing period, once rather forbiddingly termed the Dark Ages, is now referred to as the early medieval period. It is conventionally seen as extending to the end of the tenth century. This was a period of social and political flux, marked by economic decline, by vast barbarian migrations and by struggles to establish sovereignty in the vacuum left by the collapse of Roman rule. It was, however, a period in which Christianity extended its hold across Europe and features we now consider as distinctively medieval, such as the feudal system and the establishment of monasteries (which were often charged with an educational role) came into being.

The two centuries after 1000AD are usually designated as the High Middle Ages and the period extending from the fourteenth to the fifteenth centuries (and, in the view of some scholars, on into the sixteenth century) as the Late Middle Ages. The high medieval period was a time of economic expansion, population growth, theological schism and, with the establishment of kingdoms and city states, the foundational period of European statehood. It was also the period in which Western Europe came to see itself as Christendom, a pan-European community which identifies itself as standing in distinction from Muslim and pagan peoples and, indeed, after the East–West schism of 1054, as separate from the fellow Christians of the Orthodox church. The first universities were founded and intellectual life thrived, most pertinently for our purposes with the development in the eleventh and twelfth centuries of the system of thought known as scholasticism.

The Late Middle Ages saw the continued advance of knowledge in science and philosophy, prompted in part by the arrival in the West of Ancient Greek writings after the fall of Constantinople. However, this later period was also one of economic stagnation, depopulation caused by famine and plague and subsequent social unrest. Despite these problems, the fourteenth and fifteenth centuries saw great technological advances – most notably perhaps with the invention of the printing press – and an orientation of trade away from the hostile Ottoman East. This led to the opening of trade routes to other parts of the world and thence to the European colonialist enterprise. Towards the end of the Late Medieval period developments in commerce led to the replacement of feudal economic organisation by the mercantilism that some have seen, in its aggressive pursuit of wealth, as an early form of capitalism. This later period is perhaps best viewed as a time of transition, when the intellectual and cultural ferment which is referred to as the Renaissance gained increasing momentum, and the medieval worldview gave way inexorably to an outlook that was shaped by the methods of scientific enquiry and by the growth of capitalist logic and calculation, which is to say that the European world entered modernity during this period. In Chapter 5 we focus in particular on the period from the twelfth to the sixteenth centuries and the passage in thought from scholasticism to Renaissance humanism. For now, we turn to the matter of the first great systematisation of knowledge production and transmission in the West, the medieval university.

Medieval education

The account of medieval education, begun here and completed in Chapter 5, follows on from Chapters 2–3 which described the rise of the ancient Greek philosophical schools and their decline during the Roman period. In the current chapter we investigate what happened next, as thought organised according to Christian belief (its view of humankind's position in the universe, its ideas of the good and meaningful life) came to dominate much of Europe.

In the centuries that followed, education was slowly redefined and reconfigured in the context of medieval Christianity. From the outset there was considerable disagreement concerning its central dogmas and prescriptions. And yet, while there was no single understanding of the divine order, and hence, no single understanding of the nature and pursuit of education, there was basic agreement throughout this period that education would further the ends and purposes ordained by God. This ordering of thought and its consequent influence on social being was dominant until the early modern period when the power and influence of the Church weakened. Its hold on thought and the organisation of society was eventually undermined by the cultural, economic and scientific turbulence of the time. But the authority of religion in the social realm was most decisively weakened by the schism that has come to be known as the Protestant Reformation. During the sixteenth century dissension over religious doctrine, the authority of the Papacy and the forms and conduct appropriate to the worship of God led to socially devastating religious wars that traversed Europe, particularly Central Europe. Ultimately, the notion that societies, a whole civilisation, should be ordered on religious principles did not survive the carnage and ruin incurred by confessional division. With the rise of humanism and the dawn of modernity (see Chapters 5–8), religious zealotry became something to be guarded against and a new social and educational order would have to be constructed along secular lines. Before considering this secular modernity, however, it is necessary to understand its Christian precursor. Our argument is that modernity and modern education was built, sometimes despite itself, on the philosophical and educational frameworks established by medieval Christianity.

From pagan to Christian philosophy

During the medieval period, Christianity absorbed philosophy, providing the framework for its development across much of Europe. Although it was now dominant, Christianity hardly represented a complete break with past ways of construing the world. There were important continuities with the pagan philosophies of ancient Greece, where here again we are dealing with a distinctly pre-modern conception of philosophy. As such, Christian philosophy could not be studied without the student also adopting its way of life.

There were some important changes, nonetheless. Where each school of thought in classical times had its distinct recommendations for how one should live, with Christianity this range began to narrow. Philosophy was now attached to the Christian belief in a monotheistic God. Though there was variation in how the Christian way of life was interpreted, Christian philosophy was nevertheless constrained to the ideal of a single organising vision, that of ordering society in ways that would advance the Kingdom of God. In other respects, however, Christianity extended the remit of ancient philosophy. Its scope now expanded far beyond the narrow realm of the individual philosophical schools of ancient Greece. Its remit also extended far beyond its later role in serving the cultured elite of the Roman Empire.

In principle, Christianity was committed to the idea that the way of life its philosophical deliberations dealt with should apply to everyone. And so, if we define education at this point in history as being that mode of training which delivers members of a school into its way of life, we can see how Christianity, in disseminating its core principles across the social whole, also eventually developed the idea of a popular education. Since Christianity was in principle for everyone, a Christian education could be too. Of course, a great mass of the medieval population did not receive this kind of attention through institutionalised schooling. Such work was the responsibility of the priest, whose pastoral care and vigilance were central to the Church's social and theological mission.

This new universalising tendency had important repercussions. In principle if not in practice, from now on nothing was permitted to exist outside education or outside philosophy. Once education and philosophy had been pushed to encompass everything, once they served a Christian worldview, it became difficult to entertain doubts about their respective worth or relevance. From now on, to doubt education or to doubt philosophy (interpreted loosely as reasoned thought) is to doubt everything. This is why the question posed by Nietzsche at the end of Chapter 3 is as radical as it now appears. Following the transformation effected by medieval Christendom, it becomes almost senseless to ask if education itself might be nothing more than a convenient distraction from the pain of existence, a mere diversionary activity, designed to offer consolation before a cold and indifferent universe. It has become difficult if not impossible to imagine a world without education.

The Bible and the liberal arts

In medieval Europe the Bible became the supreme authority on all worldly and otherworldly matters, with ancient secular knowledge now subordinate to religious teachings. Much of it, indeed, had been forgotten and lost following the collapse of the Western Roman Empire in the fifth century. Secular teachings, such as those of the ancient Greek philosopher Aristotle, were retained and preserved outside Europe by Arabic scholars. These ancient secular texts were only gradually reintroduced to Western Europe centuries later. And this was on the condition they were carefully adapted to Christian tradition.

It is important to emphasise this break in the influence of classical culture. It allows us to see how classical teachings were later reabsorbed on very different terms. Their influence would now have to pass through Christian theology, with classical teachings repositioned as moments in the unfolding of a divine plan. The written word was no longer subordinate to the spoken word in this context, but was now the medium that transmitted authoritative knowledge over time. Philosophical and theological texts had become revered objects and teachers were followed not simply because they were authorities, or because they were accomplished philosophers. Teachers were people who were in possession of authoritative texts. They acted as mediators, appealing to the authority of others as recorded in writing.

Reading was considered a moral act, an idea that derived from the early Christian theologian, Augustine of Hippo. Augustine – part of a group of ancient and highly influential Christian theologians who became known as the Church Fathers – taught that correct textual interpretation depended on the moral capacities of the reader. This moral bearing would enable the reader to distinguish between the literal meaning, and the deeper, spiritual and metaphorical meaning of secular and sacred texts. The reader would come to understand that everything that was read pointed towards something greater, to something beyond itself. Reading curricula were consequently ordered in a way that was thought to mirror the growth of the soul, beginning from an understanding of worldly things and moving on to an appreciation of the divine in the mundane. In this way, secular or pagan knowledge (the so-called liberal arts) was carefully subordinated to the pursuit of the divine. For Augustine, the basic problem facing education was the fact that humanity is born in sin (the sin of Adam and Eve). Sinful humanity could nevertheless elevate itself through education, overcoming original sin by following a carefully prescribed educational path. Drawing from Augustine, a lesser-known twelfth century figure, Hugh of St Victor, devised an educational scheme that would do exactly that; it would elevate the soul. This demanded subservience, requiring the humility of the learner, and a willingness on behalf of that learner to proceed with great patience. Presumably, it would take considerable effort and time to progress from such low beginnings towards a closer relationship with God. Here it was necessary to stipulate 'what to read, the order in which to read it, and how to read it'.[1] All knowledge, sacred and secular, was to be conveyed through an ordered system that would interrelate all understanding, and subordinate it to an appreciation of the divine. Such reading exercises were designed to guide a programme of study that would work towards the moral and spiritual improvement of those engaged with them. This educational method was not generalised across populations – as a formal procedure, education and the spiritual exercises it involved, remained an elite training.

The twelfth-century bishop and educator John of Salisbury made an important addition to this scheme of work. His emphasis was on the necessity of *habituation*, where wisdom would only be achieved through regular practical exercises. In isolation, it was believed, reading could be dangerous, since excessive reading would cultivate eloquence without wisdom. To avoid this outcome, reading would always have to remain subservient to the cultivation of the spirit, where the spirit would be nourished through practical exercises. The influence of Greek philosophical methods can be detected here, though there was a concern in these endeavours – as Basil Bernstein put it – to make the dangerous energies of Greek thought safe for Christianity. An enterprise, he adds, in which medieval thought was unsuccessful.[2]

These educational techniques may sound far removed from the present and appear of only marginal interest to today's educator. They are, nevertheless, critically important to our understanding of the continued significance in the history of education of a form of moral training that, through various adaptations, still influences us today. We can see how in the medieval era education continued to function as an activity, which, at its core, was concerned with the spiritual formation of its pupils. Pedagogical procedures had changed, objectives had been

Christianised, and the nature of the pupil's soul was now understood differently. Yet education was still considered to be a type of training designed to form individuals and subjectivities. It was explicitly designed to constitute individuals so that they would adopt and embody a particular way of being and way of viewing the world.

Scholasticism and the medieval university

The cultivation of the Christian 'soul' was achieved in part through the educational movement known as *scholasticism*. This offered a form of moral training to those destined to fill superior roles in society. The history and development of medieval scholasticism are closely tied to the birth of the European university, the institution traditionally tasked with furnishing higher positions in society with distinguished and competent occupants. Since their inception in the mid-twelfth century, universities developed and established traditions that have been transmitted in adjusted form to the present. Indeed, the university today represents a unique mixture of influences, some of them medieval, others modern, yet others notably 'post-modern'. Typically, when universities are either criticised or defended, there is a tendency to mix principles and values that have very different historical origins and meanings. For this reason, it is important to have a clear notion of the distinct educational practices of the medieval university in order to track how these influences have been transmitted and translated, eventually becoming absorbed within the odd institutional amalgam that defines our educational present.

Formal education before the eleventh century

Before the eleventh century, formal education was largely confined to monasteries and cathedral schools. These were designed to teach future monks and priests to read the Bible and transmit its tenets. This was a minority education with a singular purpose: to serve God and to spread his word. As we have seen, while some secular (or non-religious) knowledge was admitted, this was on the condition that it remained carefully subordinate to the teachings of Christian religion. Hence, while selections from the so-called 'liberal arts' had indeed been transmitted from classical antiquity, they were translated into forms that would not unsettle Christian doctrine. In their original Greek and Roman context, these arts were far more common than the curricula of the philosophical schools considered in Chapter 2. They were deemed to be those subjects of study essential for the education of the 'free' man of paideia (a designation which excluded, of course, women as well as the large slave populations of that era). To the extent this emphasis on the education of the 'free' man remained in medieval Europe; it referred to a very different entity, and to a very different kind of freedom.

The ideal of an education in these arts, which came to be known as a 'liberal education', has been remarkably persistent (we review its continued adaptations beyond the medieval period in a later chapter). For medieval purposes, the teaching of these arts was divided into two successive stages. The so-called *Trivium* (from which the word 'trivial' is derived) offered a basic training in (i) grammar, or the mechanics of language; (ii) rhetoric, or the use of language to persuade; and (iii) logic, or the mechanics of thought. The Trivium later became the main undergraduate course in the medieval university. It was followed by the *Quadrivium*, a secondary stage that prepared the student for the study of theology. This stage was itself divided into an education in (i) arithmetic; (ii) geometry; (iii) astronomy; and (iv) music. Crucially, then, subjects traditionally associated with philosophy were now subordinate to theological training. One would acquire the nuts and bolts of philosophy before moving to the real object, which was to study theology.

During the twelfth century, the established role of the monasteries as the key institution of formal education was challenged by two major developments. Firstly, during this period, the rapid growth of cities and trade generated various administrative positions, recruitment for which required a new 'educated' class of people. The newly established professions of law and medicine were also expanding, requiring their own educated trainees. There was, in effect, a rising demand for elite vocational training. Secondly, the influx of 'ancient learning' into Western Europe meant that a new mode of teaching and a new mode of scholarship were required in order to reconcile classical knowledge with established theology. These demands were met by the medieval university.

Origins of the medieval university

If the following account seems heavy on history and procedures and light on ideas, it is a necessary reminder that education is always a practical matter, embedded in social contexts that shape the forms of thought, the philosophical ideas, to be transmitted. Philosophy is sometimes described as 'underpinning' curricula, when it might be more accurate to say that it is administrative structures and pedagogical technique which underpin education and permit the formation and transmission of philosophies.

The medieval university initially took the form of spontaneous gatherings of students and teachers. Indeed, the word *universitas* from which the more recent term 'university' is derived merely referred to a number, aggregate or group of people. It simply described a selection of teachers and students who had gathered together. In its original usage, the word 'university' had nothing to do with the cultivation of universal knowledge, or the idea of an institution in which all branches of knowledge are represented.[3] It was only much later that the word acquired this modern meaning.

As the spontaneous gatherings grew larger, various conventions were adopted and procedures formalised, these being imported from the dominant institutions of the time. The church provided 'the idea of an organisation which transcended national boundaries as well as a fetish for mysterious rituals'. The monastery lent 'the idea of a self-governing community which made its own rules and developed its own way of life'. And from the medieval guild system universities adopted 'the idea of a community of individuals bound together for mutual support and with the authority to determine its own membership'.[4]

Medieval guilds were associations of craftspeople, such as masons or carpenters or shipbuilders, who grouped together to protect and preserve the secrets or 'arts' of their craft. To become a master carpenter, for example, you had to demonstrate that you had mastered your woodwork skills. To do this you would serve a period of time as an apprentice, learning the skills of your craft from your master crafts-man. Eventually you would submit your 'masterpiece' upon which you would be assessed. Those who passed would enter the guild.

The educational scheme of the medieval university followed a similar logic. The life of a medieval student was divided into two main phases leading up to the sub-mission of a masterpiece. Students of the first phase were called 'scholars'. They spent four or more years listening to lectures delivered from a list of prescribed texts. The sequencing of these texts, and the number of times they were to be read, were again specified in advance. This was still an oral education. The authorised books were rare and laboriously written by hand. The printing press, which revo-lutionised communication, did not arrive until the fifteenth century.

In the medieval university teaching was divided between so-called 'ordinary lectures' that were delivered by masters, and 'cursory lectures' that were given by bachelors. Ordinary lectures were more detailed in that the master would pre-sent and explain the text. In cursory lectures the bachelor would provide little more than a running commentary upon it. Lectures were also accompanied by 'disputations' in which the master would resolve any difficulties raised between the text in hand, and other authoritative texts, such as those passed down from the Church Fathers. Scholars would attend these lectures and disputations for a period of two years or so, gradually learning from the example set by their master. The scholar would respond to questions, when invited, and would receive train-ing in the delicate art of textual reconciliation.

The second phase in the apprenticeship of the student was that of the 'bach-elor'. This borrowed from the terminology of the guilds, designating a candidate for mastership. After several more years of practice and study, the bachelor could be admitted to the master's guild, provided he successfully exhibited a master-piece. In the university, this took the form of a public display of the candidate's learning in which he would give an inaugural lecture followed by a disputation. The disputation effectively performed two functions. It was a method of teaching used to train scholars and bachelors, but it was also a demonstration of the skills and aptitudes that scholars and bachelors were expected to acquire. The supreme objective was the ability to achieve a harmonious interpretation of the prescribed sacred and secular texts. For the medieval theologian and his student followers faced a basic dilemma: the various church canons contradicted one another. Clearly this could not be permitted for these contradictions would cast doubt on the wisdom of those that were most revered. Facing such difficulty, medieval scholasticism could be seen as a rather heroic effort to put off the prospect of disintegration. It sought to harmonise divergent ideas by bringing them into a uniquely Christian alignment.

Scholasticism has been retrospectively ridiculed for its diligent pursuit of harmony, for its ability to argue away inconvenient and contradictory ideas. To some extent, this failure to judge scholasticism on its own merits is understandable. The scholastic preference for scriptural reconciliation clearly offends more contemporary notions of rational discourse. We intend, however, to suspend these modern prejudices and offer a more sympathetic account of the scholastic worldview, one that locates it carefully in its medieval context. This follows the work of the philosopher Alasdair MacIntyre. The key figure for MacIntyre was the influential thirteenth-century theologian Thomas Aquinas. Aquinas helped develop a mode of scholastic debate that coupled deep respect for authority with an effort to resolve contradiction and thereby reaffirm the wisdom of the Church Fathers. The university disputation in its most advanced form attempted exactly this, sorting out scriptural difficulties through scholastic debate. These carefully orchestrated disputes provided a certain amount of freedom to develop counterarguments before the final resolutions were applied, and the difficulties reconciled. Those engaged in scholastic debate, in particular those undergoing a public disputation, were thereby provided with an opportunity to demonstrate in discursive form the faithfulness and subtlety of their understanding of received tradition. Tensions were reconciled, disagreements resolved, and the harmony of scripture maintained.

There was no pretence that truth is an independent or neutral entity. Knowledge of the truth did not emerge from empirical sources or the application of a mathematical logic. Truth was arrived at by way of the correct reading of texts, whereby only those who had mastered a tradition of thought and belief could produce such readings. The level of subservience involved here and the kind of priority given to tradition are, undeniably, an affront to modern sensibilities. The Enlightenment belief that rational thought must emancipate itself from the 'tutelage of authority' still endures.[5] According to an Enlightenment worldview, to be rational one must think for oneself (and this idea persists even now, though there are many good reasons for contesting the notion that one could ever be in a position to think with the independence implied by the phrase 'thinking for oneself'). By contrast, scholastic rationalism could be said to be more honest in recognising that it depended on an external framework that made thought and debate possible. This intellectual framework was not rigidly enforced; its transmission was relatively subtle. The dogmas of scholastic tradition largely took the form of tacit or unspoken understandings and principles. These were absorbed gradually through, for example, attendance at and participation in the disputations that followed lectures. The medieval student would slowly learn through experience how to apply the acknowledged standards of his craft, and identify mistakes. The apprentice for mastership would also gradually learn to locate his efforts within the wider orbit of the scholastic universe, distinguishing between the 'kind of excellence which both others and he can expect of himself here and now, and that ultimate excellence which furnishes both apprentices and master-craftsmen with their *telos*', where the telos is their highest object or aim.[6]

In the scholastic university, intellectual and moral virtues were deemed inseparable. Of particular concern were the effects of personal desires and inclinations. These were to be guarded against when it came to textual interpretation. And they were to be governed through an education in personal conduct. The apprentice would learn to regulate the self, working towards an ideal that was, in part, exemplified by the work of the masters in whom the scholar was expected to place all trust. Personal 'defects and limitations in habits of judgement and habits of evaluation' that were 'rooted in corruptions and inadequacies of desire, taste, habit and judgement' would become evident through training. The individual concerned would develop a thorough appreciation of those personal attributes that were to be managed, and put right.

This process was not individualising; it would be a mistake to read it as such. Increased self-knowledge did not separate the individual from their environment as an increasingly distinct self-referential unit. Rather, the opposite was intended. The scholar was to become absorbed into the particular rationality or worldview of the craft, adopting it as his own. Like the guild apprentice, the scholar would learn what it is about himself 'that has to be transformed, that is, what vices need to be eradicated, what intellectual and moral virtues need to be cultivated' if he was to become a master practitioner and so be accepted into the company of like-minded peers.[7] The effects of medieval pedagogy were deeply formative in this sense, bringing individuals into alignment with tradition. It involved a whole series of everyday personal reflections, inspections and petty ordeals.

The constraints of scholastic debate were not static. Traditions gradually changed with time; new interpretations replaced old ones. The internal transformation of tradition was, nevertheless, restrained by the existing rules of debate. On MacIntyre's reading, the superiority of a new interpretation was demonstrated only if a later stage was 'able to transcend the limitations and failures of an earlier stage', according to 'the standards of rationality of that earlier stage itself'.[8] An earlier tradition could only be overthrown according to arguments that made sense to it, according to attacks that were advanced in its terms and according to its rituals of judgement. This placed unique demands on those working to advance scholarship. Those seeking adjustment would have to be fully conversant with the existing tradition in order to negotiate such complex transitions.

Changes to tradition demanded a far deeper understanding and appreciation of the constraints and possibilities of the governing discourse than was required when merely submitting to its existing mores. The critical (as we would say today) scholar who wished to advance a new reading of a text or one of its statements, would need to be the most faithful and skilful practitioner of his tradition. Hence the medieval scholar, whatever his reforming zeal, was essentially willingly subservient to, enfolded within, the doctrines of established authority, unlike the modern critic who typically adopts a stance of scepticism towards the received wisdom of traditional authorities. Only the vanity of Enlightenment thinkers allowed them to believe that if thought was to have any value it needed to be entirely deracinated, which is to say removed from the effects of power imposed by its formative environment.

Philosophy assimilated

In the medieval period, then, ancient philosophy was assimilated to a Christian order of discourse, which redefined the moral purpose and practical nature of education. Forms of personal training associated with ancient philosophy were now adapted to Christian ends. This developing array of Christian spiritual exercises came to define a new all-encompassing way of life, one that swallowed up education in its entirety. Reading was seen as a moral act requiring prior training and cultivation.

During this period the practices of Christian education constrained philosophy to a single organising vision. And yet, Christianity extended the remit of philosophy far beyond the narrow realm of the individual philosophical schools of ancient Greece, and far beyond its latter role in serving the cultured elite of the Roman Empire. Christianity was committed in a way that was radically new to the idea that its teachings should apply to everyone. In disseminating its core principles across the social whole of European Christendom, it began to develop the notional possibility of a popular education. Since Christianity was in principle for everyone, a Christian education would be too. Of course, the great majority in the Christian medieval world did not receive this kind of attention through institutionalised schooling, receiving its education from the church and its intermediary, the local priest.

Though philosophy lived on in the guise of Christian spiritual exercises, with the advent of medieval scholasticism its secular enquiries were carefully subordinated to the study of theology. The essential components of philosophy (an understanding of grammar, rhetoric and logic) were relegated in status, becoming just the necessary grounding for a more advanced theological training. In other words, from this point theology 'became conscious of its autonomy *qua* supreme science, while philosophy was emptied of its spiritual exercises' – for these had been thoroughly Christianised. Philosophy was 'reduced to the rank of a "handmaid of theology,"' its role now being 'to furnish theology with conceptual – and hence purely theoretical – material'.[9] As we now know, philosophy would not remain subordinate to religion forever. In modernity it became increasingly secular in outlook, regaining some measure of autonomy, and in some areas reviving its earlier ambition, which was to address the task of how we might live differently. In the next chapter we deal with the Renaissance's development of what would in later times become the secular religion of humanism.

5

Education and Humanism

The Renaissance

In this chapter we investigate how the Renaissance established the foundations of modern humanism, and hence set in place the basic framework out of which modern education was constructed. In so doing, we nevertheless consider the Renaissance in its own terms, as a period in which the pre-modern humanism that was established took a distinctly tentative form. This earlier humanism will be contrasted to its modern successor, which was to become far more assertive, and confident, in its attempts to place 'man' at the centre of philosophical enquiry, and, more specifically, educational philosophy.

The Renaissance is popularly viewed as a moment of rupture, a new secular humanism suddenly producing startling achievements in philosophy, the arts and sciences, sweeping away the shackles on thought that held medieval societies in subjugation to the authority of the church. This would be a misunderstanding. Since the early Middle Ages a submerged interest in non-religious texts, particularly the literature of the ancients, had survived amidst the theocratic orthodoxies of the medieval state. It was this tendency that fed into the cultural and intellectual transformations that we think of as the Renaissance. No sudden break with the past took place. It was the case that many, perhaps most, early humanists had received a scholastic education. As well as studying the texts of the ancient world they devoted great attention to the Bible, although their interest was at least as much philological as spiritual. They treated holy texts as they did the classical writings of Rome, as works of literature which were in need of philological clarification. They sought to rescue them from the corruptions that had accreted across centuries during which early scribes had modified the texts in order to 'improve' their sense and after successive translations had rendered them unreliable as true expressions of the originals.

We should remember that Renaissance means rebirth and what happened between the 1300s and the early sixteenth century is best viewed as the re-emergence of a tradition of thought that derived from the classical period. We have already seen that in ancient Greece grammar, rhetoric and logic formed the basic education for the citizenry, those free men (as opposed to slaves or women) who were to engage in the public life of the state. In Roman times the term *humanitas* was associated with a liberal education in what we would now describe as 'arts' or 'humanities' subjects – language, literature, history and moral philosophy.[1] It is clear that a scholarly interest in the humanistic texts of Rome runs in a continuous line from late antiquity to the Renaissance, achieving its educational niche in the liberal arts curriculum taught in the schools and universities of the Middle Ages.

Throughout the Middle Ages there was, then, a struggle, or rift, between a literary, classicist and humanist curriculum, and that of scholastic studies. Scholasticism, as we saw in Chapter 4, mixed speculative philosophy with dialectics, where the latter involved a series of carefully orchestrated discussions that were intended to advance and affirm the basic tenets of tradition. This rift between these two rival traditions was not absolute, however. Interactions occurred between the two pedagogies whereupon scholasticism, for example, benefitted from the methodological innovations of humanist scholarship.[2] This was not necessarily a two-way exchange, but more of a scholastic incorporation of certain humanist methodological innovations. However, by the early part of the thirteenth century, scholasticism – which is essentially the outcome of the Christian church's engagement with the newly arrived 'Greco-Arabian'[3] corpus of knowledge and ideas,[4] particularly the philosophy of Aristotle and its interpretations – had become the educational method that dominated the university curriculum, providing the rigorously Christian training required for a life as a priest, a lawyer or a physician. This curriculum, with its exacting, intense focus on dialectic and logic, had its heyday between the early part of the thirteenth century and the middle of the fourteenth, although it continued, albeit in a less speculative, more empirical mode, through to the late Middle Ages. At the level of the universities it appears to have survived into the seventeenth century by accommodating aspects of humanist education. In Renaissance schools, however, humanism and the *studia humanitatis* 'came to dominate completely'.[5] Hence, scholasticism and Renaissance humanism were concurrent for a time. As we explore in this chapter, throughout the Renaissance a growing humanism would establish the groundwork for that distinct modern cultural edifice which we now inhabit – namely, the edifice of modern liberal humanism.

Civility and virtue

We begin this chapter by exploring some important differences between scholasticism and Renaissance humanism. The latter was distinct in that it looked beyond the confines of scriptural debate, and towards the formation of a new civic order.

This more worldly and humanist outlook can be observed in the context of late thirteenth and early fourteenth-century Italy.

If scholasticism was the educational programme required to produce the class of intellectuals who would administer the hierarchical structures of feudalism, regulating the morality that sustained the spiritual–cosmological order of that society, it is in the sweeping social upheavals occurring in Renaissance Italy that we may discern the material conditions for the development of a renewed humanism and, eventually, the seventeenth-century rationalism of Galileo, Descartes and Newton. A new mercantile class had risen to prominence. This increasingly powerful group, which drew its influence from a rise in trade and commerce, was now driving a whole sequence of social and cultural changes that challenged the moral and theological resources of traditional scholasticism. This class demanded new forms of education and training considered appropriate to the new economic realities within which it moved and to the social ambitions it had acquired. At the same time, new conceptions of government in the city-states of northern Italy required personnel trained in law, history and rhetoric in ways that might provide practical and ideological service to the princes who had assumed control of what had previously been communes governed by a decidedly republican, anti-monarchical spirit.[6]

In this context, some scholars emphasise the practical, professional and vocational nature of humanist study and teaching. They point to its role in shaping the sensibilities and moral perspectives of the future rulers and leaders of society; its provision of the trained secretarial support and the historiographical expertise required by powerful secular and ecclesiastical figures; and its servicing of a vigorous book trade both before and after the invention of the printing press.[7] It is possible, indeed, to trace a line of development in this pragmatic function of humanist education to its culmination in the mid-sixteenth century in what some would describe as the frankly utilitarian curriculum of the French humanist Petrus Ramus.[8] This curriculum was geared to the social aspirations of an ambitious mercantile class. By the sixteenth century, then, a form of humanist education had been developed that was considered appropriate to the pressing needs of a changing society.

The humanists were repelled by what they saw as scholasticism's arcane jargon and its devotion to theoretical and logical hair-splitting. They claimed that scholasticism had nothing to offer to the practical resolution of the moral problems confronting society. Humanism responded to a changing society's need for 'a straightforward and effective language of civic administration suitable for political and ethical discourse' by offering a training in the arts useful to civic life.[9] The models for this language, for this discursive environment, were to be found in the past, in those classical texts of ancient Greece and Rome that were concerned with promoting civility and the art of living well. However, it would be wrong to assume that humanism was a purely pragmatic school of thought offering ideas for keeping the wheels of state turning smoothly, a fifteenth-century precursor of twentieth-century management theory. It undoubtedly presented itself as providing solutions to the kinds of problems that preoccupied the rulers of the time. Indeed, the role it came to perform in securing social distinction and career advantage as late as the nineteenth century was summed up by Thomas Gaisford's comment that a classical education 'not only elevates above the vulgar herd, but leads not infrequently to positions of considerable emolument'.[10] And yet, for all that the acquisition of a humanist education offered very practical benefits, it was undeniably informed by far loftier aims and convictions.

Alongside its emphasis on a training in arts useful to civic life, humanists sought to produce an education that would elevate man's cultural and spiritual condition. If scholasticism put God and the world he had created at the centre of its studies, the central preoccupation of the humanists was man, his hope of salvation and his place and role in fulfilling God's plan. Civic virtue, man's active engagement in securing justice and order in this life, became central to the achievement of his spiritual goals. The fourteenth-century poet and classical scholar Petrarch, sometimes referred to as the first master of humanism, sought precisely that; to develop a philosophy that placed justice as the supreme civic virtue. The form of justice Petrarch had in mind could only be secured by a simple and pure moral commitment that was acted out in contemplation of man's struggle to achieve the nobility, the quest for moral and spiritual perfection, that Christianity held out as the guarantee of the soul's immortality.

Petrarch, like other humanists, was keenly alive to man's vulnerability to the vagaries of fate, and rather than focusing on how personal salvation might be achieved through solitary contemplation, he and his followers' interest lay in how, through the exercise of reason and virtuous government, humanity might be shielded from the vicissitudes of fortune and the unpredictable effects posed by natural forces. Civic order provided the necessary condition within which man might use the freedom, given out of God's love, to take responsibility for his actions and live his life for good or ill. Education would in turn provide the training that would equip Renaissance men to participate in building the civic order that would protect them from the vagaries of fate and allow them to live virtuous lives. With humanism we encounter 'celebrations of man's constructive capacities and of the dignity which raises him to ... the level of a dignity'.[11] Effectively, early humanists viewed man as having his fate in his own hands as he strives for the kind of perfection that was embodied in the life of Jesus.

It will be apparent that Renaissance humanist thought was as devoutly Christian as scholasticism. And yet, humanism operated very differently in that it historicised philosophy. Philosophy no longer dwelt in the placid and uniform calm of God's eternity, but had entered the time of 'man' with all its attendant unpredictabilities. Humanism placed 'man' at the centre of its inquiries in a way that became attentive to the changes to which he and his thinking has been subject through human history. In this way, Renaissance philosophy became 'swept up in the transience and mutability of human existence', concerning itself in a way quite unlike scholasticism with the more immediate concerns of daily life.[12] The destiny of man's soul was not to be determined by resignation to the prescriptions and prohibitions of priestly authority, but by active struggle for moral good amidst the threats and insecurities of this world.

An air of subjectivity

Humanists displayed in their writings a form of introspection that was largely absent from the work of the classical writers they so admired. Their writings exhibited a 'tendency to take seriously their own personal feelings and experiences, opinions and preferences'.[13] This 'air of subjectivity' was noted in the nineteenth century by Jacob Burckhardt, who observed that whereas medieval man was conscious of himself 'through some general category',[14] such as race, family or corporation, in Renaissance Italy he saw himself as a 'spiritual individual' who stood over and against a world which was regarded objectively. First announced in the mid-fourteenth century – according to some scholars – this subjective focus can be found in Petrarch's well-known redirection of the inquiring gaze. It is to be redirected from the outer, physical world to contemplation of the 'soul': *'We look about us for what is only to be found within'*.

It is tempting to see this tendency to introspection as the moment at which modern individualism and the idea of the modern self – the sovereign, self-constituting subject – came into being. However, there are important differences between Renaissance humanist self-understanding and the more confident self-awareness of the thinkers of the Enlightenment. Pre-modern humanists were acutely conscious of the wretchedness of man before forces beyond his control – fate, fortune, Nature – and of man's weakness, his puniness, before the might of the supernatural being who would eventually stand in judgement over him. They were vividly aware of their uncertain place within a divinely ordered cosmos, ultimate knowledge of which was beyond human understanding. They urged the claims of reason, but not to exalt man's capacity for control of his destiny. Rather than seeking to throw off the shackles of superstitious belief they committed reason to the exploration of how man, if he was to be free and achieve immortality, should behave in accordance with the will of God. Nevertheless, there is some truthfulness to the suggestion that the Renaissance saw a significant shift in humanity's sense of itself and its relation to the world. Arguably, this moved man away from that rootedness in a common culture which, it has been claimed, marked pre-modern societies. There was a shift in emphasis towards an idea of the individual human being as capable of making decisions and having ideas that were not entirely governed by tradition, that is, governed by fealty to some general, communal morality and worldview.

It might be argued that introspection was not something new. Earlier Christian confessional practices were also aimed at shaping individuals' interiorities, regulating their thoughts and feelings in accordance with Christian morality – which is to say, developing a Christian conscience. Augustine's *Confessions* would seem to be a prime example of such introspective engagement. There were also, as we saw, in Chapter 2, Hellenistic 'cultures of the self'. But there were differences too. See, for example, the later work of Michel Foucault who puts some distance between Christian and pagan practices, clarifying the difference between, for example, Stoic exercises designed to help the soul achieve self-mastery, and Christian practices designed to attach the subject to a project of neverending introspection in order to drive out the devil.[15]

What was different in humanist writing of an introspective nature was that, rather than seeking simple subjection to the precepts of a particular moral code, humanist self-culture was more discursive, anecdotal, more observant of the material world and its pleasing or troubling distractions. Humanist writing was conscious of the bonds of personal relationships and the transience of thought and feeling and it was more questioning of how faithfulness to the Christian ideal might be achieved. It may not be too extravagant a claim to say that the moral universe explored by Petrarch anticipated the sixteenth-century French essayist Michel de Montaigne's much stronger expressions of personal judgement. The introspection of early humanists like Petrarch and those who followed was not practised as an attempt to apply a moral code to personal thought and action but rather it was an exploration of how the individual soul might orientate itself to the good. It would seem, therefore, that Burckhardt's nineteenth-century depiction – of a Renaissance man who saw himself as separate from a world that he contemplated from within an enclosed subjectivity – was surely premature. That notion of the individual who stands apart from an observable reality, an objective reality – an *out-there* – awaited, as we shall see, a full development that took place through the scientific revolution of the seventeenth and eighteenth centuries. It followed the growth of capitalist economies and the philosophical humanism of the Enlightenment when it seemed that modern man saw that he must now free himself, not only from superstition, ignorance and tyranny, but also from the depredations of time and the natural constraints that were bearing down upon his existence.

Rhetoric and education

It would be untrue to say that during the Renaissance education reduced to the teaching of rhetoric, but it is certainly the case that humanist education attached extraordinary importance to the teaching of eloquent and persuasive language. Humanists had no suspicion of rhetoric – the deployment of language to shape an audience's thoughts and feelings in relation to some issue – as a morally dubious enterprise. In modernity, however, rhetoric has acquired pejorative connotations.

The modern antipathy towards rhetoric – 'empty rhetoric', language calculated to deceive by disguising its full meaning (or absence of real meaning) – no doubt originates in the Romantic[16] insistence on sincerity and authenticity in expression, the quest for the true voice of the individual soul uncontaminated by the corrupting moral compromises involved in day-to-day existence. This distaste has presumably been subsequently intensified by the way in which the modern critical gaze has laid bare the vast work of deception and manipulation – through language and image – undertaken by apparatuses of persuasion in advertising, the media and government. As we have seen, Renaissance humanist educators embraced the day-to-day and part of its scorn for scholasticism was based on what it saw as the latter's failure to address mundane reality. The philosopher Alasdair MacIntyre was to deplore the twentieth-century acceptance, as a matter of governmental pragmatism, that individuals and populations need to be influenced to think from premises that will ensure agreement with the governing agencies' prior conclusions.[17] This is the acceptance that agreement in moral judgement is to be secured by working on the emotions or attitudes of those who are seen as standing in need of government or control. The humanist educator certainly wanted to instruct his students in the methods that were effective in exerting control over potential listeners and readers. However, in doing so, he saw himself as acting quite rationally, in accordance with a universally shared moral philosophy which sought to attain, in the perspective of Christian faith, the virtuous society. He thus had no qualms about propagating the use of persuasive language. A command of the resources of rhetoric was a practical requirement if a politician, a philosopher, a teacher or, indeed, a poet or writer of fiction was to be effective in terms of the impact he – occasionally she – wanted to make on an audience. There was no embarrassment about using language to persuade people to think and act in ways that perhaps contradicted their existing beliefs and assumptions. For the Dutch priest and humanist Desiderius Erasmus, rhetoric enabled the orator or priest to manoeuvre his audience or congregation in the direction of God's truth. Martin Luther's stern Protestantism conceded the necessity of a training in rhetoric as a basic requirement of preparation for the priesthood. Indeed, it is argued that humanism took from Cicero the idea of the orator as cultural hero, defending justice and ethics.[18] The teaching of rhetoric had an elevated, indeed elevating, purpose – it was vital to the development of virtue, in that eloquence ('properly developed language') was the proof of humanity and 'a condition of social health'. Rhetoric displayed the nobility of the thought it conveyed, and virtuous life and conduct were considered to be impossible without it. Eloquence was language cleansed of the ignoble and was regarded as 'the most important accomplishment of man'.

The humanist curriculum which flourished in the classrooms of the grammar schools of the late sixteenth and early seventeenth centuries operated to a pedagogy which contained a number of distinctive features. Some of the schools used the textbooks on rhetoric and the teachers' manuals produced by humanist figures like Erasmus and Ramus, and they all used guides to letter-writing – a central focus which had been inherited from medieval rhetoric teaching. The texts read in the humanist classroom were taken from classical literature and the scriptures and were mined for what the school pupil could learn of grammar, style and structure. Such study combined rhetoric and dialectics, although the latter was yoked to the practical purposes of an education in the use of language rather than the scholastics' metaphysical inquiries. Students were required to keep commonplace books – dictionaries of quotations organised under subject headings – which could be drawn upon for their own compositions. They compiled lists of tropes – words and phrases used metaphorically to produce a striking image – and handbooks of proverbs and comparisons.

A more controversial practice was that of *imitatio*, the practice of emulating the writings of classical models, which was apparently not universally accepted. Slavish copying of models was condemned for narrowing vocabulary and expression, although the practice might have been of value when analysis of rhetorical models was accompanied by more inventive and challenging written outcomes, such as pupils producing writing in the same style but on a different topic.[19] Erasmus and the novelist and poet Francois Rabelais, both major humanist intellectuals, satirised the excesses of humanist pedagogy. Erasmus ridiculed the fashion for an exclusive focus on the writings of Cicero, considered to be one of Rome's greatest prose stylists, whilst Rabelais mocked the formulaic absurdities of humanism's oratorical style. If, as moderns, we feel inclined to ridicule the repetitive, didactic nature of humanist education, its apparent denial that the learner was bringing anything of usefulness to the classroom, its insistence on subjugation to authorities, its scant valuing of creativity, its apparent willingness to murder by dissection, we should perhaps recall that Shakespeare and Milton enjoyed the benefits of such an education (although Isaac Newton and the poet Shelley were amongst its less grateful recipients).

The humanist educational programme was essentially a training in reading and writing, a rigorous, exacting textual analysis aimed at providing the future leaders and the professionals of its society with valuable knowledge and intellectual discipline, as well as cultivating moral standards and aesthetic refinement. It survived, continuing its educational mission, into the early part of the twentieth century, only recently to be replaced by what one commentator loftily describes as 'less demanding forms of education'.[20] Emerging as a critique of scholasticism, a critique which celebrated the moral capacities of humanity and practical engagement with social matters, school-level Renaissance humanist education came eventually (and ironically) to be seen as the dry and dusty examination of texts whose relevance to the challenges of the modern world was not obvious and whose pedagogy was hostile to the innate creative capacities of learners. But humanism did not die. Rather it was transformed, one might say turbo-charged, by a period of intellectual, social and economic upheaval that stretched from the late sixteenth to the nineteenth century.

A descendent humanism

The descendent humanism that amounted to a shift in Western thought from top to bottom, from shifts in philosophy to shifts in common sense, is what has come to be known as liberal humanism. A range of factors have been adduced to account for the development of this idealist variant of humanism. It has been described as the self-serving, self-justifying ideology of the bourgeoisie (the property owning, wealthy class that emerged with the dynamic expansion of capitalism through the seventeenth, eighteenth and nineteenth centuries). Some have seen the disempowerment of monarchies, in particular England's execution of its king in 1649, as a crucial event, in which identities formed in subjection to a sovereign – identity subsumed within the monarch's identity – opened the way for the individual to understand himself as the author of his own history. A parallel and surely more decisive decentring was effected by the great scientific and technological advances of the age, which seemed to hold out the possibility that man was in control of his destiny. He no longer occupied a universe in which his fate was entirely in the hands of a supernatural being about whose purposes he needed to have regard, nor need he be entirely powerless before the assaults of Nature. The philosophies of Descartes and Locke (see Chapter 6) proposed the figure of the knowing, self-possessed individual, and the great idealist philosophical systems, such as those of Kant and Hegel, affirmed man's capacity to take hold of and shape his being (see Chapters 7–8). These latter, it is worth noting, were philosophies that, in contrast to medieval and Renaissance humanism, had, with occasional exceptions, little to say about how education or, indeed, the moral life of societies should be organised. They were, what have been called, university philosophies, and they rarely dipped a toe into the murky waters of everyday life. Nevertheless, in university and school, disciplines that stand in a line of descent from the *studia humanitatis* of the Renaissance continue to this day in that area of the curriculum known as the humanities – literary studies, history, philosophy, the arts and associated fields.

Liberal humanism clearly differed from its predecessor Renaissance humanism in all the respects mentioned above. The most profound difference between the two humanisms was with regard to their respective positions on the 'sovereignty' of the human subject. Liberal humanism asserts this 'sovereignty' in a way that differs radically from Renaissance humanist conceptions. A more assertive, liberal humanist definition of human sovereignty can be found, for example, in the writing of the twentieth-century humanist Ernst Cassirer.

In *An Essay on Man*, Cassirer wrote that '[h]uman culture taken as a whole [could] be described as the process of man's progressive self-liberation'. Following Schiller, he notes that this self-liberation was to be achieved 'through symbolic forms like language, art, religion and science'. For Cassirer, the biological limitations of 'life' are overcome by man's cultural creations – 'what is non-genetic in his being and gifts'. Man's capacity to symbolise, to represent reality through language, mathematics and the arts, frees him to produce 'enduring creations' which indeed have a material being, but also a spiritual content which transcends his 'physical soma' and which can endure after the perishing of man's material creations. Humanity's 'creative will and power', Cassirer argues, are embodied in man's work, in his speech, his religion and in all his 'forms of culture', and defy time and decay by continuing to produce effects upon cultural development through the ages, 'call[ing] forth ever new creations'.[21]

One can see here what might be taken as recurrent themes of this kind of idealism: an assertion of the superiority in human affairs of the cultural, the spiritual and the reflective over the biological, the contingent and the material; an urge to escape, to rise above embodied existence, its constraints and mutabilities; a drive to identify a reassuring continuity in human experience, a historical coherence (cultural productions become 'the "monuments", the symbols, of recognition and remembrance of human kind'[22]); an emancipatory faith in man's capacity to control his individual existence and his history; a conviction that man is engaged in a journey of ethical advance. And, as we shall see, it engendered the belief that interpretation can recover meaning from the symbolic forms that enshrine and yet conceal it.

With Cassirer, we encounter humanism of a particular kind. This humanism is yoked to what Foucault, after Heidegger, called anthropologism. This seeks 'to preserve, against all decentrings, the sovereignty of the subject'.[23] It takes 'man' as its 'starting-point in ... [its] attempts to reach the truth'. It insists on 'refer[ring] all knowledge back to the truths of man himself'.[24] This is the form of humanism that, according to Foucault, came into full being between the late eighteenth century and the earlier half of the twentieth century, and which governed philosophical thought during that period. Considered in this light a book like Cassirer's *The Logic of the Humanities* is a spirited and scholarly attempt to defend the figure of Man against scientific determinism and the reductions of empirical, positivist knowledges. It works towards a transcendental knowledge that surpasses the limits of what can be empirically known, hoping to 'penetrate to an understanding of the universal principles according to which man gives structure to his experience'.[25] It will be apparent that this is, considered against the earlier history of humanism, a strange outgrowth, a transmutation from a pragmatic to an idealist mode of thought.

The legacy of humanism

As we shall see in the following chapter, humanism continues to have a pervasive influence and its champions, some of whom echo the humanism of Erasmus, Montaigne and Rabelais are determinedly down to earth, reasonable and open-minded. Scientific enquiry – when it accounts for itself in the public arena – almost invariably adopts a language that is humanistic, a language that speaks of progress, of the advance of humanity's knowledge of itself and the universe and of man's successes in overcoming or ameliorating many of the effects of the adversities – disease, natural disaster, famine – that have besieged it throughout history.

The common sense of our age – at least in 'developed' countries like the United Kingdom – has tended to assume that humanity has embarked on a journey of betterment, of meaningful progress towards a future in which suffering, pain and cruelty are either eliminated or exceptional. And, of course, one of the most vocal expressions of progressive thought describes itself as humanist. This is the secular humanism that finds a militant form in the British Humanist Society which defines humanists as people who discount religious explanations of man's existence, who believe that the scientific method offers the only route to an understanding of the universe and that the exercise, in social and political life, of reason and 'humane' values can lead human beings towards a happier and more rewarding existence. Finally, with the United Nations' adoption in 1948 of the Universal Declaration of Human Rights, world governance has enshrined human rights as the inalienable property of all human beings, the embodiment in quasi-law of the universal moral principles that define humanity. The principles of dignity, liberty, equality and brotherhood generate a profusion of documentation, some of it statutory, designed to guarantee fundamental freedoms in relation to the individual, civil and political life, matters of conscience and religion, and cultural and economic rights. However sceptical one might be of the Declaration's claim to the universality of its system of rights, and its attempts to implant those rights by decree, it must be acknowledged, as Tony Davies has written, that:

> Some variety of humanism remains, on many occasions, the only available alternative to bigotry and persecution. The freedom to speak and write, to organise and campaign in defence of individual or collective interests, to protest and disobey: all the prospect of a world in which they will be secured, can only be articulated in humanist terms.[26]

Humanism is at present 'an inescapable horizon' that limits our notion of the possible. There are extensive critiques of what is involved in these manifestations of a surviving and influential humanism, for example in relation to the consequences of taking man as the starting point of attempts to reach truth, and critiques directed at the notion that somehow fundamental rights are 'inherent in all human beings'. Subsequent chapters will address such issues. This chapter will conclude with a brief reflection on humanism's need to invoke an 'other' against which it opposes and defines itself, and with observations concerning humanism's flexible political affiliations.

Humanism and the other

As Heidegger observed in his 'Letter on Humanism', anyone preparing to criticise humanism experiences a certain trepidation lest the reader think that the writer is going to argue for inhumanity – for barbarity and brutality.[27] The word humanism is freighted with a sense of the deepest and most precious values and to oppose it as an idea may seem a destructive and malign act. Heidegger's argument, however, is that questioning the concept opens up 'other vistas', different ways of conceiving what 'man' is in his essence. And this is one of the suspicions that has been expressed about humanism, that far from defining man in his full possibility, the term circumscribes, limits, what it is possible to think and say about humanity. It works to narrow what it is to be human.

Davies describes all humanisms as 'imperial', as speaking 'in the accents and the interests of a class, a sex, a "race"'.[28] All humanisms assert the universality of their values, even though a consideration of each humanism in its historical materiality reveals that they work in the interests of a particular fragment of a society, of a world, and that they identify and exclude from full humanity 'others' who, at various times and in various places, have included slaves, peasantries, women, those of a different religion or race and the uneducated. Erasmus, for example, is for many the greatest humanist and the educator who anticipated much of the pedagogy of progressive education. He believed that the 'children of commoners are human beings as much as those of royal family',[29] he opposed corporal punishment and urged that teaching should be observant of and respond to children's individual talents. He wanted the teacher to work through kindness and praise and to encourage play as a tool of learning. He thought that languages were best learned by using them, through speaking and listening, rather than by dinning grammatical rules into children's heads. He wanted to lift the mass of people out of ignorance and thus create a harmonious society in which all would become one and share freedom in Christ. Yet Erasmus also repeatedly expressed the conviction that those lacking in an education of his design would be 'less than human'.[30] It seems that here and with later humanisms, being human requires full compliance with a specific, strictly boundaried and policed system of thought and belief. To repeat, all humanisms are local, historically contingent, yet see themselves as embodying universal truths. All humanisms have others, often plural, who do not qualify as human and therefore fall outside the grace of God or the mercy of the civilised. It is worth pondering who the others of modern secular humanism might be.

Political associations

Medieval humanism was at times at odds with the dominant Aristotelian and scholastic culture of the period. It was a genuinely critical presence, a more or less tolerated irritant in the mainstream, and its criticisms of scholastic university education also embodied a social critique which sometimes placed humanists in difficult and dangerous positions. They could be accused of heresy and the dissemination of seditious ideas, for which they might be imprisoned, tortured and burnt at the stake. However, what is notable about the humanism of the later Renaissance and all subsequent humanisms is how comfortably they have sat with power, how adaptable they have been to the ruling dispensations of their times.

This claim, that Renaissance humanism was generally accommodating to power, seems perhaps to contradict a conventional impression of Renaissance humanists as an intellectual vanguard that brought about the destruction of a stifling, restrictive worldview – scholasticism. In this view, humanist innovations were designed to let the light of practical reason in on an enclosed, inflexible system of thought, and this was a liberating enterprise. There is truth in this conventional perspective. However, the historians Grafton and Jardine, humanist scholars themselves, contend in their somewhat heterodox book, *From Humanism to the Humanities*, that the Renaissance humanists' literary education, far from constituting 'the natural triumph of virtue over vice', achieved its success not by way of argument but because it produced a biddable subjectivity, 'a properly docile attitude towards authority'. Scholasticism, 'a system far better adapted to many of the traditional intellectual and practical needs of European society', offered talented members of the lower orders pathways to high office. And yet, its traditions of vigorous debate on issues of state and church governance were, they argue, ill-suited to a new Europe of the Counter-Reformation and a hardening Protestant orthodoxy, within which increasingly closed-off elites sought to limit and control political and social debate: '[S]cholasticism bred too independent an attitude to survive'. Humanist education, by contrast, furnished the powerful with 'an indelible cultural seal of superiority', providing a model of culture as given, something produced and owned by an elite, 'to be mastered, not questioned'.[31]

This is a severe judgement on Renaissance humanism, but it is not an isolated one. Indeed, one may detect in Grafton and Jardine's analysis commonalities with Marxist and sociological critiques of nineteenth- and twentieth-century liberal humanism. These criticisms are similar, in that they claimed that culture had been enshrined by humanism as cover for the iniquities of an unjust system of power, as a political sedative, and as an ideological naturalisation of class distinctions.

Liberal humanism: doing good in the world

In this chapter we contrasted an earlier Renaissance humanism to the liberal humanism of modernity. In Renaissance humanism we traced a form of self-understanding, a type of introspection, that was acutely conscious of the wretchedness of man before forces beyond his control, and of his weakness before the might of the supernatural being who would eventually stand in judgement over him. Renaissance humanists were vividly aware of their uncertain place within a divinely ordered cosmos. Their educational philosophy was a practical one, attempting to bring human affairs within the control of a civic order that would allow men to realise their virtues in a relatively controlled environment. By contrast, modern liberal humanism is, as we shall see in later chapters, far more optimistic, idealistic and assertive, when it comes to human potential.

If this chapter seems to have ended by sanctioning a negative judgement of the humanisms that it has described, it is in part because a version of humanism has, since the early modern period, been the ethical resource by means of which Western civilisation has justified its actions, its forms of government and its often violent contacts with other cultures and civilisations. It is the enlightened face that it presents to the world, a face that bespeaks a moral superiority. It invites critique precisely because it presents itself as a system of thought that is more purely rational and moral than any of the alternative ethical, philosophical or spiritual systems that exist in the world – and yet it has failed to restrain, has at times licensed, acts of national and international cruelty, exploitation, conquest and larceny. Under the banner of humanist values, Western powers have freely engaged in acts of inhumanity towards their own populations and those of other nationalities. In this, it might be pointed out, it is no different from other dominant belief systems throughout history which have proclaimed a moral right to deal violence to those who have thought or believed differently. However, it is doubtful that any other dominant system of thought has been quite as ready to portray its imperial enterprises as philanthropic projects. Where earlier imperialisms invaded, plundered and slaughtered because it would bring glory or wealth to their nations or because they wished to punish unruly populations, governments operating on a liberal humanist licence to invade, plunder and slaughter do so because they wish to bring civilisation to benighted lands, because they wish to confer the benefits of freedom, justice and the light of reason upon savage or benighted peoples. Liberal democracies claim that their violences are enacted for benevolent reasons – it is a way of doing good in the world.

Liberal humanism is the official value system of the so-called developed nations that still largely dominate global economics and politics and it is the system of values which, as citizens of the liberal democracies, we are obliged to live by. These factors alone make it necessary that we call it to account and submit it to critique. However, although liberal humanism does not always work as well as it claims, it would be foolish to ignore its achievements. Davies, we will recall, warns that it would be dangerous to 'abandon the ground occupied by the historical humanisms' since humanism often offers the only available bulwark against 'bigotry and persecution'.[32] Humanist values have been incorporated into law in many countries and the institutions that have been created to defend and promote the rights that humanism espouses – such as freedom of speech, equality before the law, freedom of expression, the freedom to associate with others, the right to political protest – are important and valuable achievements, for all that these institutions often struggle to assert and realise those values in opposing the various barbarisms that abound in the world. It is also the case that humanism, in concert with capitalism, delivered European societies from the bondage of dogmatic religious thought and the tyrannies of feudal society and, as Marx and Engels put it, in their paean to the achievements of the bourgeoisie, rescued whole segments of populations from 'the idiocy of rural life'.[33] Education has been a key instrument for transmitting the values and postulates of liberal humanism. As we shall see this has been a role and responsibility that has not only been touched by the higher goals of humanism but one that has also inherited its contradictions.

In the following two chapters we consider the developments in thought which may be seen as building on the Renaissance's innovations in terms of critical enquiry and on its fascination with the human self, its nature and capacities. It was, however, a period which saw the acceleration during the seventeenth century of the scientific insights that surfaced during the Renaissance, a period in which philosophy was obliged to confront the radically disturbing ontological implications of this new knowledge. This is the period that has come to be known as the Age of Enlightenment. The intellectual ferment that characterised the seventeenth and eighteenth centuries could not, we decided, be crammed into one chapter, so we have divided our account of the period of the Enlightenment and the inauguration of modernity into two parts. Chapter 6 describes the tension between the rationalist and empiricist views of the nature and powers of human reason through an examination of the ideas of two of the major thinkers of the seventeenth century, Rene Descartes and John Locke. Chapter 7 focuses on the eighteenth century and deals with David Hume's radically sceptical empiricism and the response – so influential on subsequent philosophy – that it incited from Immanuel Kant. Both chapters will offer a view of the implications of the philosophical turbulence that characterised Enlightenment thought.

6

Enlightenment and Modernity: Descartes and Locke

And new philosophy calls all in doubt,

The element of fire is quite put out,

The sun is lost, and th'earth, and no man's wit

Can well direct him where to look for it.

Tis all in pieces, all coherence gone

(John Donne, 1612)

The Enlightenment, enlightenment and modernity - a clarification

The terms enlightenment and modernity are often used interchangeably. The two terms are indeed interrelated and cover similar semantic fields. However, their casual identification can obscure, or indeed efface, points of distinctively different cultural and historical signification. We therefore open this chapter with brief explanations of what we mean when we use these terms here and in subsequent chapters.

The Enlightenment is a retrospectively defined period in the history of thought which is heavily identified with the ideas of eighteenth-century philosophers like John Locke, David Hume and Immanuel Kant, and French intellectuals like Voltaire, Jean-Jacques Rousseau and Denis Diderot. Such thinkers argued, with varying degrees of stridency, against the unreflecting acceptance of traditional authority and for the creation of a rational and just social system which honoured individual liberty. It is worth noting that this dominant view of the Enlightenment has been challenged by writers who locate its origins at an earlier date or who identify its essential character as quite different from conventional accounts. A striking example of this is Jonathan Israel's work on what he calls the Radical Enlightenment.[1] Israel argues that the central figure of the Enlightenment was the Dutch philosopher, Baruch Spinoza, whose argument that the potency of reason must be applied not only to scientific matters but also to human affairs led him to insist on the moral equality of all human beings and on republicanism and democracy as the only rational and just forms of government. Israel sees Locke, Hume, Voltaire and Kant as essentially wary of radical social and political change and he argues that conventional accounts of the period ignore the influence of Spinozan thought on figures, like Diderot, who have been under-regarded and whose intellectual activities were the real driving force behind the Enlightenment.

Enlightenment without the definite article refers to a way of thinking about human existence which was concerned with constructing forms of knowledge and a morality – based on an idea of the autonomous rational individual – that would produce a just and rational society. The thought of enlightenment did not spring spontaneously into being in the eighteenth century since elements of such thinking can be traced to earlier periods, but it was in the eighteenth century that it acquired the critical mass that led it to become the paradigmatic 'modern' mode of thought, a way of understanding human beings and the meanings and purposes of their lives that has been dominant into the present period, although we shall see that it is a mode of thought that has been questioned with increasing intensity since the twentieth century.

Modernity is a term that suggests a temporal change, an awareness of a historical shift in consciousness and the experience of individual and social being. It makes a statement about change and transition to a new way of ordering thought and understanding the nature of humanity's supposed destiny. Modernity is the period in which man sees himself casting off customary and superstitious belief and instead ordering his existence on the basis of reason modelled on the intellectual procedures of scientific enquiry. In its most vigorous stages, during the eighteenth and nineteenth centuries it was possessed by a notion of progression towards a system of knowledge that would offer a complete representation of objective reality, including the nature of man. If the late modern period that we inhabit has lost something of that confidence in progress to a final goal of complete rationality, it is still haunted by the prospect. Ideas of progress, social improvement and the gradual removal of obstacles to a fuller humanity still characterise modern thought. Modernity is the social, cultural and political project that embodies the goals of the Enlightenment.

The promise of Enlightenment

Modernity, then, marks a rupture, a radical division in history. This is a break, real or imagined, that separates all that is modern from all that came before. Modern thought stands at this moment in opposition to medieval – pre-scientific – understandings of the world, which it rejects as being too ready to believe what has been traditionally believed and too much governed by superstitious concerns. The 'modern' thought that was incubated during the Renaissance and assumed its distinctive form in the seventeenth and eighteenth centuries was marked by a resolve to resist habitual and traditional formulations. It intends to shine the brilliant light of reason upon the relation of human beings to their world. This is not a reason that seeks to discern the will of God, but one that brings the disinterested gaze of science to bear upon the question of humanity and its relation to the universe. It is a project of reason whose logic commits it to questioning every conventional understanding, every assumption about man and the cosmos, in order to comprehend the truths of human existence. It was a turn in thought that had the effect, at least amongst educated classes, of casting all in doubt, thus destroying the coherence of a world once ordered by religion and tradition.

Enlightenment thought was not however an enterprise of mere destruction. Most of the early thinkers of modernity were keenly aware of the potentially destabilising social and moral implications of their speculations and were content to situate their thinking about the emancipation of mankind within the frame of the decidedly undemocratic states in which they lived. They took upon themselves the daunting task of generating a new idea of how the world might be ordered out of the intellectual disarray and the possibilities for social disorder caused by the practices of critical thinking. The promise of modernity was that free of tradition and superstitious belief, humanity would achieve autonomy, finally becoming the master of its destiny. This is an idea that continues into the present to have a considerable hold on political, cultural and philosophic imaginations. It is an idea that has also had weighty consequences for education, charging universities with responsibility for producing the knowledge required to guide the formation of an enlightened society and burdening all levels of education and schooling with the task of forming the individuals required for such a society.

In this chapter we will consider some of the moments in thought that were decisive in forming the distinctively modern perspective from which, in large part, we continue today to see the world. The so-called Enlightenment project was never, of course, a planned or co-ordinated undertaking, but a trajectory in thought, a current that buoyed thinking which took radically different forms and worked to very different purposes. We shall see that the Enlightenment also, from its origins, carried within it the seed of a self-critique that has grown to a point where the central assumptions and goals of the enterprise have been tested near to destruction. What was at stake in the transition from what was essentially a medieval to a modern conception of the world is captured in Jonathan Swift's moral tale about the spider and the bee.

Doubting modernity: a parable

In 1704 Swift was busy lampooning the intellectual and social climate in which he found himself, a climate distinguished by what he saw as the rise of the 'Moderns'. Swift was particularly taken by their conceit, by what he viewed as their excessive pride and self-confidence. In a parable involving a spider and a bee, Swift contrasts the modern attitude, represented by the spider, to a more venerable attitude represented by the bee, which he identifies with the 'Ancients'.

The spider dwells upon a high shelf in a library paying little attention to the surrounding books. Having used them only as a support for his web, he has grown to a considerable size from the 'destruction of infinite numbers of flies, whose spoils lay scattered before the gates of his palace'.[2] After insulting the bee that accidentally destroyed part of his web, the bee replies with insults of his own. In his attack upon the spider, he defines the modern attitude: 'You boast indeed,' he says, 'of being obliged to no other creature but of drawing and spinning out all from yourself.' The problem with this self-resourced attitude, however, is that all the spider brings forth from himself is poison and dirt.[3] It is true that the spider displays great skill in architecture and mathematics, yet if you 'judge of the great genius or inventions of the Moderns by what they have produced, you will hardly have countenance to bear you out in boasting of either'. You Moderns, he says, may erect 'your schemes with as much method and skill as you please; yet if the materials be nothing but dirt, spun out of your own entrails ... the edifice will conclude at last in a cobweb'. This cobweb swiftly becomes forgotten in a corner, only to be replaced by the next modern scheme. As for the Ancients, they are content like the bee, 'to pretend to nothing of our own beyond our wings and our voice', remaining wilfully subservient to tradition.[4]

Both the spider and the bee in this parable are, of course, rough and ready (although, one might feel, apposite) metaphors for ideas that were already in currency in the late seventeenth and early eighteenth centuries. The bee is just as much a parody of the 'Ancients' as the spider is a parody of the 'Moderns'. Nevertheless, Swift's parable makes a point which has been levelled at Enlightenment thought up to the present day, in that his depiction of the spider is an attack on the arrogance of those who believe that the application of reason to human affairs must necessarily bring about a better – or a perfected – world. The modern attitude, here with Swift and in subsequent commentaries, comes under attack for its excessive faith in the human intellect; for its presumption that a stage has been reached in human history where 'man' is on the verge of coming to rule over himself and nature; by the idea that all problems can be solved with sufficient effort, that all mysteries are merely examples of ignorance and that all misfortune can (eventually) be prevented. The bee refuses to be duped by the spider's sense of self-importance, and insists that the spider be judged not by how he describes himself, but by what he has achieved. He is surrounded by waste, the bee observes, and his 'great' achievements are quickly forgotten as other webs are spun, only to gather dust themselves. His material wealth depends upon exploitation and suffering; he kills flies with poison, only in order to develop more poison to kill yet more flies. According to the bee, this is a futile endeavour without value; it is a pointlessly destructive activity designed only to resource more destruction. Retrospectively, we might say, this kind of doubt about the ultimate value of modern achievements has only intensified throughout the modern era. Modernity intermingles a seemingly unassailable confidence in human ingenuity and a basic and persistent doubt about the ultimate cost and value of all this 'progress'.

Scientific knowledge, scientific thought

The ideas that in their early stage caused John Donne to feel that the world had lost coherence and, in their fuller development prompted the unease of the deeply conservative Swift, were simmering in Donne's sixteenth century, and no doubt earlier. In the seventeenth century they were carried forward to a fruition that threatened the complete overthrow of traditional thinking. The eighteenth century was to see the culmination of what amounted to a transformation in humanity's understanding of how knowledge was to be acquired, how and for what purposes that knowledge might be used, and in its apprehension (in more than one sense of that word) of its place within a reordered universe. This was not an intellectual revolution conducted by a few great thinkers, but a process carried forward through fierce debate amongst the educated citizenry of the times. That debate, however, was shaped by the major contributions – philosophical and scientific, but also cultural and political – of many figures. In this chapter and the next we will refer to some of these thinkers but our account of the Enlightenment will be built around an examination of the writings of four philosophers whose ideas are often cited as the most influential in determining the directions and the contours of modern thought – the Frenchman René Descartes, the Englishman John Locke, the Scot David Hume and the German Immanuel Kant.

René Descartes

Doubting everything

Descartes lived from 1596 to 1650, his most important texts being published between 1637 and 1644. A notable characteristic of his thought is its refusal to begin from the ideas of earlier thinkers. His approach was summed up in a later work where he wrote of being 'obliged to write here as though I were treating a topic which no one before me had ever described'.[5] This resolve amounted to a rejection of scholasticism's reverence for philosophical tradition and its assumption that knowledge could be attained by way of a detailed, rigorous examination and clarification of the canonical texts of the past. This apparently minor decision to write as if in innocence of previous thought announced a departure from a literary–historical approach to the acquisition of knowledge in the direction of a scientific perspective. It had another significance. Descartes was conscious and wary of the personal hazard occasioned by displays of intellectual dissidence – he seems to have been keenly aware of his contemporary Galileo's treatment at the hands of the Catholic Inquisition – but his apparently purely methodological decision not to defer to the authority of thought that had been sanctioned by time (and, in effect, authority) may also be seen as a shrugging off of the intellectual ascendancy of Christian scholastic doctrine.

In his *Meditations on First Philosophy*, Descartes conducts an inspection of his own thoughts in order to determine what he may be able to identify as irreducibly true and certain knowledge of the world. His aim is to give the sciences firm metaphysical foundations, something which he believes has not been achieved hitherto. In part, Descartes' endeavour may be seen as stemming from a troubled recognition that the scientific discoveries of Copernicus, Galileo and others cannot be reconciled with the traditional Christian understanding of a cosmos ordered according to the will of a benevolent God. Along with such figures he was engaged in the final demolition of the medieval worldview and Descartes was clearly uneasy about the shattering effects of this new thinking on the reassuring assumption that human beings existed in a universe that had been constructed and maintained by a supreme being who loved humanity. Thus, as we shall see, Descartes, along with seminal thinkers of the time like Locke and Newton, was at pains to account for the place of God within the dizzying perspectives of the new order that was being mapped. Science offered exciting new possibilities, not least in reconfiguring the idea of man and what he might be and might do, but it also gave humanity a glimpse of a void, a chillingly impersonal universe quite unlike the anthropomorphic cosmos of the medieval world with its divine guarantee of meaningfulness. Considered in this context Descartes' philosophical masterwork, which might otherwise appear as an exercise in solipsism, emerges in its full urgency.

The *Meditations* are, then, not simply an exercise in consolatory philosophical introspection, an attempt to win for the lonely human self safe harbour within the intimidatingly vast and inhuman dimensions of the universe. Descartes' objective is to establish true and certain knowledge of the universe and humanity's place within it. This would involve the final demolition of the classical and medieval view of the cosmos. Science had not just shaken confidence in this model, but made it plain to educated people that this was not how the universe worked. Faced with the collapsing foundations of scholastic cosmology, Descartes offered a method of enquiry that he intended to enable the construction of certain, clear and distinct knowledge of the world – a physics – and a new metaphysics, a supporting structure accounting for the nature of the new reality described in physics.

Descartes' physical theory is largely set out in earlier works, principally in the *Rules for the Direction of Mind*, an unfinished treatise presenting his views on the correct method of scientific study, and *The World* which contained approval of Copernicus's idea that the earth moved around the sun and which was also an assault on the conception that things have a hidden and foundational substance which cannot be directly perceived (the scholastic theory of substances). Aware that in that same year Galileo had been summoned to appear before the Inquisition for endorsing 'heliocentrism', Descartes chose not to publish, although he rewrote *The World* toning down its offensiveness to traditional metaphysics and scholastic theory, and published it as a textbook in 1644. The *Rules* presents Descartes' reductionist theory of scientific procedure which argues that scientific enquiry should aim to reduce composite 'natures' or entities to the simplest natures in order to discover the fundamental properties of matter. (It will be seen that Cartesian reductionism shares commonalities with his philosophical method for arriving at clear and distinct knowledge). Cartesian physics aims to reduce phenomena or objects to their most basic parts, or particles, and thus to determine the universal properties of matter. In order to explain how these simple natures interact to form composite or more complex things, like pieces of wax, the human body or the universe, he formulated laws of motion by means of which he can account for the operation of the entire cosmos. The universe is thus explained in terms of the dimension of matter and the dimension of motion combining to form a perfect mechanical system.

In the First of his *Meditations*[6] Descartes sets out a project of conducting his reflections on the validity of his beliefs according to a method of doubt. He resolves to 'scrupulously withhold my assent from what is not fully certain [as much as from] what is blatantly false' and to 'attack the very principles that form the basis of all my former beliefs'. He does this in an attempt to arrive at knowledge that cannot be doubted and thus to 'construct something lasting and unshakeable in the sciences'. He begins by saying that what he has learned so far has been 'from or by means of the senses' but that he now realises that such knowledge can be unreliable because the senses can deceive. He concedes, however, that some things which seem beyond doubt are true on the evidence of the senses – that he is here sitting by a fire in a warm winter gown, handling some paper and that his hands, his body exist. Surely only a madman would doubt these things and – he concludes rather summarily – he is not a lunatic. He moves on to consider the possibility that he is dreaming. Yet the unreal things that he sees in dreams are evidently derived from real things and could not be formed except on the basis that these things – 'such as eyes, head, hands, and the rest of the body' – are real and exist. Even if these things are doubted there are, surely, more simple, universal realities that cannot be called into question, like 'bodily nature in general' and its extension (the dimensions of matter in space), and things like shape, quantity and the time and place in which they exist. Arithmetic, geometry and similar disciplines that deal with things at their most simple and general level contain truths that cannot be doubted. Awake or asleep, two and three always make five, a square always has four sides. However, Descartes then introduces the notion that God might have concocted the world as a dream or illusion that appears to humans as a reality or that God has willed it that he should be mistaken about even simple things such as the result when he adds two and three. If God can will it that he is sometimes deceived, then logical consistency suggests that it is likely that God can permit him to be 'perpetually deceived'. And if, as some people might believe, there is no all-powerful God to impose this deceit, it seems to Descartes that the obvious imperfections that lead him to misperceive the world must be so ingrained that it is likely that he is indeed constantly deluded. He admits that he has no answer to these arguments and the only course open to him is to doubt – systematically, rigorously – all that he once held to be true. He must break with his enslavement to that 'long experience and familiarity' with all that he saw as true – even if he denies those things which in all reason he holds as true – so that he might eventually arrive at a balanced assessment of 'the correct perception of things'. He will proceed, therefore, under the supposition that an evil spirit, 'supremely powerful and cunning', has undertaken to deceive him so that all that he thinks exists in the world is an illusion, 'traps [the evil spirit] has laid for my credulity'. He will consider himself as having no body and no senses, although falsely believing that he has these attributes. He will, however, resist giving his assent to anything false and will refuse the demonic deceiver in his attempts 'to impose upon me in any way'.

In the next five meditations Descartes develops themes that set the agenda for philosophy down to the present day. In the Second meditation he repeats his resolve to take the path of doubting everything until he discovers something certain or discovers that nothing is certain. He quickly concludes that a supremely powerful demon may deceive him as much as it wishes but it can never cause him to doubt his own existence 'as long as I think I am something'. He feels that he can be sure that whenever he utters or thinks the proposition, 'I am, I exist', that it must necessarily be true. He concedes that he does not yet know what this 'I' may be and that he must be careful not to relapse into thinking as the 'I' he once was. What he once believed himself to be was a body and a soul, but this certainty cannot be sustained in the face of the regimen of doubt he has implemented. He turns to a consideration of bodies in general – 'those things that are commonly thought to be more distinctly grasped than anything else'. He takes as an example a piece of wax. His senses seem to give him reliable knowledge of what it is, but if he holds it close to a fire it seems to change and all its properties – smell, colour, shape and so on – disappear or change. Yet the wax remains. He concludes that what this wax is cannot be apprehended by the senses or 'imagination', but only by the mind, by the intellect, which may be confused or 'clear and distinct' according to the degree of attention he gives to the object's properties. This returns him to his 'long-held opinion' that objects, bodies, are not perceived by touch or sight but because they may be understood, recognised by the intellect.

The Third Meditation reaffirms what Descartes knows to be certain – that he is 'a thinking thing', that 'modes of thinking ... exist inside me'. He is thus faced with a problem: how can he be certain of the existence of things distinct from himself? How can he escape from this imprisonment in the self to engage with what he can be certain are true things in an outside world? His solution is one that may seem unconvincing to many modern readers. He offers proofs of the existence of God whom he describes as 'an infinite, independent, supremely intelligent, supremely powerful substance, by which I myself and whatever else exists (if anything does exist) was created'. His first proof is based in the notion that men know they are imperfect but have in their minds an idea of supreme perfection. He argues that it is beyond the capacities of an imperfect being to produce such an idea of per-fection since 'a cause must contain as much reality as its effect'. This intriguing (some would say, distinctly strange) cause and effect principle has been subject to much criticism and it was pointed out almost immediately, in the Replies to the Meditations, solicited by Descartes from eminent thinkers of his time, that this proof contains a circular argument: God's existence is taken to guarantee clear and distinct perceptions, yet the proof of his existence relies on the exist-ence of clear and distinct perceptions. Descartes' second proof, presented in the Fifth Meditation, is a version of what has been called the ontological argument – that existence, as a perfection, cannot be detached from the notion of a supreme being whose essence is perfection. These notably similar proofs have appeared to many (but not all) commentators as unpersuasive, even facile, and from a modern secular viewpoint must appear as interesting more for historic than philosophical reasons. If, however, we consider Descartes' decidedly abstract definition of God as an infinite, supremely intelligent and powerful *substance*, we can see how his argument for the existence of a supreme being is necessary to establishing the possibility of scientific enquiry. His belief that he has demonstrated the existence of a benevolent God who does not deceive secures confidence in the existence of a rationally ordered exteriority that is susceptible to investigation through the intellect and, with due precaution, the senses. 'God' here is the necessary condi-tion, the 'substance', that serves the function of guaranteeing that there is an objective reality with which 'I', the thinking thing, can engage. Truths other than the single certainty that I exist, truths about the world – the cosmos, the universe, nature – can be discovered and an ordered, systematic representation of reality is made possible. This is not to suggest that Descartes was engaged in a blind-siding manoeuvre aimed at concealing his atheism. He was a conventionally religious man, although his intellectualised version of the deity offended other thinkers, such as the mathematician and philosopher Pascal and, perhaps surprisingly, Sir Isaac Newton.

As will have become obvious, Descartes' enquiries into the possibility of know-ing reality are predicated on a thoroughgoing separation of the mental and physical capacities of human beings. The Sixth Meditation takes up again his ideas about the division of mental and bodily faculties. It amounts to a dogged attempt to pin down the relationship (if there is indeed one) between the powers of intellection and the sensory experiences afforded by physical embodiment. The intention is to arrive at a final certainty that 'material things exist' and to identify how human beings might go about securing clear and distinct knowledge of the material world. He begins by saying that he knows that material things exist since he can clearly and distinctly perceive the objects of pure mathematics, but he remains troubled about the validity of the knowledge that he receives through the senses. He reiterates the unreliability of such knowledge although he does not wish to discount all that he learns from the senses. However, his essence lies in the fact that he is a thinking thing. The mind is distinct from the body and he states that he can exist without the body, which is to say that the soul can exist after the body has perished. The mind and body form a composite, but only the mind is capable of knowing truth and the separation of mind and body is evident in the fact, as he sees it, that the mind is indivisible whereas the body is evidently divisible. When he considers the mind, his understanding of himself as a thinking thing, he can identify no different parts – he understands himself, his essential self, his mind, as 'entirely one and complete', whereas the body can be mentally (and actually) divided into parts. Moreover, not only the faculty of sensory perception, but also those of willing and understanding can be classified as parts of the mind, since it is the mind that senses, wills and understands. The elevation of the mind above all corporeal or practical faculties could not be more clearly stated. Descartes concedes that the brain 'or perhaps only ... one small part of the brain' has an effect on the mind. The one small part is the location of 'common sense' (this is not what we commonly understand by the term, but in scholastic theory the faculty that connects and organises the perceptions of the five senses). Descartes concludes the Sixth Meditation with an excursion into physiology. He traces the route by which the sensation of pain is transmitted from the foot by way of the nerves, through the spinal cord to the brain, which 'gives a signal' to the mind to experience pain. He notes that the sensation of pain can be stimulated in the mind by 'one of the other parts through which the nerves run, or indeed in the brain itself'. The significance of this observation is that it demonstrates the liability to error of the composite of mind and body and the need for vigilance in assessing the evidence of the senses. More interestingly, it also marks the dissonance between the potentially imperfect information offered by bodily sensation and the scientific account of what actually occurs in the physiological process, the mechanism by means of which the experience of pain is transmitted to the brain. As such, it touches on a theme of present day analytic philosophy – the relationship (or conflict) between two rival conceptualisations of man: everyday 'folk' understanding of man and his place in the world (the manifest image) and the scientific image of man which claims to offer a complete account of the world and its operations as they really are.[7] This is an image of reality constituted by physical systems imperceptible to the everyday framework of understanding by means of which we negotiate the world.

Descartes' legacies

Descartes bequeathed a controversial legacy. He has been attacked for being a rationalist, a thinker who took too little account of experience, a philosopher who saw human beings as prisoners in their own heads. He has been accused of instantiating, or at least, kick-starting, the modern pathology of individualism, a view of the world that is damaging to the possibility of sociality and civility. His elevation of the mind as the supremely human substance is linked, particularly in a critique developed within continental philosophy, to a nostalgic humanism that falsely installs man as the sovereign subject of history. His rationalism and his insistence on the divide between the human intellect and the material world have been seen as inaugurating a catastrophic hubris concerning humanity's capacity for controlling human and natural worlds. His physics was quickly overturned by Leibniz and Newton, his scientific method put into question by empirical thinkers like Locke and Hume. Newton had contempt for the sloppiness of his experimental work. Indeed, some scientists today remain puzzled by the significance attached to Descartes by philosophers and historians of ideas. Later philosophers saw him as a naive realist who believed that the human intellect could directly engage with and report the truths of a non-human reality. As we shall see, this view of the relation between the human knower and the natural world was for most of the next three centuries after Descartes relegated to the status of an intellectual error, like geocentrism or scholastic theory. Some commentators believe his achievements are limited by his failure to break free of scholastic concepts. Others have argued that Leibniz and Newton were the real innovators of the seventeenth century and that Spinoza's thought was more radical and perhaps of more applicability to the times we live in.

The above charge sheet is not an exhaustive catalogue of Descartes' real or alleged deficiencies. He has not for some time been a fashionable philosopher, although there has recently been a revival of interest in his realist epistemology. Nevertheless, it can be argued that he is the single most significant figure in the development of modern thought in that he set the terms of philosophical debate – the key issues for enquiry – for almost all subsequent philosophy. He formulated, more systematically than earlier thinkers, an anthropocentric focus on the relationship between man and the cosmos. Where the emphasis had been on discerning and conforming to the revealed truth of the Godhead and the doctrines and interpretations authorised by the Church, Descartes made the decisive shift to a human perspective, to an understanding of being grounded in the rational autonomy of the human subject. Arguably, the emancipatory trajectory of Enlightenment thought was thereby launched. Although he was not himself a sceptic, his reductive method – the method of doubt – instituted a form of scepticism that has been crucially influential on intellectual enquiry and particularly on the quintessentially Western practice of critique. The various and differently inflected philosophies of mind and consciousness – from Kant to Husserl to Heidegger and the modern analytical philosophy of consciousness which draws on cognitive science – can be said to stand in a direct line of descent (or ascent) from the problems opened up by Descartes' mind–body dualism. Continental philosophy often quite explicitly traces its preoccupation with ideas of the self and subjectivity to Descartes' self-investigations. Critiques of reason from Kant down to the present day may be said to be based on the provocations of Cartesian thought. Although he did not participate in the debate, it may be claimed that the philosophical and scientific method that he espoused gave new life to thinking about the relative merits of theoretical and empirical enquiry.

This is not to say that Descartes was fully aware of the likely impacts of his thinking, nor that he was never mistaken in his speculations, but it is to say that he exposed problems that have since his time been central to philosophi-cal enquiry. We have not considered his contribution to mathematics but it was considerable. Perhaps his greatest achievement was that he articulated with clarity the thought that the universe, all its observable phenomena, was composed of a ubiquitous matter, particles whose interactions were governed by a few simple laws of motion. The supposedly immutable perfection of the medieval cosmos became a dynamic system susceptible to scientific investigation. As many com-mentators have said, Descartes passed on to (a less than grateful) Newton a physics that accounted for the structure, composition and interrelation of everything that could be observed on earth and in the heavens. Perhaps the distinctive quality of Descartes' philosophy, observable not in explicit statements but present in the scrupulous delicacy with which he clears a way for the scientific gaze through the thickets and snares of established thinking, is consciousness (no pun intended) of the cultural consequences of the scientific revolution to which he made such a significant contribution. There are also those who would see his determination to put everything – all thought, all that is held as knowledge – into doubt as an admirable starting point for philosophising.

Empiricism

Descartes' rationalism was soon energetically contested by thinkers who opposed what they took to be his idea that the truths of the world could be attained through philosophical reflection and that the reliability of evidence derived from sensory experience was doubtful. The history of ideas often divides late sixteenth to early eighteenth-century thought into two camps – the British empiricists like Bacon, Locke, Berkeley and Hume and the Continental rationalists like Descartes, Spinoza and Leibniz. This distinction has some usefulness in that it identifies observ-able and significant differences between two traditions of thought, differences which some would say have continued to the present day. A couple of caveats are required, however. The empiricist/rationalist distinction is retrospectively applied and none of the philosophers on either side would have thought of themselves as contouring their thought to the boundaries of either a rationalist or an empiricist 'school' or faction – in some cases, as we have seen with Descartes, they might have combined theoretical enquiry with 'experimentalism'. It is also the case that European thinkers like the eighteenth-century French political intellectuals Voltaire and Jean-Jacques Rousseau were deeply influenced by British empiricism and Sir Isaac Newton, the single greatest figure in British empiricism, was both a theoretician and an experimentalist.

We will now briefly consider what has been meant by 'empiricism' and the ways in which its method of enquiry differs from that of rationalist (or theoretical) reasoning before moving on to the philosophies of John Locke and David Hume, both of which questioned Descartes' understanding of how knowledge was acquired and, particularly in the case of Hume, undermined the notion that 'clear and certain' knowledge could ever be attained.

Empiricism is usually defined as the idea that all knowledge is derived from experience. The crude common sense view of what empiricism means has often been illustrated by an anecdote concerning the eighteenth-century essayist and critic Dr Samuel Johnson. He was asked by his friend and biographer, James Boswell, how he might refute Bishop Berkeley's 'immaterialist' philosophy, which denied the existence of matter. He responded by kicking a large stone and saying 'I refute it *thus*'. It will be apparent that this does not amount to a refutation since it does not engage critically with Berkeley's notion but simply dismisses it as ridiculous. However, Johnson's tetchy response does encapsulate an important feature of empirical thought – its conviction that knowledge of the world, the truth of things, is won through sensory experience rather than theoretical enquiry. The empiricism of philosophers like John Locke and David Hume rejects the notion that the human mind is innately equipped with *a priori* knowledge – innate concepts preceding experience and enabling the formulation of ideas. Locke saw the neonate mind as 'white paper' to be written on by experience. (Rationalists have pointed out that this presents a problem since it does not explain how ideas which lie beyond the realm of sensory experience, such as logical and mathematical concepts, can gain entry into human thinking.) A brief reflection on Descartes' insistence on the priority of intellection over experience will suggest why arguments between empiricists and rationalists (or empiricists and idealists) have been such a feature of philosophical debate down to the present day.

The distinctive feature of empirical thought is its application of inductive thinking to philosophical problems, induction being the inference of general laws from particular instances. The empiricist observes specific phenomena, notes recurring features – a pattern – and forms general conclusions or inferences which amount to an explanation or theory. Inductive reasoning stands in contrast to deductive reasoning which typically begins with a theory about the topic under study, predicts what the consequences of the theory might be and then makes observations to test the validity of the predictions and the theory. Deduction starts with theoretical speculation and moves towards observation of reality, whilst induction starts with what can be observed through the senses and moves towards general conclusions or theories. It should be noted, however, that some have pointed out that this is an overly tidy division of method which does not always survive the actualities of scientific and philosophical enquiry.

John Locke

Clearing the ground a little

John Locke's political thought, based around his formulation of social contract theory, stands as a significant, and still influential, contribution to liberal philosophy or doctrine. We will touch on these ideas in what follows, but for now we will focus on his account of how human beings acquire understanding of the world.

Locke is entirely resistant to the idea that human beings are born with *a priori* knowledge that enables them to make sense of the world (although he is put under challenge on this conviction when it comes to mathematical concepts). In Book I of his treatise *An Essay Concerning Human Understanding* he acknowledges that there are natural inborn faculties which operate as the means by which humans can acquire knowledge, but these, he says, do not amount to innate knowledge. They are simply the faculties of sense. In infancy, ideas – 'whatsoever is the object of the understanding when a man thinks' – are the first impressions imprinted on the mind by external things.[8] These impressions become, with familiarity, lodged in the memory and names become attached to them. He goes on to say that, although the greater part of our ideas come by way of experience or 'sensation', other necessary materials of thinking are provided by 'the internal operations of our minds perceived and reflected on by ourselves'.[9]

Reflection is the mind taking notice of its own operations 'and the manner of them, by reason whereof there come to be *ideas* of these operations in the understanding'.[10] Locke lists as examples of ideas produced in this way, perception, thinking, doubting, believing, reasoning, knowing and willing. He also includes under the heading of the mind's operations the 'passions' aroused by the ideas formed by the mind, such as 'the satisfaction or uneasiness arising from any thought'. Locke goes on to distinguish between simple and complex ideas. Simple ideas enter by the senses – a piece of ice, for example, produces the distinct ideas of hardness and coldness and these ideas are 'uncompounded', sufficient to themselves and resistant to further reduction into even more simple and basic ideas. More complex ideas may be formed by virtue of the understanding's 'power to repeat, compare and unite' simple ideas.[11] He offers as examples of complex ideas, 'beauty, gratitude, a man, an army, the universe', which – although compounded of 'various simple ideas' – may be summoned to thought as 'one entire thing, and signified by one name'.[12] The mind, although passive in its reception of simple ideas, has the power to exert 'several acts of its own' upon the ideas it receives; it can combine, compare and separate ideas one from another to form general ideas.

(A rationalist or, indeed, anyone interested in how the human individual acquires knowledge of the world, might observe that the notions of 'internal operations' and the mind's 'powers' are doing a lot of undisclosed work here in bringing the kinds of ideas Locke identifies to conscious understanding. These operations look suspiciously like innate rational capacities).

Locke makes the important observation that, with due respect to Descartes, man cannot invent a single idea that has not been given to him through his senses or by reflection. Just as in the material world man cannot fashion 'the least particle of matter',[13] but must work with what the world has given him, so in 'the intellectual world' he cannot make an idea that has not originated from sensory impressions or reflection on the ideas formed by such impressions.[14]

Locke's notion of the self is, as one would expect, intimately linked to his material-ist view of how human beings acquire knowledge of the world, although he somewhat warily treads a line between scientific materialism and conventional religious ideas about the immateriality of the soul. 'The body too goes to the making of man', he says, and it is the body that determines a man's consciousness.[15] Personhood or per-sonal identity is equated with the consciousness that ultimately derives from the individual's embodied experience – his sensory experience and his reflection on those experiences. The self is 'that conscious thinking thing'[16] which can unite the indi-vidual's past and present, conferring 'an internal infallible perception that we are',[17] that we exist as autonomous individuals, thus securing 'the sameness of the rational being'.[18] The self 'is a forensic term, appropriating actions and their merits and so belongs only to intelligent agents, capable of a law, and happiness and misery'.[19] The self – the conscious, thinking thing – 'owns all the actions of that thing as its own'.[20]

Locke's thinking about the self has been seen as a founding formulation of the classical liberal idea of the individual as an autonomous, self-possessed agent, a notion that underpins liberal (or capitalist) economic and political theory. The twentieth-century Canadian political philosopher and social scien-tist C.B. Macpherson identified Locke's ideas about the self, along with those of other seventeenth-century thinkers like Thomas Hobbes, as seeding the notion of the individual as the sovereign owner or proprietor of skills and capacities which could be traded on the open market.[21] This is the 'possessive individualism' that sees self-interest and a thirst for the accumulation of possessions as the essential components of human nature, an outlook that entails a diminution of the indi-vidual's responsibility to society. Macpherson's ideas are relevant today to debates in political and economic theory, but two points need to be made here. Firstly, Locke, although his thought clearly contributed to its development, would almost certainly have been horrified by the libertarian individualism of twentieth-century free market economics (he disapproved, for example, of the over-accumulation of personal property); and, secondly, the idea of the autonomous, self-governing subject became essential to more socially literate versions of liberalism and also to humanist socialism, as we shall see when we deal in more detail with the notion of the self-possessed autonomous self in later chapters.

Locke's empiricism, as we have seen, amounts to a rejection of the rationalism of philosophers like Descartes. Cartesian thought was confident in the powers of the human intellect to penetrate to the reality of 'things', to know the essential truths of all that exists in the universe and the laws that govern their relations. This is what is meant by Cartesian certainty – that the mind can formulate ideas about objects or entities which are true representations of those objects. Locke had a more modest view of what human reason was capable of. In part this could be attributed to the unavailability to him of a subsequently developed scientific knowledge concerning, as Locke understood it, the constitution and 'internal' relations of the particles of matter that form entities. He observes that 'our faculties are not fitted to penetrate into the internal fabric and real essences of bodies'.[22] Additionally, in Book III of *An Essay Concerning Human Understanding*, he devotes the final two chapters to the unreliability of words and in particular men's use of words, for expressing the truth. Words are merely the signs of our ideas and should not be taken 'for things themselves'.[23] Although he argues for rigour and precision in the use of language he recognises that imprecision, slippage in meaning and the possibility of wilful misuse (problems which he refers to as 'these *inconveniences*') are – whether it be in the rhetoric and disputation of the Scholastics or in the everyday exchanges of speech – inherent to language. The final chapter of Book III, for all that it is a call for clarity, accuracy and plain, uncomplicated communication through language, harbours a residual pessimism about the power of language to communicate or represent ideas – to penetrate to the absolute truth of things. Locke's thoughts about language articulate concerns that resurface as a major issue in twentieth-century philosophy.

It seems clear that even if Locke had been vouchsafed the findings of modern particle physics and general relativity, he would still have retained doubts about the human intellect's ability to discern the ultimate truths of the universe. In his tract on the education of young men he wrote:

> the works of nature are contrived by a wisdom, and operate by ways too far surpassing our faculties ... for us ever to be able to reduce them into a science.[24]

He was also an early representative of the distinctively modern kind of philosopher who cannot commit to the Cartesian idea of certain knowledge because he viewed ideas about reality as representations which needed to be judged as to their veracity – in Locke's case, judged on the basis of what our senses can make available to us. This activity of reflection or judgement, necessary as it is, stands between us and certain knowledge of the objective realm. In analytical philosophy, this has come to be known as 'the veil of perception' and has been much debated. Locke may thus be seen as positioned at that moment when Western thought began to question the reliability of ideas as mental representations of objects. This was the dilemma that Kant addressed and attempted to overcome in his *Critique of Pure Reason*, launching what Michel Foucault called the analytic of finitude, the distinctively modern investigation into the limits of man's ability to know the world and the possibility of transcending those limits. This 'analytic' has, in the view of many, dominated modern philosophy, for good or ill, as we shall see in Chapter 9.

Locke has been described as holding the middle ground between scepticism and rationalism, rejecting both and believing in the possibility of a limited, but nevertheless valuable and useful, knowledge of the universe of mind and matter. We will shortly encounter a much more vigorous scepticism in the empirical mode when we consider the philosophy of David Hume, but firstly we will consider Locke's ideas about education.

Virtue and a well-tempered soul

Locke's chief contribution to educational thought is not an intellectually rigorous treatment of the subject. It is in fact a manual of advice for the parents of male children born into the gentry, setting out what to do and what to avoid if such children are to be 'set right' for the calling of gentleman. Locke never married or had children but had had experience as a 'governor' or tutor. A good deal of *Some Thoughts Concerning Education* is given over to opinions that might strike the modern reader as quaintly old-codgerish. He warns against excessive tenderness and coddling (better that parents should instil respect and awe in their male offspring) and is concerned about children being encased in too tight clothing. He goes into considerable detail concerning the conduct and content of children's eating habits, favouring a plain diet and warning against over-eating, especially of meat. He is keen on cold baths, exposure to the open air, hard beds and keeping children away from the unpredictable and possibly unsuitable behaviour of servants. He reluctantly approves beating, but only in the case of 'obstinacy or rebellion', and the point of the punishment should be to produce shame in the child rather than to cause pain. He is dismissive of children's play, has little time for children writing poetry and thinks that learning to play a musical instrument takes up time that could be spent on more useful activity. He also writes at some length about the importance of parents establishing a regime within which their children 'go to stool regularly'.

However, Locke was decidedly not an advocate of education based on fear, privation and harsh discipline. He in fact urged a variant of the 'sympathetic' method that was formulated in greater practical depth in the nineteenth century by Christian educators. (This pedagogy was subsequently disseminated within a national system of popular education by politicians and bureaucrats concerned with schooling and 'gentling' the children of the potentially unruly urban populations of the Industrial Revolution, as we shall see in Chapter 11.)

Locke's thinking on education was driven by a concern with the production of virtue rather than academic learning and by a consciousness of the need to develop a ruling class that would ensure the welfare and prosperity of the nation. His aim was that education should serve the ancient purpose of subduing the passions so that reason might master natural inclinations (the 'native propensies') and guide the subject into the ways of virtue. Unlike many progressive educators Locke has no qualms about exerting authority. He is unembarrassed by the inequalities of power contained in the tutor–pupil relationship. The parents' or tutors' task – the task of education – is to bring about in young children 'a compliance and suppleness of their wills',[25] so that this conformity to adult authority 'will seem natural to them'. He urges parents:

> to observe your son's temper; and that, when he is under least restraint, in his play, and as he thinks out of your sight. See what are his predominate passions and prevailing inclinations.[26]

Like nineteenth-century pastoralist educators he saw play not only as a necessary break from study, but also as a pedagogical opportunity, since play, as an expression of liberty, was the condition in which children's real or natural characters were laid bare before the parent or tutor. Subsequent teaching and learning could be tailored to the particular disposition of the child. Moral deficiencies 'are not to be cur'd by rules, or a direct contest' and least of all by corporal punishment.[27] His counselling for gentleness and kindness in the teacher's treatment of children had a practical purpose in that 'rules' and 'contest' would be likely to build resistances to the acquisition of virtue and reinforce children's natural moral weaknesses. In essence, Locke proposed a moral–psychological approach to education, working on children's subjectivities, their passions, with the teacher, whether it be a tutor or parent acting as a moral exemplar whom the child would aspire to emulate. However, beyond this sort of moral management, he had firm opinions on how children might be led to a fuller knowledge of the world. He desired the tutor 'to raise in [the young gentleman] a love and esteem of knowledge; and to put him in the right way of knowing and improving himself when he has a mind to it'. Children 'are to be treated as rational creatures' and their ideas should be taken seriously, with parents and tutors engaging them in discussion:

> [A]nswer all his questions, and explain the matter he desires to know, so as to make them as much intelligible to him as suits the capacity of his age and knowledge. But confound not his understanding with explications or notions that are above it; or with the variety or number of things that are not to his present purpose. Mark what 'tis his mind aims at in the question, and not what words he expresses it in: and when you have informed and satisfied him in that, you shall see how his thoughts will enlarge themselves, and how by fit answers he may be led on farther than perhaps you could imagine.[28]

Locke suggests that the content of the curriculum – the subject knowledge that should be taught – should include the sciences, history, chronology and languages (the latter in moderation) but he is more concerned with furnishing the student with knowledge as to what is 'convenient and necessary to be known to a gentleman',[29] so that he may participate in conversation with other educated men, rather than with developing scholarly habits and interests. '[V]irtue and a well-tempered soul' are preferable to 'languages and sciences and all the other accomplishments of education'.[30]

It will be apparent that Locke's ideas about education are based on his anti-innatist belief that the newborn child offers a *tabula rasa* for society to write on. They also lay bare what is more muted in his philosophical writings, that man is a creature who will be governed by his appetites and desires, his natural inclinations, unless he is submitted to the control of reason. Rational understanding is not to be acquired by meditation on the conditions of knowledge. Rather reason is to be applied to the practical task of making man a more civilised creature. Significantly, he recommends that young men should read the legal theorists and political philosophers Hugo Grotius and Samuel von Pufendorf, whose writings on government and civil law are decidedly non-speculative and guided by the application of practical reason. They will thereby 'be instructed in the natural rights of men, and the original and foundations of society, and the duties resulting from thence'.[31] No urging here to engage with theory and philosophical conjecture. Such metaphysics as is necessary should be confined to the consideration of spiritual matters and led by reading of the bible. The truth of revelation needs to come before engagement with the truths of scientific discovery, 'the study of matter and body'.[32] The reader may recall Basil Bernstein's remark (Chapter 4), which relates to the trivium being a kind of inoculation against the dangerous, more theoretical knowledges of the quadrivium, in an effort to make Greek thought safe for Christianity. Reading Locke one has a sense of nervousness about his young gentlemen being exposed too soon to the more disturbing ideas thrown up by the scientific and philosophical revolution. The correct reading of the bible is a necessary protective armature for the young student.

Locke did not believe that humanity could come to a full and certain knowledge of the universe, but he did believe that such knowledge as we could acquire, about ourselves and the world, might be brought to bear upon the matter of improving humanity's lot. In his Epistle to the Reader which introduces *An Essay Concerning Human Understanding* he said that he aspired only to act as an 'under-labourer ... clearing the ground a little, and removing some of the rubbish that lies in the way to knowledge'.[33] He thought that knowledge could benefit man by giving us some control over nature and that the application of reason to human affairs could produce a more civilised and well-ordered society. Thus Locke, who has been described as a mitigated sceptic – rejecting the Cartesian conviction that human reason can attain to absolute knowledge of nature, but rejecting as well the sceptical claim that we can know nothing – might also be described as a mitigated optimist concerning human possibilities.

In the next chapter, the second part of our account of the Enlightenment and modernity, we will move on to the eighteenth century to consider the more radically sceptical philosophy of David Hume and the response it called forth from Immanuel Kant.

7

Enlightenment and Modernity: Hume and Kant

David Hume

There is something comforting about John Locke's philosophy, something reassuring. He is down-to-earth, has no time for speculative flights and appears to say that for most purposes the world is very much as it appears to us through our senses and although there are things which must elude our understanding this should not trouble us too much. He strongly endorses the idea of a deity who set the world in motion and who maintains, indeed guarantees, the order and harmonious operation of the universe in which humanity finds itself. When reading Locke a particular kind of reader (one like the present writer) is assailed by a set of impressions which resolve themselves into descriptive terms – bluff, no-nonsense, pragmatic, commonsense, even parochial – that one irresistibly associates with a certain stereotypical Englishness. Here is someone who thinks the world is pretty much as it is bound to be, but that it can be made better by the judicious application of good sense – no need to overthink problems and certainly no need for radical change. This kind of reader, assailed by such impressions, might then feel a little ashamed because they amount to an unfair caricature of Locke, an obviously kindly man who recognised the iniquities of this world and wanted to see society operate on more liberal principles, a man who, indeed, argued that revolution was in some circumstances legitimate. Nevertheless, one is left with a sense that Locke's thinking is, to turn a phrase, philosophical empiricism with the handbrake on. A very different kind of empiricism is to be found in the writings of the eighteenth-century philosopher David Hume, a Scot, something which may or may not be significant. Hume is often described as the most important philosopher to have written in English and his is a philosophy which allows free rein to the scepticism that is inherent to the empirical cast of mind.

An anatomy of the mind

Hume, like Locke, firmly believed that humankind could know nothing beyond what can be experienced through the senses. He was opposed to any form of hypothetical thinking which claimed to penetrate to the allegedly deeper truths concerning the world and human nature. In his view a regrettable consequence of this kind of thought was that it based conclusions about human nature on speculation that was no more than guesswork about the nature of reality and the knowledge that human beings might aspire to. Knowledge, whether of this fanciful sort, or knowledge that had a more credible claim to offer an accurate representation of the world, had implications concerning the ways in which humankind should conduct its affairs. Referring to himself in the third person he confides the 'delicate satisfaction' he, the writer, derives

> from the free confession of his ignorance, and from his prudence in avoiding that error, into which so many have fallen, of imposing their conjectures and hypotheses on the world for the most certain principles.[1]

Arguments about whether Hume was an atheist, an agnostic or some kind of qualified theist continue to this day, but what seems clear is that there is no place in his philosophy for a supreme, all-knowing being around whose existence questions about human nature and the conduct of human affairs had necessarily to be organised. Hume's thinking – about how human nature was constituted, what humankind might know about the universe and his ideas about morality – is conducted without reference to God. Hume, as a philosophical naturalist, rejected the idea that we can usefully access realities above or beyond those of nature and the physical laws that govern the universe. He aimed to bring the scientific gaze and its procedural rigour to the task of devising a 'moral' philosophy, on the model of Newton's natural science. Hume applied the term 'moral' not just to ethical matters but to everything that went to make up the nature of human beings. He set out to construct an empirical science of human nature, 'explaining all effects from the simplest and fewest causes'.[2] Thus, he eschewed *a priori* assumptions about innate human capacities, relying instead on facts and observations. He accepted limits to human reason and understanding, desiring to establish what our faculties enabled us to address and what was beyond their scope:

> 'tis still certain that we cannot go beyond experience; and any hypothesis, that pretends to discover the ultimate original qualities of human nature, ought at first to be rejected as presumptuous and chimerical.[3]

In *A Treatise of Human Nature*, he alludes to the successes of anatomists whose dissections have revealed the structures and operations of human and animal bodies and announces his project as 'apply[ing] this method of enquiry, which is found so just and useful in reasonings concerning the body, to our present anatomy of the mind, and see[ing] what discoveries we can make by it'.[4]

Impressions and ideas

Book I of the *Treatise* examines how the human mind produces understanding. Hume divides the perceptions of the human mind – its contents – into *impressions* and *ideas*. Impressions are those perceptions 'which enter with the most force and violence' into the mind; they include what he calls our sensations, passions and emotions. Ideas, the essential units of thinking and reasoning, are the 'faint images' of impressions.[5] Hume further divides impressions into two kinds – impressions of sensation, which are originary and have 'unknown causes',[6] and impressions of reflection, which are derived from ideas: the mind takes 'a copy' of the original impression, forming an idea and this idea, 'return[ing] upon the soul', produces an impression 'of desire and aversion, hope and fear' which is the impression of reflection. These are in their turn copied by the mind and become ideas which may trigger further impressions and ideas.[7] Hume identifies two 'faculties' by means of which the mind can recall ideas to consciousness – memory and the imagination. Memory is closest to the vividness of the original impression, preserving it in something like its original form, whilst the imagination, which deals in pure ideas, may 'transpose and change' those ideas, producing, if it wishes, winged horses, dragons and giants.[8] We see, then, that in Hume's analysis, all ideas are copies of original impressions or they are put together from ideas that are copies of impressions.

Hume emphasises that ideas and impressions do not just come to us in entirely random ways but that there are principles governing their appearance in our minds. The force governing and ordering our thinking is *association*. Association is a natural endowment, 'a gentle force', which usually ensures that ideas connect with one another in a coherent way. There are three associative principles: *resemblance* (similar ideas running easily together), *contiguity* in time or place (the tendency to link ideas on the basis that they occurred at about the same time or are closely spatially situated), and *cause* and *effect*. Of these relations, causation is the strongest[9] and the only one which can take our thinking beyond our senses, 'inform[ing] us of existences and objects, which we do not see or feel'.[10] However, the principle of cause and effect, so important to our reasoning, is not the product of reason itself. Every causal inference depends on the associative principles which are 'natural' and can be traced ultimately to some sensory impressions. Hume gives as an example of how ideas are always dependent upon some original impression, the belief that Caesar was killed on the Ides of March. He traces the 'characters or letters' that signify this occurrence, down through the chain of testimonies of historians to the witness of those present at this event, the 'spectators' whose perceptions are the necessary fixed point which sustains the chain of reasoning and give it authority. This authority for belief or evidence, or for the validity of reasoning itself, derives from some event which was observed, taken in by the senses. Thus, 'all reasonings concerning causes and effects are originally deriv'd from some impression'.[11] He goes on to argue that philosophers have mistakenly looked for some power or force, 'that quality which makes [causes] be follow'd by their effects'.[12] However, all such efforts are chimerical since all we can perceive is the 'constant conjunction' of cause and effect. Hume's detraction of reason is spelt out in his assertion of two 'very obvious' principles: that 'reason alone can never give rise to an original idea' and that it alone, without reference to experience, can never convince us of a necessary connection between cause and effect.[13]

Book I of the *Treatise* is a relentless assault on conjectural thought – 'hypothetical arguments, or reasoning upon a supposition'[14] – during which he examines and refutes every claim for the existence and operation of any productive powers in nature or in thought which lie outside, beyond or above what can ultimately be traced to sensory experience. Reason cannot give a satisfactory answer to the question why we should, observing the constant conjunction of two objects, 'extend that experience beyond those particular instances' to infer a relation of cause and effect between them. Reason cannot identify a 'power'[15] or force that animates such a relation; it is custom, the frequent contiguity of objects, which 'determines the imagination' to infer a connection.[16] Human beings have a natural tendency to anticipate the same outcome and our beliefs are formed, not by way of rational deduction, but as the result of an instinctive, automatic 'propensity'.[17] Thus, the notion that one kind of event is always and necessarily connected to another is something that is located within ourselves and not in the objects themselves or in our ideas of cause and effect.

Hume's uncompromising naturalism concerning causation appears to lay waste to the claims of rationalist–metaphysical thought, by saying that human reason does not exist and operate in some realm distinct from or above the experience given to us by our senses, nor can it produce any new idea or belief – it is limited to a mediating role between the evidence presented to us by our senses and the formation of our beliefs about the world. Reason sets out the evidence of previous experience – and the ideas so produced – for comparison with new evidence presented, so that a belief may be confirmed or challenged. (To repeat, what is key here is that reason cannot produce a belief; a belief can only be generated by feeling or sentiment, which is to say the emotional–psychological predisposition of any individual.) However, if Hume's sceptical empiricism clips the wings of speculative ontology, it also has worrying implications for scientific reasoning itself, that is to say, for the method of inductive reasoning that Hume employs. In the Humean sense, induction, 'the experimental method', consists in reasoning from the previously observed behaviour of objects to their behaviour when unobserved. Put differently, it is prediction or inference on the basis that '[t]he same cause always produces the same effect, and the same effect never arises but from the same cause'. He goes on to say that '[t]his principle we derive from experience, and is the source of most of our philosophical reasonings'.[18] Indeed, as we have seen, faith in such an assumption underlies Hume's experimental method, which is to say the scientific method that Hume himself employs in his philosophising. This approach depends on the belief that things will continue to be as they have been in the past – effectively, that nature will always be uniform, its laws always the same, with similar causes always producing similar effects – but this is an argument that cannot be proved inductively since one would be assuming an effect or outcome about what remains to be proved.

Hume seems relatively untroubled by this dilemma – that belief in causation cannot be supported rationally – and is content to carry on with his enquiries according to the methods of inductive reasoning. In fact, in his *Enquiry Concerning Human Understanding* he compounds the offence to reason by saying that causal inference, which is 'essential to the subsistence of all creatures' is an 'instinct or mechanical tendency' implanted by nature and that we must remain ignorant of the powers that operate in cause and effect.[19]

A voluminous literature has been produced on Hume's problem of induction, discussing whether he was really resigned to the notion that the principle of cause and effect could not be rationally supported; whether, in relation to the powers of reason, he was an uncompromising or more conditional sceptic, or, indeed, a sceptic of any hue. It has been argued that, lacking the conceptual armoury developed by twentieth-century philosophy, he was not equipped to fully understand the notion of induction (a term which, by the way, he never employed). Analytic philosophy, committed to finally establishing certainty in the matter, has produced acreages of meticulous reasoning concerning Hume and induction, an enterprise that, in its subtle gradations of meaning and its effort after refinement, would not have shamed the scholastics. It remains the case, however, that Hume's naturalistic empiricism, so positive in its contribution to later, particularly Anglo-American, philosophy, presents perhaps unresolvable problems to philosophy understood as enquiry into the truth and the nature of reality. Hume's impact may be summed up as follows.

He relegates reason to a service role within an otherwise naturally determined process of knowledge acquisition. He demonstrates, persuasively, that it is the passions (emotions, desires, feelings) which govern our thought of cause and effect – the essential motor of everyday thought and of scientific and, in his view, philosophical enquiry. Causal inference is an instinctive, mechanical 'tendency' which cannot be attributed to rational thought. Reason's scope and power are severely contracted – on its own it 'can never produce any action, or give rise to volition'; reason 'is, and ought only to be the slave of the passions, and can never pretend to any other office than to serve and obey them'.[20] Hume extends his scepticism to the notion of the self. Contrary to Locke, Hume had real doubts about the human sense of personal identity:

> For my part, when I enter most intimately into what I call *myself*, I always stumble on some particular perception or other, of heat or cold, light or shade, love or hatred, pain or pleasure. I never can catch *myself* at any time without a perception, and never can observe anything but the perception.[21]

He describes the self as

> a bundle or collection of different perceptions, which succeed each other with inconceivable rapidity ... in a perpetual flux and movement.[22]

As we have seen Hume insists that there can be no idea that does not derive from some impression and since identity cannot be linked to any of our actual impressions it is a fiction. It is merely a relation imposed by the imagination, creating a sense of a self unified over time where there would otherwise be an incoherent series of impressions. It is memory that enables the imagination's work in 'discovering' personal identity by pointing to relations of resemblance and cause and effect among our perceptions. The self is a notion that is necessary to human subsistence, but it cannot be grounded philosophically. So much for Descartes' identification of the self as the anchor point of philosophy. In a remarkable anticipation of the considerations of some twentieth-century, language-based philosophies, Hume states that personal identity is best regarded as a 'grammatical' problem rather than a philosophical one.[23]

Hume's rebuke of rationalism echoes down to the present, but his conclusions had no more significant impact than their effect on a contemporary, the German philosopher, Immanuel Kant, who, it seems, was so disconcerted – or stimulated – by Hume's ideas (he credited Hume with awakening him from a 'dogmatic slumber') that he published nothing for eleven years as he thought his way through the problems set by the discordance between the ideas of Hume and those of rationalist philosophers like Descartes and Leibniz. In the next section we will consider the transcendental philosophy of Kant, an endeavour that is often cited as the most original and influential body of philosophical work since that of the Ancient Greeks.

Immanuel Kant

Kant's endeavour was to make sense of the divide between rationalism and empiricism, to effect a synthesis of the two competing conceptualisations. He recognised the strengths of the empiricist case but thought that reason had a far more significant role in constructing human understanding than empiricism allowed. In his three Critiques (*of Pure Reason, of Practical Reason* and *of the Power of Judgement*) he set out to establish a new epistemology – explaining how the mind structures experience to produce knowledge – and a new metaphysics – a 'speculative science'[24] concerning itself with the ultimate nature of reality and the relation between a mind-independent reality and the human intellect and human morality. We shall see that Kant's metaphysics also addresses the limits of human reason in apprehending the world as it exists in itself. We will focus on the first of the Critiques, the *Critique of Pure Reason* (*CPR*), although we will make reference to his thinking as expressed in other texts.

Kant and the project of Enlightenment

The background to Kant's Critiques is the prodigious success of scientific discovery in sixteenth and seventeenth-century Western societies. Newton's astonishing account of a systematically ordered, law-governed universe invited confidence in the powers of human reason to control nature and bring about a rationally ordered society free of the ignorance, superstitions and corrupting effects of power that had constrained and disfigured human life throughout history. This was the project, as it was later termed, of Enlightenment. Humankind was to emancipate itself from its immemorial state of servitude, its immature reliance on its rulers to do its thinking, and thus assume intellectual and moral autonomy. However, Kant was faced with a problem in that scientific reason had indicated a universe that operated like a machine, programmed (predetermined) to function in the way it did. There seemed to be no room for freedom, for human autonomy, and none for that vital spark of humanity, the soul. Some of the anxiety attending this revolutionary scientific discovery may be observed in the remark of Blaise Pascal, the French mathematician and theologically inclined philosopher, that 'the eternal silence of these infinite spaces frightens me'. The universe was no longer arranged in a comforting anthropocentric way, overseen by a loving, paternalistic God, but had acquired a vastness that intimidated thought as much as it excited wonder. In his preface to the first edition of the *CPR* Kant had been unequivocal in his statement of the consequences for established religion and power if they sought to escape the scouring light of reason. 'Our age', he said, 'is the age of criticism' and religion and 'the authority of legislation' cannot be exempt from 'the test of a free and public examination' if they are to retain respect.[25] However, it seemed possible that the free use of reason – enlightenment – would lead to the obliteration of traditional morality and the social anchoring that came with a belief in God. Kant, like other thinkers of the time, was wary of the 'scandal' that was sure to be provoked by 'metaphysical controversies' and the impact upon 'the masses' of any 'perversion of … doctrines'. If metaphysical philosophy was to be saved from unwittingly producing the evils of 'Materialism, Fatalism, Atheism, Freethinking, Fanaticism, and Superstition' (and made safe for public consumption) it was vital that the rights, the just scope and limitations, of reason 'be established on a firm basis'.[26] The task Kant undertook was to construct a new science of metaphysics which would demonstrate the harmony of natural science and traditional morality and religion. Kant intended to justify the claims of reason and to defend the Enlightenment vision of the rational, just social order that would be brought about once human beings took responsibility for their own destiny.

The 'a priori'

In the *Critique of Pure Reason* Kant set out to reveal how it was possible for human understanding to correspond to things themselves, how certain principles of reason could produce intellectual representations that agreed with a reality that was independent of human consciousness. Kant's project was clearly shaped in response to the problems set by David Hume. The latter's flat refusal of the idea that reason might function in a supersensible realm beyond experience and his conclusion that the human mind was not equipped to penetrate to the true nature of reality set a challenge that Kant met by offering a critique of reason itself, an enquiry into the scope and powers of reason and the limitations it must recognise. He states bluntly in his introduction to the CPR

> that certain of our knowledge rises completely above the sphere of all possible experience, and by means of concepts, to which there exists in the whole extent of experience no corresponding object, seem [sic] to extend the range of our judgments beyond its bounds.[27]

However, Kant does not, as we shall see, argue for the existence of a transcendent reason that floats free of experience to confront an unmediated reality. His vindication of reason relies instead on the idea that what enables us to both construct our experience intelligibly and to think and know beyond the limits of experience are certain conceptual categories that are given to us *a priori* – innately and before all experience.

Kant argued that objects are given to the mind, enabling it to 'receive' representations, by way of sensibility (or sensation) which 'alone furnishes us with intuitions' which are then 'thought' by the understanding,[28] giving rise to concepts. Thus, all thought relates directly or indirectly to intuitions and before that to sensibility. However, if the empirical 'appearances' of sensation are to acquire form, if they are to be 'arranged under certain relations' that enable thought – conceptualisation – such a 'pure form of sensible intuition' must exist in the mind *a priori*. If everything that belongs to sensation is stripped away from the understanding what we are left with are two 'pure forms of sensible intuition', two principles of knowledge that are given *a priori* – space and time.

Space is not an empirical concept derived from external experience. If we are to represent objects in space as outside ourselves, sometimes next to each other and sometimes in separate places, this can only be managed through an antecedent, *a priori* representation, or idea of space, which 'already exist[s] as a foundation'.[29] In a similar way, time is also not an empirical concept since without this fundamental representation, or idea of time, we would not be able to represent things existing together at the same time or at different times.[30] The principles or rules related to time 'instruct us concerning experience', so that axioms such as:

> 'Time has only one dimension', 'Different times are not co-existent but successive' (as different spaces are not successive but co-existent). These principles cannot be derived from experience, for it would give neither strict universality, nor apodeictic[31] certainty. We should only be able to say 'So common experience teaches us', but not it must be so.[32]

These innate forms of sensible intuition underlie our ability to structure and order experience, to come to an understanding of the world. They are (clearly) not empirical, nor are they concepts. They are simply the means by which the world appears to us in an ordered, systematic way.

Kant deepens his account of *a priori* intuition when he considers the 'manifold' contained in the *a priori* forms of space and time. The manifold consists of the entirety of the sensory intuitions presented in space and time which must be *synthesised* – joined together and organised – so as to produce meaningful and useable knowledge. He defines synthesis as 'the process of joining different representations to each other, and of comprehending their multiplicity in one act of knowledge'.[33] Synthesis is not a calculated activity of the mind:

> Synthesis, generally speaking, is ... the mere operation of the imagination - a blind but indispensable function of the soul, without which we should have no knowledge whatever, but of the working of which we are seldom even conscious.[34]

But if the process of synthesis is to produce knowledge, if it is to bring about a unified conceptualisation of an object, it must be submitted to what Kant calls the 'pure concepts of the understanding'.[35] These are the 'categories', the concepts belonging to the understanding *a priori*. Kant identifies twelve such categories, dividing them into four groups: Quantity, Quality, Relation and Modality. These are the concepts according to which acts of synthesis conform, the rules which make cognition possible.[36]

Kant's thesis was and remains controversial. What he says is that entities that are independent of the human mind, things in themselves, can only be experienced by human beings as appearances and not in their immediate reality:

> We have intended, then, to say, that all our intuition is nothing but the representation of appearances; that the things that we intuit are not in themselves the same as our representations of them in intuition, nor are their relations so constituted as they appear to us; and that if we take away the subject, or even only the subjective constitution of our senses in general, then not only the nature and relations of objects in space and time, but even space and time themselves disappear; and that,

these, as appearances, cannot exist in themselves, but only in us. What may be the nature of objects considered as things in themselves and without reference to the receptivity of our sensibility is quite unknown to us. We know nothing more than our own mode of perceiving them, which is peculiar to us, and which, though not of necessity pertaining to every being, does so to human beings.[37]

Kant places a severe restriction on human understanding, but at the same time confers upon it extraordinary powers: human reason constitutes the only world that we can know. It is important to recognise that Kant is not saying that there is no objective reality existing independently of the human mind. It is simply that we cannot have direct, unmediated experience of it. In the preface to the second edition of the *CPR* he writes:

The estimate of our rational knowledge *a priori* at which we arrive is that it has only to do with appearances, and that things in themselves, while real in themselves are nothing to us.[38]

It will be apparent that Kant adopts a strongly subjectivist position on the relation between humanity and the world; human subjectivity constructs our knowledge of external reality (and, in some sense, constructs the objective realm of things in themselves) which, for us, can only exist as appearances. Argument continues to this day concerning the validity and coherence of Kant's ideas about the constitution of human cognition and the division he imposes between mind and world, but what is clear is that his analysis offers the necessary grounding for his belief in the social and historical necessity of human autonomy and the possibility of freedom. 'God, Freedom and Immortality' are placed firmly in the realm of things in themselves, removing them from the kind of critical examination that pertains only to 'the objects of possible experience'.[39] Science, because it is limited to appearances, is unable to threaten faith or the condition of freedom required for moral autonomy.

Kant's philosophy is systematic in that his ideas about epistemology and metaphysics, about ethics and about aesthetics and teleology are bound together by the same essential principles. In truth, it is his thinking about the conditions of possibility for knowledge, expressed in his greatest work, the *CPR*, which governs his conclusions in the two subsequent Critiques. In what follows we will consider how the fundamental conclusions contained in the *CPR* play out in terms of his ideas about the self, morality and his political thinking.

The autonomous self and the legislation of nature

At first glance Kant's thinking about the constitution of the self, what he calls self-consciousness, appears somewhat insubstantial, not possessing the heft required for the heavy work he builds into his notion of human autonomy. For he defines it as occurring in our mind's work in 'join[ing] one representation to another' and thus being conscious of their synthesis:

> I am, therefore, conscious of my identical self, in relation to all the variety of my representations given to me in an intuition, because I call all of them my representations.[40]

What this means is that the mind doesn't, as Locke thought, carry around something that we call consciousness which informs the representations I make of the varied experiences I encounter in life, thereby conferring a sense of an unchanging self, a personal identity that threads across and threads together – as belonging to me – the various experiences I have. Rather, consciousness of myself arises from an awareness of the mind operating in a consistent way. The sense of an 'I' that persists across the variety of my experiences is an effect of the synthesising process by which the *a priori* concepts of the understanding produce cognition. We see, then, that this 'identical self' and its autonomy are firmly grounded in and guaranteed by the *a priori* concepts – the categories, the pure concepts of understanding. What may seem a flimsy notion of self-consciousness actually proclaims the sovereign power of the moral subject, the autonomous individual who 'is subject to no other laws than those he gives himself',[41] engaging with other such subjects who are his moral equals. The sense of a self is something that is constructed by the human cognitive faculties and not something granted by some general consciousness that hovers around the different 'actions', as Locke calls them, that I undertake. This is a self, a moral subject, fit to carry out the work of freedom Kant prescribes as the duty of the self-determined subject.

We become aware of the distinctive and radical nature of Kant's thought when he spells out the implications of his thesis that the categories, the faculties of understanding, construct the world as it appears to us. As we have seen, Kant argues that we can have no direct, transcendent knowledge of the objective world – nature – but that the powers of our understanding can produce a reliably consistent and ordered systematisation of the world as we experience it. In the Analytic of Concepts, a section of the *CPR*, he states that 'Categories are concepts which prescribe laws *a priori* to appearances, consequently to nature as the complex of all appearances'.[42] He goes on to ask how it can be that nature can be said to regulate itself according to categories which are concepts inhering in the human mind and not concepts existing in and given by nature. His answer is that we can only have cognisance of nature, of the sum of things as they are in themselves, by way of the structuring effected by the categories. Nature, as we understand it, is simply a complex of appearances, given order and lawfulness by our *a priori* conceptual apparatus. He states the case even more unequivocally later in the Analytic:

> ... the understanding is itself the legislature facing nature, that is to say without understanding there would be no nature at all, i.e., a synthetic unity of the manifold of appearances according to rules.[43]

Kant seems to recognise the startling nature of this statement when he admits that it must sound 'exaggerated and absurd ... to say that the understanding is itself the source of the laws of nature, hence the formal unity of nature'.[44] It is, he goes on, nevertheless correct, since all appearances (which are all that the mind can make of experience) conform to the laws or rules of human understanding. In his preface to the second edition of the Critique, he sets the issue out in terms which assert the positive value of the limitations imposed on human reason:

> ... reason only perceives that which it produces after its own design; that it must not be content to follow, as it were, in the leading strings of nature, but must proceed in advance with principles of judgment according to unvarying laws, and compel nature to reply to its questions.[45]

It would be difficult to imagine a more uncompromising expression of faith in the powers of reason to interrogate nature and build knowledge.

Once again, it is important to state that Kant is not denying the existence of a reality independent of human thought. His frequent insistence that we can have no knowledge of things as they really are in themselves makes clear that he accepts that there is a realm beyond the reach of human apprehension. Self-consciousness, awareness of our own personhood, is the product of separating ourselves from objective reality. Thus, the formation of an idea of the self is also the recognition of a realm inaccessible to our subjectivity and only susceptible to representation by our *a priori* faculties as appearances.

Freedom and morality

The idea of an autonomous subject and the possibility of moral action are conditional on the capacity of human beings to exercise freedom in their decision-making. For if a causal action on the part of an individual is the necessary result of a previous cause then all human actions are predetermined and therefore can never be free. For example, if I choose to vote for a particular political party – a causal action which will have certain effects (however unpredictable) – I may choose to see this decision as freely made upon judgements about the relative merits of the various policies of different parties. In other words, I will have made free and unconditioned use of my reason in making this decision. However, it may be objected that I was disposed to vote in this particular way because of influences in my prior experience, the circumstances of my upbringing or a particular event or events that coloured my judgement. It may be that I have a psychological disposition that inclines me to favour one party over others and, of course, since I could not have freely chosen this disposition (I acquired it through nature or nurture) my voting decision was not freely made. You can apply this argument against freedom to any of the decisions – minor and major – that you make in life, from giving or not giving money to beggars, to the subjects or courses you opt for during your education, to the choices you make in your style of dress and, if modern behavioural and cognitive psychologies are to be believed, whether, on a recreational evening walk, you choose to turn left or right as you enter the park. If his great emancipatory idea of the autonomous moral subject is to stand up, Kant has to detach reason from the determinations of the natural laws of causality which govern our experience. His solution to the problem is contained in some densely argued pages in the *CPR*.[46]

In summary, what he does is to remove freedom and reason from the realm of nature, the latter being the sphere of inescapable determinations. He argues that there are two 'modes of causality' – nature and freedom, freedom being 'in the cosmological sense, a faculty of the *spontaneous* origination of a state, the causality of which, therefore, is not subordinated to another cause determining it in time'. Reason, he claims, creates this idea of spontaneity, 'which can begin to act of itself, and without any external cause determining it to action'. This is managed by the capacity human beings have to make judgements and apply reason to problems, which places such ideation, or formation of ideas, outside the system of causal necessity – the natural law of causality that exists in what he calls the phenomenal world. He argues that reason's ideas can operate free of the determinations applying to natural phenomena since they deal in appearances, which are nevertheless 'nothing more than mere representations' which means that 'they must have a ground which is not phenomenal'. There is nonetheless interaction between a free use of reason and the actions of man. Hence, we discover that sometimes 'the ideas of reason did stand in a causal relation to certain actions of man; and that these actions have taken place because they were determined, not by empirical causes, but by the act of will on grounds of reason'.[47] This seems to muddy, or at least complicate the relationship between the realm of reason and the realm of nature, since one is informing the other, and vice versa. Indeed, Kant concedes that this distinction between the idea of appearances as being simultaneously empirically conditioned and giving rise to the action of unconditioned, free thought, 'must appear in the highest degree subtle and obscure'.

Reason, Kant argues, is 'distinct from all empirically-conditioned faculties, for it employs ideas alone in the consideration of its objects',[48] determining or causing the understanding to make empirical use of its *a priori* conceptual armoury. Thus, reason is a mode of causality – it can originate actions and cause effects. Kant exemplifies this causal faculty of reason by reference to 'the imperatives, which in the sphere of the practical we impose as rules on our active powers'.[49] This is where Kant intrudes his notion of the distinctively human proclivity to think what *ought* to be, 'a species of necessity' connected 'with grounds that nature does not contain'.[50] It would be absurd to ask what ought to be the properties of a circle. All we can ask of nature is, 'What *are* the properties of a circle?' As reasoning human beings, we are bound by 'laws, which are imperative or objective *laws of freedom* ... which tell us what *ought to take place*'.[51] Our reason cannot pretend to a speculative insight into the reality of things as they are but it can aspire to speculative knowledge in the sphere of the practical use of reason. It is in this sphere that reason can be said to be free – free to inquire into the character and remit of the moral laws[52] that govern our conduct.

Kant sets out his thinking on ethics or moral law more fully in works like the *Grounding for the Metaphysics of Morals*[53] and the *Critique of Practical Reason*[54] where he argues that all actions, whether we are aware of it or not, are made on the basis of a principle or maxim and never on the urgings of a desire or impulse. Thus, if I want to get rid of a headache (my desire) I will act according to the maxim that some paracetamol will relieve me of my discomfort; if I want to find out what Reykjavik has to offer in the way of night-life I will act on the maxim that Google will inform me; if I want to enjoy some mindless activity and release from the ennui or stress of life in a society where value and meaning are in scarce supply I will go paint-balling. Maxims are principles of rational action. The class of maxims that apply to moral conduct are *categorical imperatives*. Kant's earliest and most well-known formulation of this notion, in the *Grounding*, was that we should resolve to 'act only according to that maxim whereby you can, at the same time, will that it should become a universal law'. A categorical imperative commands that an individual act in a particular way regardless of their motivations or desires. A categorical imperative cannot be escaped, although it can be transgressed; it is unconditional. For example, if I act on the maxim that I should not seek to gain advantage at the expense of another's disadvantage I am acting according to a categorical moral imperative that has universal application; however, if I decide not to seek advantage at another's expense because I want certain people to think well of me, I am not acting on a maxim that could be universally applied, except at the cost of severe social and moral disorder. I would be acting in pursuit of a goal that would satisfy a desire, whilst categorical imperatives apply without reference to my personal desires. I may not want to act considerately and fairly on a particular occasion because to do so would conflict with my own interests, but if I overcome my selfish desires and behave decently I am acting on a categorical imperative, a universal moral law.

Furthermore, if I am to act freely I can only do so on the basis of the moral law, since if I act according to desire I am moved by impulses that are beyond my control because they are ultimately determined by nature rather than by reason. Kant's key principle of human autonomy thus depends on the notion of the categorical imperative. He believed that subordination to the moral law, the full realisation of moral imperatives, would lead to a perfected world, a world of complete virtue and happiness and he believed that if such a world was to be brought about it was necessary – a duty – to believe in the possibility of such an outcome. He did not think that human beings were bound to act on categorical imperatives – if this were the case they would not be capable of free action – nor that the ideal world he envisaged was destined to come into being, but he did believe that it was the individual's moral duty to act in ways that would bring about the desired end of a virtuous and happy world. Kant's thinking strains after a way of rendering this ideal world as the inevitable outcome of conformity with the moral law but is constrained by his doctrine that human understanding, limited to the representation of appearances, cannot make out the true nature of the universe and any laws which may govern it. And, of course, such an inevitability, such a determination, would transgress the idea he has been at such pains to establish, that of the freedom granted to the human will through the individual's possession of the faculties of pure reason. He argues that

> since reason commands that ... [moral] actions should take place, it must be possible for them to take place; and hence a particular kind of systematic unity - the moral, must be possible.[55]

Thus, in the sphere of the practical use of reason, 'especially in its moral use ... the principles of pure reason possess objective reality'. He envisages a world which constitutes 'a system of happiness', incited and regulated by the principles of moral law, in which 'rational beings, under the guidance of such principles, would be themselves the authors both of their own enduring welfare and that of others'.[56] This is as clear an expression of the Enlightenment ideal as one might find, but it is, as Kant acknowledges, 'only an idea', what he later calls 'the effect of the practical teleology, which pure reason imposes upon us'.[57]

The practical use of reason would clearly require the continued guidance of Kantian philosophy, though Kant himself largely wrote *CPR* for a small group of specialists.[58] Together this group of apostles (or 'excellent men'[59]) would work on the further refinement of his philosophy, serving too as teachers, who would explain the consequences and necessary implications of this complex philosophical synthesis for those who must remain (due to its difficulty) uninitiated. These specialists would provide further philosophical elaboration on the sovereignty of human reason, to which all else must relate. The critique, or critical project announced by Kant, would continue then, but only at the level of its further refinement. Kant was the last great philosopher in this sense, with subsequent philosophy consigned to the role of 'perfecting those things which are here defective in their presentation',[60] and elucidating any obscurities. This may sound conceited, Kant admits,[61] but that is what happens when you inaugurate a philosophy of such scope and rightness. The rest of the population would serve, if they were sufficiently educated, as lesser participants in the unfolding of rational knowledge, a project which must, by definition, always exceed individual mental states and be subjected to the tribunal of reason, itself guided in its construction by Kantian philosophy. These lesser participants would also learn to apply categorical imperatives as well as other ideas derived from Kantian philosophy to their lives and professional activities. To some extent, subsequent history bears this out, with the modern university in particular (to which we return in Chapters 11–12) attempting to fulfil the critical project Kant inaugurated, forming citizens who are able to act freely in the public realm but who nonetheless respect its necessary laws, and forming a professional class of academic researchers who would labour in pursuit of the progressive generation of knowledge and scientific understanding, knowing that full understanding of the world in itself would always remain just beyond their reach.

If Kant has, to his own satisfaction, demonstrated the objective reality of the moral law and the human potential, allowed by the faculties of pure reason, to act freely in the practical realm, and if he has also conceded the unbridgeable gulf between the powers of human cognition and the existence of a sphere beyond the objects of possible experience – a sphere in which nature operates according to the laws imposed by an inscrutable supreme intelligence – it might be asked why he spends so many pages in examination of the relation between the moral world and the divine will. It would seem that his case has been made quite adequately without reference to the possibility of the existence of 'a sole Primal Being, as the supreme good'.[62] One answer to this question was touched upon at the beginning of this section: that Kant, like other intellectuals of his time, was concerned that science presented a picture of the universe as mechanical and fully determined in its operation, a view that leaves no room for God or free will – in other words, a soulless world, empty of meaning and purpose. Kant may have felt that this was a rather cheerless prospect that offered little in the way of challenge to – and none of the consolations of – the conventional religious belief that, in his view, obstructed mankind's progress towards maturity. The scientific and religious imaginations had to be reconciled. Another possibility is that Kantian teleology – the inevitable progression of humanity to a completed rationality – was no more than an 'idea', an abstraction lacking the sensuous attraction, the vivid, visceral penetration into hearts and minds of the complex, anciently sedimented worldview of folk and religious belief. Furthermore, it seems that Kant wanted for his idea – the teleology implied in his meticulous conceptualisation of human autonomy – some guarantee of its necessary unfolding, that it had to take place once reason was applied to the practical affairs of the human condition. His solution to the problem he identifies is to posit the hypothesis of 'a supreme original good',[63] which, although 'hidden from the world of sense' is, it seems, implied by the principles of pure reason which produce the idea of a systematic moral world, the idea of 'moral unity as a necessary law of the universe'. In his two subsequent Critiques Kant continues and develops his thinking concerning the necessity of God to the possibility of a moral world, leading to the conclusion that Nature itself was divinely created in order that human beings might fulfil the moral ends imposed by the granting of moral autonomy. This is a departure into speculative reason which some would say fails to enhance the credibility of Kant's critical enterprise.

Kant's legacy

Kant's philosophy has had incalculable influence on subsequent thought. As he says in his preface to the second edition of the CPR[64] he aimed to effect a

Copernican revolution in human thought. Where Copernicus contradicted the established view that the sun and stars revolved around the Earth, suggesting a more truthful account of the cosmos would have the human observer revolving around the sun. Kant rejected the empiricist idea that, as Locke thought, the mind was a blank sheet on which impressions of the external world were imprinted. He also rejected Humean scepticism about the possibility of deriving any reliable knowledge beyond that supplied by the senses. The mind was not blank but had at its disposal powerful *a priori* operative faculties without which rational thought would be impossible. On the other hand, he rejected the rationalist conviction, first articulated by Descartes, that knowledge relayed by sensory experience was entirely unreliable and that it was the mind that exercised pre-formed ideas that enabled it to penetrate to the reality of the external universe and its organisation. Thus, Kant's transcendental method offered a corrective to the passivity and scepticism of the empiricists and a denial of the rationalist claim that human beings could acquire direct, unmediated knowledge of things in themselves. All subsequent philosophy has had to deal with his mapping of the territory. Responses have ranged from general conformity with his ideas to critiques that have attempted to modify or radicalise his conceptualisations and on to outright rejection. His meticulously detailed account of the capacities and limitations of human cognition, in particular his idea that human beings can only arrive at representations of reality, rather than achieving direct engagement with it, has been extraordinarily influential on culture, giving systematic form and weight to an intuition that has an ancient heritage. In other words, Kant provided a more systematic framework for a kind of metaphysical thinking which positions true understanding of reality above and beyond us, as something to strive for, but never fully achieve. His demonstration of the powers granted to humanity by its possession of rational faculties has given intellectual underpinning to mankind's drive to harness and control nature for its own ends, whilst ideologies of progress, economic growth and social and personal betterment are an outcome of Enlightenment, and particularly Kantian, analyses of the human condition, of humanity's nature and destiny. The achievements of Western civilisation, in science, technology and the material well-being of national populations, have been remarkable. Modern 'developed' societies display an outwardly efficient orderliness in meeting the essential needs and in satisfying the desires of its citizenries. They enshrine in their constitutions, in the form of human rights, a moral law that is intended to offer dignity and justice to all citizens. These achievements are indisputably the outcomes of Enlightenment thought, an edifice that was given its most influential form by Immanuel Kant.

Despite Kant's legacy, his claim to effect a Copernican revolution in thought is a little misleading. For Copernicus achieved something very different. He decentred the human perspective on the cosmos. As a result of his work, the earth and the human gaze were no longer the still and certain point from which to view the universe. Kant, by contrast, conceptualises the human mind as the very active originating point of knowledge, albeit with a recognition of the limitations bearing upon human cognitive faculties. Kant's enterprise might thus be seen as an effort at retrieval, from scientific determinism and philosophical scepticism, of Renaissance confidence in the powers of the human intellect to form a rational structuring of the world. As such, Kantian thought has attracted the criticism that it underpins a hubristic faith in humanity's capacity, and right, to exert control over the natural world and to shape it to human needs and desires, with calamitous consequences. There have been other assaults on the Kantian inheritance. He has been seen as casting unwarranted doubt upon the capacity of the human intellect to know the world – according to this argument, thought was functioning quite happily and productively until he suggested that it was unaware of its limiting conditions and that its claims to knowledge required justification. Kant has been seen as ultimately responsible for the idea that cognition is naïve and untruthful unless it confronts and brings into consciousness its concealed underpinnings. Another accusation focuses on Kant's confinement of reason to the practical and moral realm, his insistence that the human mind cannot aspire to pure cognition of the natural order, that it can only manage representations of appearances. This is seen as an intellectually disastrous shackling of the Enlightenment's project of disenchantment, its resolve to apply what has been termed 'the coruscating potency'[65] of scientific reason to the nature of reality. At an extreme, this argument sees Kant's accommodation between empiricism and rationalism as leading philosophy – most of it – to focus on the parochial, on the human, so that it becomes a consolatory activity which turns away from the forbidding dimensions of cosmic time and space and their implications for human existence. These and other critiques of Kant's enterprise will be touched upon in ensuing chapters. What cannot be gainsaid, however, is Kant's transformative effect on subsequent enquiry in philosophy, the humanities and the social sciences. His life's work amounts to an answer to the question 'What is Enlightenment?' – What are the uses and the purposes of rational enquiry? – and his response continues to set the framework for argument on this theme down to the present day.

8

Modernity and its Problems

The age of critique

Kant's pronouncement that 'our age is the age of criticism'[1] spoke of something at work in Descartes, Hume, Kant and many other thinkers, even the more conservative Locke, writers who felt ideas as they were expressed by earlier thinkers were not to be taken at face value, that statements needed to be validated by way of a process that tested them by putting them into doubt – they could not be taken to simply express bare truth. This was the procedure of critique and in a later chapter we examine the cultural impact on thought and, in particular, on education, of the elevation of what was formerly a method or technique (for restoring corrupted texts to their original authenticity) to the level of a principle as 'the essential activity of reason'.[2] We invoke Kant's words now because they herald the arrival of a new thought about the human condition, that of modernity.

The case can be made – and we have made it – that in classical and medieval times man was conceived as a creature who had scant control over his destiny. He was conceived as a being who, forever faced by the inscrutable and threatening forces of nature and the unpredictable violences likely to be inflicted by human power or human wickedness, was compelled to seek how best he might align himself with the will of a benevolent but exacting supreme being. With the rise of modernity this changed. During the seventeenth and eighteenth centuries, a new confidence grew that humanity could exert control over nature, that it could awaken a slumbering human reason and build not only a better world but also one that was governed by reason rather than tradition and superstition. This was to be a world in which scientific knowledge would compel nature to the service of human ends and in which critical reason would relieve humanity of its reliance on mere appearance and illusions, freeing it for the pursuit of truth and the full realisation of its hitherto shackled potential. This was a utopian project but one which was to be undertaken on the apparently practical and secure foundations of science and critical reason. Its goal is signalled by one of the earliest of Enlightenment thinkers, Sir Francis Bacon, as:

> the knowledge of Causes, and secret motions of things; and the enlarging of the bounds of Human Empire, to the effecting of all things possible.[3]

Enlightenment thought ushered in what has come to be seen as the era of modernity, the period in which 'man' forms an idea of himself as a historical being, a creature with a past that could be distinguished, marked off, from a present and future which he could shape to his own needs and purposes.

Modernity's achievements

The title of this chapter might cause some understandable puzzlement. After all the period of modernity, say, from the mid-seventeenth century to the present day (although some would say – we wouldn't – that we have moved into an era of postmodernity[4]), has produced astonishing achievements that have brought about immeasurable benefits to human society. Problems? What problems? Men and women, across vast regions of the globe, now have freedoms – of conscience, speech and movement – and opportunities to build their lives as they wish that would have been unimaginable to the great mass of medieval peoples. Even in those countries and communities where such freedoms and possibilities are under severe restriction, the very existence of polities in which they are guaranteed as civil rights, offers example and hope. Prosperity, the increase of wealth and its sharing, has come about in developed countries and appears to be spreading to less economically advanced societies. The great majority of the citizens of the Western world enjoy levels of material well-being that in some respects surpass those of the aristocratic classes of previous ages; in Africa, we are told, the widespread possession of mobile phones is transforming its economies. Communication technologies, from the radio, to newspapers and television, have increased the possibilities of human interaction, a progression and enhancement of human capacities that has been given wings by the development of digital media. These technologies – binary and digital – make available information and knowledge more accessible than at any other time in history. The modern age has brought an orderliness to those modern societies which have embraced one of the key objectives of the Enlightenment. They offer a guarantee of freedom under the law that earlier times were never able (or disposed) to provide. Such liberties and the extension of legal rights and protections to all citizens regardless of wealth or status, along with the economic productiveness that is the result of good governance, may not yet be available in all countries, but the liberal democracies offer a model that other societies might aspire to. Indeed, they have a magnetic attraction to the citizens of less justly and efficiently governed nations. Perhaps above all, science and engineering have brought about advances in medicine, systems of sanitation and dietary improvement that have brought increased longevity and previously inconceivable benefits to the great mass of people in the world.

Finally, almost as the jewel in the crown of the project of Enlightenment, we come to education, the means by which men and women were to be raised from ignorance and a state of humiliating dependency to the level of autonomous intelligence required for the construction of a just and rational social being. In the nineteenth century, the modern university was developed as the master institution for completing a full reckoning of what could be known about man and the universe, an edifice of knowledge that would be a comprehensive and systematised representation of the universe in which humanity found itself. Such a perfection of knowledge would offer mankind, guided by the light of reason, the kind of control over the natural world that would allow the completion of its full humanity. The social technology for bringing enlightenment to the mass of people took the form of the national systems of education that have been instituted across the world since the nineteenth century. They have offered access to knowledge and paths to self-realisation and empowerment denied to previously benighted, disenfranchised populations. However grandiose we might find these Enlightenment aspirations, it cannot be denied that the systems for the production of knowledge and its dissemination, invented in the nineteenth century and driven by (one is tempted to say, under the enchantment of) eighteenth-century rationalism, have been instrumental in shaping the world to one in which individual opportunity, personal freedom and a more just and egalitarian social dispensation have come into being.

In the modern period, human life has indeed been marked by progress from superstition and a state of unquestioning dependence on authorities – secular and spiritual – to maturity and an autonomy founded in the use of reason. Human history is now a narrative of progress in the human condition, marking what might be called a change in consciousness – in human beings' understanding of themselves and what they might make of their lives and in their apprehension of where they stand in relation to the powers, human and natural, that order the world. If problems remain, if the promise of modernity has not been met in full, it is only because we find ourselves in the midst of what was always going to be a struggle. We may be confronted by threats and problems that could not have been anticipated when the thought of man as an autonomously rational creature came into being, but with renewed effort and commitment (and faith in the project) we will eventually arrive at the end point of a social existence governed by reason, one which confers a harmonious and happy liberty, justice and dignity on all.

And yet

The story of modernity outlined above forms the backdrop to the world we live in. In a sense, it is a narrative that forms part of – to adopt an overused term – the prevailing ideology, the often taken-for-granted, unquestioned commonsense understanding, of our times, or as Stuart Hall puts it:

> the mental frameworks - the languages, the concepts, categories, imagery of thought, and the systems of representation - which different classes and social groups deploy in order to make sense of, figure out and render intelligible the way society works.[5]

As we have seen, there are good reasons why this is the accepted narrative within which, in varying ways, we locate our own personal histories and hopes. It is an account based on solid achievements, undeniable progress. And yet there has been no shortage of dissent from the project of Enlightenment. It has been seen, *inter alia*, as an enterprise that has failed or strayed from its original blueprint; a project that was mistaken from the start; a naive and unworldly or, alternatively, a cold-blooded attempt to contain human diversity within a theoretical grid. It has been blamed for draining human life of its vitality, for creating, or allowing to be created, the alienation that is said to mark modern existence, for humanity's separation from a grounding sense of purpose and belonging in the world. It has been accused of setting in train the dehumanising onward march of instrumental reason, wherein the dominant form of rationality focuses solely on the most economical and efficient means for achieving a given end, to the neglect of the human cost of deploying such means. The world is thus revealed, or made over, as a soulless, 'disenchanted' habitation, robbed of value and meaning. Modernity is associated with some of the darkest moments in human history. These include rapidly accelerating environmental degradation, human exploitation (some would say 'wage slavery') organised on a global scale, the development of modern warfare and weapons of mass destruction, and repeated genocides which have drawn heavily from the affordances of modern technology and bureaucracy, of which the most haunting, for many, remains the Holocaust. For some critics the major concern has been that modernity's progress has been conducted hand in hand with the expansion and intensification of a capitalist economic system, a relation that may have produced tremendous material benefits for humanity, but has also, in the view of such critics, perverted humanity's sense of its potential and created a world, a spectacle, of illusory desires and excitements that screen the profound inequalities and injustices that are structured into the capitalist system. For some, the worst events in recent history are symptomatic of a wider disorder: these events expose the intrinsic barbarities of modern rationality. In this chapter we will explore some of these critiques, laments and accusations in more detail.

Contrary humanisms

In his book *Cosmopolis: The Hidden Agenda of Modernity* the philosopher Stephen Toulmin offered a pithy and uncomplicated analysis of what happened in modernity.[6] His argument is this. In the seventeenth century a more assertive and doctrinaire humanism displaced the Renaissance humanism of the fifteenth and sixteenth centuries. Questioning the foundations of knowledge, it opened up consideration of the possibility of human existence being constituted exclusively on a rational basis. Though Renaissance humanists had already sought through the exercise of reason to effect a measure of control over human affairs and the world in which they lived, the kind of rationality they employed was directed to problems and challenges that were locally specific, practical and timely (in the sense of being rooted in present rather than eternal concerns) and which was intellectually modest, relatively tolerant of diversity and healthily aware of the bodily nature of human experience and understanding. As Toulmin sees it, this Renaissance outlook did not survive the intellectual events of the seventeenth century. The older, humane attitudes of openness and relaxation which informed the thought of Erasmus, Bacon, Montaigne, Rabelais and Shakespeare, the sceptical tolerance of 'uncertainty, ambiguity and diversity of opinion' which characterised the 'climate of opinion' of late sixteenth-century culture, was soon marginalised.[7] Under the influence of Descartes (and Leibniz) thought was rationed to a new order and western philosophy set on the path of an abstract, decontextualised enterprise that 'separate[d] rationality and logic from rhetoric and emotion'.[8]

Montaignean and Cartesian thought were both individualistic, but with important differences. Montaigne comprehended an individual who was conscious of his individuality in relation to a world of other independent persons with whom he had commonalities of experience. By contrast, Descartes conceived an individual who was 'trapped inside his own head', his individuality a purely intellectual phenomenon, his existence governed by a mind that sits above his embodied being, assembling an intellectual construct of his world from the data that reach him through his senses. In Toulmin's view, this was a road wrongly taken by Western thought, following a theoretical, speculative trajectory that committed reason to an abstract and idealist reaching after certainty, rather than a pragmatic, less grandiose version of reason as a guide to questions of human social existence. Modern humanism became an intellectual orthodoxy, a narrowing of the bounds of thought, which was to have consequences in terms of social and intellectual conformism, an insistence on 'respectability' in thought or behaviour and a certain narcissism, deriving from an essentially self-centred mode of understanding which has infected morality, culture and politics.

As Toulmin argues, it was the brutal, confessionally driven wars between 1618 and 1648 which put an end to the tolerant, sceptical humanism of the sixteenth century. This was a period of intense conflict in which unyielding religious dogmatisms sought the victory of their respective doctrinal certainties. Afterwards, there was not a return to earlier humanisms. Rather, the system of secularised sovereign nation states set up after the Peace of Westphalia in 1648 removed government from the sphere of ecclesiastical zealotry. As it did so, it sought to deliver society from the chaotic, violent dissension of the immediate past. It attempted to address 'the loss of all social, political, and spiritual cohesion', through a return to the stabilities of the medieval 'cosmopolis', the harmonised coherence of natural and human orders.[9] For Toulmin, this aspiration was profoundly influenced by the Cartesian project of finding the single certain thing that could guarantee other certainties, and later by Newton's comprehensive, unifying account of the natural order. The aim was to create a new, more rational 'cosmopolis' – a city inhabited by people from many different countries and faiths, but nevertheless organised according to a single unifying logic. Here was an attempt to order society along more secular lines, in accordance with the newly discovered 'systematicities' of nature.

For Toulmin, the consequences of this shift were very damaging, leading to a new direction of thought and government. A political conservatism took hold whose prime directive was achieving stability. This stability would only be secured through a fixed social order reflecting the axiomatic certainties, the fixed laws, of the Newtonian system which 'called for stable institutions, unambiguous class structure, centralized power, and defence of the state's sovereign autonomy from external interference'.[10] In philosophy, modern humanism led to a quest for global analyses, the grand narratives of modernity, and a search for the universal foundations of truth, at the expense of the practical, adaptable rationality of Renaissance humanism. In Toulmin's view, at the levels of politics, the arts, science and morality, the valorisation of formal rigour, logical certainty and systemic wholeness produced thinking and institutions that have, at their worst, tended to a form of inflexibility that has put a brake on human possibility and rendered social institutions and the subjectivities they produce unresponsive to the increasingly diverse challenges of 'postmodernity'.

We present Toulmin's analysis because it encapsulates in an easily understood way key themes – modernity's preoccupation with order and control; its reactionary character; its bleak rationalism; and its hostility to human difference and physical exuberance – which we will encounter in some of the more abstruse appraisals of modernity we are about to introduce. His account could be accused of simplification, an over-neatness in analysis, but it usefully and importantly draws attention to the fact that powerful philosophical ideas – such as modernity's experiment in the application of pure reason to human affairs – will always have social and cultural consequences.

There are clear educational consequences too, and we explore a number of these below. For example, in Chapter 11 we explore how the modern aspiration to order, certainty and systematic wholeness, was later expressed in the idea of mass education. But at a more basic, and fundamental level, the idea of education itself comes to share the modern promise of progress. Indeed, it became axiomatic that only through education could modernity be realised. And so, to the extent that modernity was always a problematic, if not contradictory project, education came to embody these contradictions in practice. These contradictions and their continued effects will be explored for the remainder of this book.

Spoilt for choice

One is spoilt for choice when considering thinkers who have expressed doubts about the Enlightenment project. These come from many distinct, often conflicting intellectual positions. As a result, each position configures the problem of Enlightenment differently.

The German idealist philosophers who engaged with Kant's thinking in the late eighteenth and early nineteenth century, the most important of whom was Hegel, offered a correction, rather than a full-blooded critique of Kant. Kant was viewed as somewhat timid in his cautious account of transcendentalism. It was argued instead that if the promise of Enlightenment was to be fulfilled a more historically aware, absolute idealism was to be embraced. We explore these ideas later in Chapter 11 when we examine the idea of Bildung.

From a rather different angle, Karl Marx's historical materialism was uncompromisingly critical of the direction modernity was taking under the twin impulses of liberalism and capitalism. His thought has spawned a vast critical literature, some of which we examine later in the book. But Marxism has been described, accurately in our view, as an in-house critique of the Enlightenment. Marx accepted Kant's idea of a teleology of progress, applied to a rationally ordered human existence. And he accepted Hegel's conception of history as powered by an emancipatory historical force. It was just that for Marx, that progressive force was thoroughly materialist, an awakening working-class consciousness, rather than an idealist spirit of history.

Turning to another very different tradition of critique, in the twentieth century the development of Anglo-American analytic philosophy, with its rejection of grand theoretical scheming and its emphasis on conceptual precision and a narrow focus on single problems, could be seen as a refusal of the totalising ambitions of Enlightenment idealism. Again, however, this is not a full-blooded critique of modernity. For it has not, on the whole, turned against the modernist notion of the efficacy and onward progress of rational thought. Indeed, much of analytic philosophy seems to take place within a silent assumption that it is contributing to such an advancement. The work of Alasdair MacIntyre introduced in Chapter 4 stands as a notable exception. It is an instance within analytic philosophy of radical scepticism concerning the project of modernity.[11]

Within continental philosophy (to switch traditions again), the twentieth century produced what in retrospect seemed a sustained assault on the central propositions of Enlightenment thought and thus the rationale of modernity. In the first five or six decades of the twentieth century structuralism appeared to abolish the idea of the autonomous self. If post-structuralism partially revived it, this self was returned as a weak, evanescent, insubstantial and shifting thing that was ill-fitted to building the empire of reason. Like their Anglo-American distant cousins, post-structuralists turned against the construction of theoretical schemes, against what Jean-François Lyotard called the grand narratives of modernity.[12]

Perhaps the two most comprehensive assaults on Enlightenment modernity came from the German philosopher Martin Heidegger and his fellow country-men Max Horkheimer and Theodor Adorno. We will return to these figures later in the chapter.

It could, however, be argued that the two thinkers who had the most penetrat-ingly corrosive effect on the narrative of modernity are not philosophers at all, but the psychoanalyst Sigmund Freud and the naturalist Charles Darwin. Freud's ideas about the fragility of our rational control over ourselves and the world, the heavily determining presence of unreason in our lives, have entered our culture and chal-lenged the notion, shared by the modernist enterprise and by traditional religions, that individually and collectively we are engaged in a consciously controlled and purposeful journey towards a fully meaningful being. On the contrary, Freud says that we are flawed, damaged creatures whose aspirations, whose very grasp on life, have been shaped by pre-conscious experiences and external forces that we will never be able to completely control. Here we might compare Enlightenment dreams of an empire of reason with Freud's conclusion that at best we may stave off debilitating anguish and learn how to live with 'common unhappiness'.[13]

Charles Darwin was never entirely comfortable with the wider social and intel-lectual implications of his theory of evolution through natural selection, but the influence of his ideas on how human beings perceive themselves has been all-per-vasive. Darwin is perhaps best known for establishing that human beings share an ancestry with apes – the common misconception is that he said we are descended from apes and monkeys. Clearly his theory of natural selection put paid, for all but the most determinedly faith-driven individuals, to the idea that man was made by God in His image. The species we know as the human being is simply the outcome, across millennia, of a random process of genetic mutation within the phenotype, the sum of the observable traits or attributes of the organism as determined by its genetic constitution and environment. Humanity could no longer claim an exalted origin or special status. If man was to have dignity it would have to be something that was constructed out of this humiliation. Furthermore, if we could no longer claim a privileged moment of creation, neither was it possible to envisage our-selves as embarked on a teleological progress towards perfection, of a religious kind or, more tellingly, of the kind that Enlightenment modernism envisaged. As the processes of evolution through natural selection continued, *homo sapiens* was not guaranteed survival, at least not in the forms we now recognise. Not only was God ejected from science (and, largely, from philosophy), man became a moment within an impersonal biological record. Like God, the figure of man could die.

The death of God

Before we turn to the idea of the death of man we need to consider the philosophi-cal entailments of what has been called the death of God. No one spelt out more clearly and dramatically the impact upon thought and the human self-image of this idea – indeed he invented it – than the nineteenth-century German philosopher Friedrich Nietzsche, in our view the most influential and radical critic of the humanism that informs modernity.

In *The Gay Science* Nietzsche tells the story of a 'madman' who enters a marketplace on a bright morning carrying a lit lantern and crying out that he sought God. The crowds in the market place, many of whom, we are told, did not believe in God, were greatly amused and offered speculation as to where he had gone. Is he hiding? Has he got lost? Has he gone overseas? The madman says that they need to know that God is dead and that 'we' – he and his listeners – have brought this about. He goes on:

> But how did we do this? How could we drink up the sea? Who gave us the sponge to wipe away the entire horizon? What were we doing when we unchained this earth from its sun? Whither is it moving now? Whither are we moving? Away from all suns? Are we not plunging continually? Backward, sideward, forward, in all directions? Is there still any up or down? Are we not straying as through an infinite nothing? Do we not feel the breath of empty space? Has it not become colder? Is not night continually closing in on us? Do we not need to light lanterns in the morning? Do we hear nothing as yet of the noise of the gravediggers who are burying God? Do we smell nothing as yet of the divine decomposition? Gods, too, decompose. God is dead. God remains dead. And we have killed him.[14]

The madman seeks to confront his audience with the consequences of this murder. He goes on to ask how humanity is to live with this event:

> How shall we comfort ourselves, the murderers of all murderers? What was holiest and mightiest of all that the world has yet owned has bled to death under our knives: who will wipe this blood off us? What water is there for us to clean ourselves? What festivals of atonement, what sacred games shall we have to invent? Is not the greatness of this deed too great for us? Must we ourselves not become gods simply to appear worthy of it? There has never been a greater deed; and whoever is born after us - for the sake of this deed he will belong to a higher history than all history hitherto.[15]

Nietzsche here spells out the full magnitude of the epochal change that the Enlightenment brought about. His images of disarray and derangement – none more than his extraordinary thought of a sponge wiping away the horizon – call attention to the full ontological convulsion that has taken place in human thought, the dislocation that had occurred, apparently without anyone noticing it. Humanity's isolation in a vast, insensate universe is chillingly evoked. His suggestion that we will be summoned to account for this crime is perhaps best seen as a perception that the burden of responsibility for the murder will weigh on us as an immiserating, unnamed guilt unless we accept that responsibility, become worthy of it, as the cost for achieving a 'higher' humanity in which we will face the cosmos alone and without need of the support and protection of gods or a God. By any measure this is a fuller, more unblinkingly honest account of what it will mean for mankind to come to *mündigkeit* – maturity – than Kant was prepared to countenance. Not the least of its virtues is its conjuring of the problems and the social and psychological harms that will result from not facing up to the implications of the revolution in thought that occurred in the seventeenth and eighteenth centuries. It is also the case that Nietzsche recognises what might be called the horror of the boundless space of the universe and the crushing insignificance visited upon humanity by consciousness of this 'infinite nothingness'. He takes up the most radical of Enlightenment reason's effects, its disenchantment of the world – as Ray Brassier has put it – its shattering of the idea that Nature can offer a home to humanity or collude with our desire for comforting meanings and values.[16] If the idea of Nietzsche as a nihilist has any merit, it lies in his readiness to look full in the face this consequence of bringing to bear the full light of reason – scientific rationality – upon the reality of humanity and its narratives within the cosmic order. We noted in Chapter 7 that this was a recognition that appalled Pascal but, as has been pointed out, it is not a thought that has much concerned subsequent philosophy. Clearly there is no natural home for humanity within that vast emptiness, and we now know that our hold on existence as a species is time-limited; we die when changes in the nuclear activity of the sun cause it to expand and engulf the Earth. In his essay, *On Truth and Lies in a Nonmoral Sense*, Nietzsche wrote this:

> Once upon a time, in some out of the way corner of that universe which is dispersed into numberless twinkling solar systems, there was a star upon which clever beasts invented knowing. That was the most arrogant and mendacious minute of 'world history,' but nevertheless, it was only a minute. After nature had drawn a few breaths, the star cooled and congealed, and the clever beasts had to die. One might invent such a fable, and yet he still would not have adequately illustrated how miserable, how shadowy and transient, how aimless and arbitrary the human intellect looks within nature. There were eternities during which it did not exist. And when it is all over with the human intellect, nothing will have happened. For this intellect has no additional mission which would lead it beyond human life.[17]

What happens to thought – all the endeavour to make sense of mankind and its struggle for meaning – in the perspective of an eternity that does not include us? In this perspective modernity's idea of progress through reason, to a state of harmonious existence in which humanity's potential for happiness is fully realised, begins to look illusory, inconsequential. How inconsequential now appears that idea of Man as 'transcendental subject, a trans-historical source of value and meaning'?[18] Man is now just a clever beast whose thoughts and frenetic activity have no meaning, no impact and no real substance within the indifference of cosmic time and space. Nietzsche thus presents a critique of modernity and its ambitions, although we will see that he did not completely resist the lure of the old idea of a supernatural being (not a god but a god-like existence) that would defy and overcome the scientific facts of human extinction and the death of thought. We would have to become gods ourselves.

Heidegger, nihilism and technology

Martin Heidegger, whose major work was produced during the middle decades of the twentieth century, registered the full destructive impact of modernity, its cataclysmic effect on what he called *Dasein* (there-being), a term which in everyday use in German connotes 'existence', but which he developed to indicate the way in which individual human beings exist in the world. Dasein is neither consciousness in the rationalist tradition – the reasoning individual's understanding of an objective world, beyond the self – nor is it a simple submission to a determining objectivity which writes itself on the human subject. Rather, Dasein is the individual's concerned engagement with the external world, their mode of existence in the world, the experience of Being-in-the-World. In his essay 'The Word of Nietzsche: "God is Dead"' Heidegger says that:

> God is [Nietzsche's] name for the realm of Ideas and ideals. This realm of the suprasensory has been considered since Plato, or more strictly speaking, since the late Greek and Christian interpretation of Platonic philosophy, to be the true and genuinely real world.[19]

Nietzsche's pronouncement means that:

> the suprasensory world is without effective power. It bestows no life. Metaphysics, i.e., for Nietzsche Western philosophy understood as Platonism, is at an end.[20]

All that remains is the imperfect, earthly domain. The possibility of belief in a suprasensory realm, hitherto taken as 'the true and genuinely real world' of ideal forms, bliss and perfection, is what has been destroyed and with it the goals, the meaningfulness that it supplied – 'nothing more remains to which man can cling and by which he can orient himself'. Nothingness is 'spreading out' and nihilism, in Nietzsche's word, 'the most uncanny of all guests', stands at the door.[21] For Heidegger, nihilism is revealed as not just another intellectual current within Western history – Christianity, humanism and the Enlightenment are the examples he offers of such movements in thought, and we might include liberalism and socialism in the list – but as 'the fundamental movement of the history of the West'. Nihilism is 'the world-historical movement of the peoples of the earth who have been drawn into the power realm of the modern age'.[22] The authority of God is replaced by the authority of individual conscience, or the authority of reason. Social goals replace the suprasensory ideas, received by Christianity from Judaeo–Hellenistic thought, about the ordering of the world. The idea of historical

progress springs up and humanity sets itself the thoroughly worldly goal of bringing about the greatest happiness of the greatest number. Creativity, previously
the exclusive property of the deity, becomes the distinctive human activity, and
finally, creativity 'passes over' into the 'business enterprise'.[23]

Heidegger sees every stage in this movement of human history as typified by a
distinctive mode of attunement to the world, a particular way in which the relationship between human beings and the world becomes organised into a distinctive
experience – their being in that world. In the period of medieval Christianity
human beings would see themselves as subject to God's will and located in a world
entrusted to their care by God; in our period, the dominant understanding is that
we exist as individuals over and against an objectified Nature which can be utilised to meet our purposes. Heidegger saw both understandings as examples of
historically situated metaphysics or ontology.

Metaphysics here is a tradition of thinking which answers the question of how
we stand in relation to the cosmos and which constructs a mode of being in the
world. It will readily be seen that the medieval peasant, tending their allotment
of land, will have a closer, more observant and, arguably, more intimately respectful relationship with the nature that surrounds them than inhabitants of what
we call the developed countries of today's world. Additionally, the peasant would
have viewed the possibilities available to them in life as shaped by the divine and
earthly hierarchies within which they were situated and their awareness of the
judgement awaiting their conduct in that life. Today's first world citizen, subject
to an intensified sense of their individuality, sees the world – of nature and the
world made and structured by human beings – as the means available for the
achievement of their own ends, as a collection of things and their relationships
which can be manipulated to meet those ends. All such suppositional constructs
are, in Heidegger's view, inadequately thought through, insufficient formulations,
failures to engage with or turn away from the possibility of humanity realising
its 'essence', its true Dasein. Heidegger's full critical armoury, however, is directed
towards the period of modernity. Despite his identification of the business enterprise as the characteristic form of the current, perhaps final, phase of the West's
unfolding nihilism, Heidegger has little to say about capitalism, although it may
be taken as the efficient motor of what he sees as the presiding danger in the
organisation of man's relation to the world – modern technology.

In short, Heidegger views modernity as 'challenging' nature, forcing it into
arrangements and orderings that will be of maximum utility to human beings.[24]
Technology transforms the essential properties of natural entities – minerals, the
water in rivers and seas, forests, the wind, sunlight, farmed produce – into an ever
available resource, a 'standing-reserve', 'on call for a further ordering', always at
hand for humanity's use.[25] Heidegger is not, of course, suggesting that previous
ages had no technologies, but that in earlier times the techniques of the farmer,
the craftsman, the builder were applied in sympathy with the natural materials
they worked upon; they worked within an acceptance of the natural properties of

things. Today those natural materials are treated with a violent disregard for their essential being. Heidegger is concerned that modern existence's mode of being alienates it from nature, that something sacred is lost in modernity's proprietorial relation to the natural world. But his predominant concern is with the effect upon human life – on Dasein – of the technological age's designation of natural entities as resources to be exploited for the most efficient and immediate satisfaction of human needs. Modern man has entered, has allowed to come into being around him, a technological 'enframing' which threatens his essence.[26]

Technological enframing

Enframing is one of those Heideggerian terms (there are several) which, for some, never quite come into a final and precise focus. It seems to connote an all-encompassing organisation of how human beings perceive and understand their place within the world, such that alternative possibilities for understanding are closed off or, at least, heavily impeded. The enframing that technology manages is to install the standing-reserve as the governing idea of modernity, a 'setting-upon that sets upon man, i.e., challenges him forth, to reveal the actual, in the mode of ordering, as standing-reserve'.[27] The word 'actual' is important here: technological modernity imposes an idea of reality – that which is necessarily the case – as a gathering together and ordering of the things of the world, and the violent transformation of their natural properties, so that we might derive from them 'the maximum yield at the minimum expense'.[28] Efficiency in the ordering of the things of the world into a ready availability for our ends becomes the all-pervasive way in which human beings understand their relation to the world. Crucially, Heidegger proposes that within this enframing men and women come to see themselves and other human beings as resources to be utilised for the achievement of their ends.

A brief reflection on the dominance in our period of the idea of the economy as the central and necessary concern and focus of human activity and government will perhaps illustrate this point. Governments seek to produce (through education and by such means as interventions in labour laws, the operation of welfare systems and incentivisation through taxation) a multiply and flexibly skilled workforce which can adapt itself with maximal efficiency to the requirements of the marketplace, a workforce whose subjects see themselves as economic units possessing certain attributes, attitudes and competences which are tradeable within the employment market (we return to these ideas in Chapter 12).

The deep subject which early modernity envisaged (and to a limited extent achieved), with its principled commitments, habits of reflective critique and rational goals, or even the proletarian subject, caught up in the early stages of mass production, whose self-understanding was rooted in the practices of the workplace and the cultural values of what seemed a secure social environment, becomes (and comes to see itself as) a more or less useful commodity within a standing-reserve. The modern subject is destined to make the most of the skills she possesses, to operate easily and flexibly in the pursuance of economic satisfactions and personal aspirations which have little or nothing of the meaningfulness afforded by earlier, more deeply moralised or culturally rooted ways of being in the world. We come, then, to see ourselves and others as resources for exploitation. But Heidegger argues as well that the technological mode of enframing, with its focus on the utility and calculability of things as resources, robs the objects of the world of their distinctive properties. Where once objects were encountered by humans in a particularity that required us to adapt our handling of them to those inherent qualities, we now treat them as undifferentiated stuff within the standing-reserve whose usefulness we can tap into through technological means. The result is that humans become lost within an all-pervading 'objectlessness',[29] drifting in a world devoid of those engagements with things in their thingness which build and enlarge our sense of being in the world, our sense of being at home in the world. Technological enframing produces the characteristic maladies of late modernity – loneliness, boredom, depression, the absence of purpose to life and the need for ceaseless stimulation to distract from that absence.

No escape

Heidegger argues that technological modernity differs from previous ways in which the world was set up – ordered – to reveal their essences, their essential truths. We have seen that in early modernity, for example, the world was revealed as consisting in subjectivities of hitherto unrecognised complexity and depth and a reality of objects external to human beings. And we have seen how this understanding led to the self-awareness of 'man' as an autonomous being capable of shaping a world that was both rational and just. These earlier modes of revealing imposed powerful restrictions on how human beings might conduct their lives, inhibiting ways of seeing things differently. But (as Toulmin argued) they did allow spaces within which alternative ways of configuring the relationship between human beings and the world of objects could be imagined, as is evidenced by the dissident literatures, the ferment of argument, the striving after fuller understanding of those periods and as is evidenced by the fact that these orderings did indeed pass. Heidegger's fear is that 'when destining reigns in the mode of Enframing, it is the supreme danger'[30] because it allows for no alternative ways of things revealing themselves; human beings are the creatures who have through history witnessed and received every new disclosure of the essence of being, but this threatens to come to a halt when technological enframing's closure is completed by man's understanding being incorporated into, taken over by that enframing. The human being – its 'essence' changed – is rendered incapable of hearing, of receiving, a new, perhaps 'more original revealing and hence to experience the call of a more primal truth'.[31]

Heidegger writes – or does philosophy – in a way that differs from any of the registers adopted by European or Anglo-American philosophy. He is considered difficult to read. He clearly resolved to think everything anew and as a result he uses very little of the terminology that seventeenth- and eighteenth-century philosophers bequeathed to subsequent enquiry, although he shares an interest in etymology with Nietzsche that takes him back to the language used by classical Greek thinkers. His style is marked by a plainness of vocabulary – which seems to be an attempt to avoid theoretical abstraction and to cleave to language which he perhaps feels is closer to Dasein's embodied experience of things. This plainness, however, is contorted by a repetitive, insistent use of key terms – denoting concepts – that he has himself coined. Some have seen such utterances as tautological (saying the same thing twice with different words). His voice as a writer can appear sententious, bordering on the prophetic, and he sometimes references a traditional German peasant way of life that he saw as his 'ground'. This can lead to an impression of Heidegger as a nostalgic ruralist, pining for old ways. It would be a profound mistake to see him as such. Heidegger was not hostile to modern technology – to electric kettles, telephones and power stations – but he was concerned about the effects on human beings of technology as an enframing, as a total closure of human possibility that could lead, as he would put it, to the destruction of the essence of human beings, an essence which is open to new ways of understanding what it is to be human in the world. Heidegger's critique of modernity is arguably the most thoroughly thought through of all the analyses of the consequences of Enlightenment revolution in science and philosophy.

Myth and Enlightenment

To complete this chapter, we shift our focus to a different school of philosophy – critical theory. It affords a similarly acute diagnosis of modernity, and can be set alongside Heidegger's critique in terms of its scope and ambition. We consider here the work of two critical theorists in particular, Theodor Adorno and Max Horkheimer, who were German Jewish intellectuals associated with the Marxist-oriented Institute for Social Research, which became known as the Frankfurt School of critical theory. The Institute was established after the First World War as an adjunct of Frankfurt University and Horkheimer became its director in 1930. The work produced by the Institute's theorists is typically opposed to the positivist strain of thought which had become increasingly influential in the early decades of the twentieth century, and is marked by a desire to rethink Marxism as a critical and emancipatory endeavour, given the challenge presented to Marxist theory by social and political developments since Marx's time. They sought to broaden radical theory and make it more sharply focused on the problems of the period by incorporating insights from a range of other perspectives within philosophy and the critical social sciences.

Adorno and Horkheimer wrote their most famous book *Dialectic of Enlightenment* during the final years of the Second World War when they were living in California.[32] The *Dialectic* is an unusual book, 'an odd book' in the words of Jürgen Habermas, the most prominent representative of latter-day critical theory.[33] It contains a highly speculative essay on the idea of enlightenment, its ancient origins and intellectual legacy, two 'excurses', the one centring on a reading of Homer's *Odyssey*, the other a reflection on morality that draws on Nietzsche and the writings of the Marquis de Sade, two further essays, the one dealing with mass culture under capitalism, the second with anti-semitism as a case study in the dialectic of enlightenment and domination (of which, more later) and, finally, about 40 pages of 'notes and drafts' more or less connected to the themes of the earlier parts of the book. The difficulties of the *Dialectic* may be accounted for by the circumstances of the book's unusual composition, the authors jointly dictating large sections as notes taken by Adorno's wife Gretel.[34] More significantly, in their introduction Adorno and Horkheimer describe the book as composed of 'fragments' and there seems to have been an intention to refuse the measured orderliness and finalities of a systematic and closed theoretical statement as inappropriate and inadequate to the task of reckoning with the fractured historical reality they were faced with.[35] They refuse also to engage 'the impoverished and debased language' of 'dominant forms of thought'.[36] Its tone is, for an academic treatise, unusually impassioned; it is often didactic in its assertions and makes free use of a speculative analysis of the pre-history of human thought. It is obvious that the book's peculiarities arise from the disrupted, precarious situation in which its authors found themselves and from the intense pressures of the historical moment in which it was composed. This was a time in which history, the movement of human social and cultural development, had, for intellectuals steeped in the Enlightenment tradition of thought, become illegible, no longer susceptible to the kind of rational conceptualisation that European thought had engendered since the Middle Ages. The world had been given over to madness. The book is a provocation to thought, an incendiary device meant to destroy intellectual complacencies and to illuminate the cultural calamity that gave birth to the varied forms of twentieth-century oppression and to mass slaughter. It is perhaps not surprising that the *Dialectic* did not attract a general readership for more than twenty years, although its intellectual influence, particularly in West Germany, was profound. Its popular moment arrived on republication in 1969 at the height of the Cold War, when Western liberal democracies were undergoing a radical questioning of their claims to embody the Enlightenment principles of liberty and justice. During the 1970s the analyses and orientation of a critical theory informed by the work of the Frankfurt School spread throughout the human and social sciences.

The central idea of the *Dialectic*, and its most quoted formulation, is first seen in the Introduction to the book's first edition: 'myth is already enlightenment; and enlightenment reverts to mythology'.[37] This is the dialectic of enlightenment. What it means is that myths – traditional stories, often involving heroes and supernatural entities, told to explain a people's origin, a natural occurrence or the meaning or purpose of a particular practice – are ways that bring light to the problems and anxieties that beset (typically ancient) societies; they are attempts to explain, to shape into understanding, the relationship of human beings to the phenomenal world. (Similarities can be observed here with Nietzsche's argument in *The Birth of Tragedy*, introduced towards the end of Chapter 3.) Myths are thus exercises in enlightenment, attempts to organise the cosmos into a meaningful whole. At the same time, they are attempts to stabilise the world, to give the cosmos a reassuring predictability and permanence. Myth employs the resources of human reason and imagination in an attempt to exert control over nature.

Human thought has gone through successive stages of enlightenment, most obviously from an animistic belief in spirits and demons which men needed to appease, to the systematised, patriarchal religious orderings of, for example, Greek or Norse myth, to the monotheisms which identified a wrathful, exigent God and which in turn, in the European context, led to the medieval anthropocentric cosmos ordered by a merciful, loving deity and to the fully rational account of man-within-the-cosmos proposed by the Enlightenment. Each of these formulations, Adorno and Horkheimer argue, involved the use of reason to give meaning to the circumstances of human existence – to enlighten a surrounding darkness – and each of them sought to exert control over nature and – the crucial point – over other human beings. Furthermore, these efforts involve a structuring and deepening of individual subjectivities that itself amounts to an action of control over the self, where sacrifice, and self-sacrifice, become the key agents of this extension of control – something we consider shortly.

The authors preferred term for this tendency towards or desire for control is domination. Enlightenment, in the sense of enhancing understanding and establishing the truth of things, is always informed by the urge to dominate. *The Enlightenment*, modernity's endeavour at cleansing thought of ignorance and superstition, is, no less than earlier ways of conceiving the world, informed by this dominative impulse, an urge to bind thought and human behaviour within certain limits. All mythologies enlighten, all mythologies seek to control; the project of modernity enlightens and exerts control. Thus the Enlightenment, originating as a labour to bring the light of reason to the world, ends up as a system of control that inhibits thought. It becomes another mythology. Myth is already enlightenment; and enlightenment reverts to mythology.

We will now briefly consider how Adorno and Horkheimer make their argument, a thesis which involves an examination of the toxicity peculiar to the *ratio* – the kind of reason – governing late modernity, a moment in history in which rational progress seems to have gone into reverse and become 'irrational regress'. It will be seen that although critical theory's analysis of modernity takes a different path, its conceptualisation of enlightenment as domination has similarities with Heidegger's concerns about technological enframing.

Sacrifice and renunciation

The idea of sacrifice lies at the heart of the *Dialectic's* argument. Here, in the first 'excursus' of the book, the *Dialectic* turns to prehistory and the ancient world, discerning in ancient notions of sacrifice important analogues to the sacrificial logics of modernity. There is substantial evidence that at certain stages in pre-history the sacrifice not only of animals, but also of human beings, was enacted as a means of placating or gaining the favour of deities.[38] Adorno and Horkheimer quote Ludwig Klages, a mystically inclined theorist of pre-history, who saw human sacrifice as 'an exchange of fluids or essences by surrendering one's soul to the supporting and nurturing life of the world'.[39] The individual is surrendered for the good of the collective. Like its related practice – the offering of gifts to the deity – sacrifice contained a prudential or pragmatic purpose. It is 'a device of men by which the gods may be mastered: the gods are overthrown by the very system by which they are honored'.[40] Sacrifice acquires the transactional intent of magical practice, the aim of manipulating nature in accordance with human ends. This is reason as deception, as 'cunning', aimed at deceiving the god to whom the sacrifice is offered, 'subject[ing] him to the primacy of human ends, and dissolv[ing] his power'.[41] Adorno and Horkheimer offer Odysseus, the great liar, as the archetype of the modern bourgeois, the calculating, self-interested man whose ruling concern is with his self-preservation in the face of the greater powers which surround him. They contend that in Odysseus we can discern the elevation of deception to self-consciousness. In his travels, Odysseus repeatedly offers himself to sacrifice but by trickery he eludes the extinction that threatens him, eludes the violences of the supernatural entities – the goddess who offers an oblivion that would return him and his men to the unreflective happiness of brute existence, the lawless giant who would consume him, the Sirens who offer bliss in exchange for the self-consciousness that gives him some measure of control over the world. Each time Odysseus sacrifices himself to superior forces, he finds an 'escape clause in the contract, which enables him to fulfil it while eluding it'.[42]

In Odysseus, we may see the aboriginal form of the ego, the modern self which 'sacrifice[s] the present moment to the future'.[43] This is the end result of the 'introversion of sacrifice' – a turning inwards – which 'has its prototype in the hero who escapes from sacrifice by sacrificing himself'.[44] Here survival becomes 'dependent on the concession of one's defeat'. The bourgeois enlightenment, Horkheimer and Adorno argue, is built on a similarly perverse sacrificial logic. It is only gained 'at the price of the abasement and mortification of the instinct for complete, universal and undivided happiness'.[45]

Adorno and Horkheimer's argument is a subtle and complicated one – that 'man' comes to see nature as a set of blindly automatic processes that cast into utter insignificance, and threaten to engulf, his existence, and that to secure his survival he must imitate this 'despiritualised' nature by mortifying what is natural within him – 'animation', the instinctual relish for life that brings undivided happiness. This renunciation of nature in himself – 'the introversion of sacrifice' – is the founding act of civilisation which for all its achievements is the history of 'domination over non-human nature and over other men'.[46] Man, in order to deliver himself from the perilous vagaries of nature, must come to view nature as 'a hopelessly closed cycle',[47] an impenetrable system oblivious to the concerns of human beings, but a system which is calculable and therefore available to human control. The cost of this wished-for domination – the necessary condition of self-preservation – is that men and women must deny nature (viewed as surrender to instinctual happiness) in themselves, and understand themselves as units within a system whose governing principle is self-preservation through that mastery.[48] Humanity objectifies and thereby sacrifices itself.

Scientific rationality and domination

This system, which Adorno and Horkheimer explicitly attribute to the Enlightenment, 'is the form of knowledge which copes most proficiently with the facts and supports the individual most effectively in the mastery of nature'.[49] The notion of 'facts' is significant here. Adorno and Horkheimer see modern thought, ruled by the standards of science, as having come under the domination of 'what is directly given'.[50] What is lost in positivist thought's elaboration of the relationships between facts, is analysis of their 'social, historical, and human significance'. Thinking becomes 'mere apprehension, classification, and calculation';[51] it is confined to what is immediately evident, blindly reproducing what is – in social terms, the status quo. The distaste of the authors of the *Dialectic* for science goes much further than Heidegger's critique of technology. Given the elevated status of science in twenty-first century culture, as the one great hope for solving the problems of humankind, this can seem to be something like blasphemy. Adorno and Horkheimer's position is best understood as a plea for the continuing relevance, indeed the centrality, to thought about the human condition of an alternative kind of intelligence or intellectual comportment which might be described as the application of historical consciousness to human affairs, a critical reflectiveness trained on the specifics of how we, as social individuals, have been formed by our attempts to understand who we are in relation to all that vast and forbidding non-human otherness which surrounds us. Such thought was active in pre-history, in the philosophy of classical antiquity, in the great world religions and in medieval metaphysics. It came into its most recent fullness with the Enlightenment but now faces extinction with the dominance of the scientific mode of cognition over other forms of rational enquiry and, as Adorno and Horkheimer see it, the crippling hold over thought of scientific rationality's criteria for what counts as knowledge. In the modern period, thought has increasingly become a closed system which simply reproduces what is – repeating and sustaining the way things are. As in previous such closures, thinking that began as enlightenment becomes mythology, a rigid and unreflective tyranny over discourse and human activity.[52]

Adorno and Horkheimer view science as the latest attempt to contain the fear of the outside that produced the magical thinking of animism and myth. It does so by bringing the daunting variousness of nature under a conceptual unity, a single analysis that explains all: 'Nothing at all may remain outside, because the mere idea of outsideness is the very source of fear'.[53] Analytic scientific reason, like earlier ways of considering the world, exists in terror of a reversion to nature.[54] Science is not a purely disinterested enquiry into the nature of things but is bound up in this irrational urge to control, an urge which is rationalised as a utilitarian desire for, in Bacon's words, 'the better endowment and help of man's life'.[55] Everything must be brought within the confines of human consciousness, of a scientific rationality which is hostile to any kind of thinking that threatens its imperium. Adorno and Horkheimer are not, it is clear, arguing for a revival of magical thinking or the readmission of superstitious belief into modern analyses of humanity's place in the world. What they argue for is a fuller notion of reason, not the computational, instrumental version of a science that has no consciousness of the origins of its will to knowledge and, as a purely technical practice, is incapable of 'reflective consideration of its own goal'.[56] This fuller reason knows its own history, is alert to the tendency of enlightenment to become domination. It is capable of critical reflection on its practices and goals. Where science strives for the final single truth of things which would assert that everything that is *is as it must be*, critical reason operates on the dialectical principle that 'everything is always that which it is, only because it becomes that which it is not'.[57] Adorno and Horkheimer argue for a dynamic idea of becoming, in opposition to the stasis of being. If they were to be asked what such reasoning looks like they might fairly say, 'Like this, like this book'.

The *Dialectic* is unsparing in its account of the social and cultural consequences of the hegemony of scientific reason. The world we live in is almost completely determined – given its goals, its concepts governing what is important, necessary and true and its self-understanding – by the instrumental reason dictated by the logic of science. Everything, including the human being, is made into object material for subjugation in the interests of the self-preservation of the species. Society is shaped on an industrial model:

> Being is apprehended under the aspect of manufacture and administration. Everything – even the human individual, not to speak of the animal – is converted into the repeatable, replaceable process, into a mere example for the conceptual models of the system.[58]

Although they do not use the term, Adorno and Horkheimer argue that this industrial, instrumental schematisation produces in the modern citizenry a common sense, a shared public understanding that the world is necessarily ordered in this way.

Thinking is 'pre-censored', determined *a priori* in accordance with dominant norms of understanding. As a result, the possibilities for individual identity are heavily circumscribed – 'no one is other than what he has come to be: a useful, successful, or frustrated member of vocational and national groups'.[59] Thinking and the possibility of action in contravention of this common sense is severely restricted since the concepts with which Kant, for example, equipped enlightenment to restrain science's inevitable tendency to the establishment of a supreme value of operational effectiveness – concepts such as freedom, human solidarity, justice – 'have no meaning in a scientific sense'[60] because they cannot be made into the indices required for scientific–rational manipulation.

Open insanity

Capitalism is conceived as the agency of domination that has thrived under this means–ends rationality in which the means, the action required for survival, becomes the point and goal of existence, its end. Human organisation – society – is understood in purely economic terms. Adorno and Horkheimer see late capitalism as 'tantamount to open insanity',[61] in part because it peddles myths about the nature and possibilities of human life which are clearly untrue, but primarily because its intense focus on means drives all other ways of conceiving what it is to be human to the margins of discourse, of what can be thought. Human life is no longer directed towards the goal of a free and harmonious social life but towards subjugation of the world and the possibilities of humanity through an exclusive focus on self-preservation.[62] By 'madness' Adorno and Horkheimer perhaps mean a form of psychosis in which the fear of extinction drives the sufferer to exclude the complexity of reality by means of a single focus on an object – here, economic security – that will, it is believed, ensure survival (though it brings its opposite, destruction). Characteristically, however, they approach capitalism through a cultural lens; the fourth section of the *Dialectic* is an essay, 'The culture industry: Enlightenment as mass deception', which deals with the ways in which popular culture – which they treat purely as state (Nazi Germany, Stalinist Russia) or capitalist (Hollywood, the popular music industry) projects of domination and exploitation – produce false representations of reality which are aimed at distracting individuals from or reconciling them to the restricted possibilities available to them in real life. Mass cultural production, they argue, 'reproduces, reinforces and strengthens dominant interpretations of reality'.[63]

As we have noted Adorno and Horkheimer view the history of civilisation as the history of sacrifice, of renunciation; capitalist economics organises the latest systematisation of renunciation which, as always, requires that the human being 'gives away more of his life than is given back to him'.[64] This statement is a clear echo of Marx's theory of the exploitation of surplus value: the worker produces more than is required for his and his family's sustenance, but in capitalist societies that surplus value is appropriated by the capitalist, the bourgeois. For all that it is an attempt to identify the cultural, social and ideological dimensions of the revolution in philosophy, science and technological capability that was the Enlightenment, the *Dialectic* is firmly based in a Marxist economic analysis. It is best seen as an attempt to supplement that analysis with an account of how the forms and practices of class domination have evolved at a level beyond the relations of production and their ownership to frustrate Marx's predicted social revolution. Their thinking thus gives greater weight than classical Marxism to the role of culture and ideology in the maintenance of the exploitation of one class, the proletariat, by another, the bourgeoisie.

Doubting modernity

Adorno and Horkheimer have their critics. Orthodox Marxists have argued that their emphasis on 'superstructural' phenomena – the realm of culture, belief and ideas – neglects the material realities of the working class's struggles to overthrow the iniquities of the class structure – the 'base' that determines what is thought at the superstructural level. They view the critical theory of the Frankfurt School as an essentially bourgeois endeavour that enervates the theory of class struggle by removing it to a purely philosophical plane. Later critical theorists have viewed Adorno and Horkheimer's work as overly pessimistic – Habermas suggests that other forms of reason are operative in the public sphere, competing with and moderating instrumental rationality and that the institutions of Western democracy contain a rational, progressive potential that can challenge calculative reason.[65] In terms of radical critique they can appear to have been outflanked by the arguments of, mainly French, post-structuralist theory. Certainly their concept of power as domination and subjugation looks inflexibly binary alongside Michel Foucault's more nuanced view of power as relational, never entirely in the possession of one actor or institution, but diffused and always in ebb and flow across the social body in relations of contestation, strategic negotiation and resistance. For Foucault power is never in itself purely negative, but as a component of social relations can be positive and constructive. A more mainstream critique came from critical rationalists like the philosopher Karl Popper who, fiercely opposed to Marxism, argued that the dialectical critique of the Frankfurt School embodied an intellectual recklessness that sanctioned extreme political action, up to and including violent revolution, feeding into the totalitarianisms of the twentieth century – the elimination of societal ills and injustices was to be better managed by cautious, incremental change.[66]

Despite these and other criticisms, Adorno and Horkheimer's achievement in the *Dialectic* was to put into philosophical discourse, more clearly – some would say, luridly – than had hitherto been the case, the notion that the ills and evils of modernity might be traceable to the moment of an Enlightenment that was supposed to usher in the dawn of social harmony and sweet reason. Their account of instrumental reason – however provocatively expressed – deserves continuing attention, particularly, perhaps, in the light of the frequent calls from social liberals for a reassertion of Enlightenment values.

Criticisms of instrumentalism in education are, of course, all too common. These criticisms are, moreover, produced by social liberals just as much as they are by those of a more radical persuasion. In educational circles, particularly in university education departments, it is hard to avoid the self-assured utterances of this kind of lament; there is too much examination, too much form-filling, too much protocol and inspection, and so on. But these criticisms often only scrape the surface. As this chapter has argued, these matters of instrumentalism are not reducible to a simple question of a little more or a little less interference, as if education could be rescued from the worst excesses of modernity by a few procedural adjustments. Indeed, the logic of this way of thinking, 'a little less instrumentalism please', is – if Heidegger, Adorno and Horkheimer are to be believed – already technologically enframed, subservient to the presiding rationality. From their perspective, to think that a little less administration or examination would free education is to indulge in a short sightedness that remains opposed to a more serious troubling of education. The problems of modernity cannot be faced by a little bit of tinkering around the edges. Educational dilemmas, insofar as they are reflective of modern dilemmas, cannot we would argue, be solved through processes of adjustment and alteration, as matters of enhanced technique and improved institutional protocol. If they demand any kind of response, it has to be one that recognises these difficulties as problems of a more fundamental nature. If Adorno and Horkheimer's analysis is accepted, the critic of this way of thinking should not be distracted by, and diverted into opposing, the heavy machinery of government that weighs on each educational setting, without at the same time realising how this machinery is symptomatic of an epoch, of an entire way of thinking that constitutes us as moderns.

9

Modernity and the Figure of 'Man'

Resituating man and reason

In this chapter we explore the educational implications of our modern humanism by examining the consequences of a decisive shift in humanist thought which occurs as the figure of 'man' is given unprecedented prominence, becoming a substitute in many cases for the figure of 'God'. We explore the consequences of this transition, focusing in particular on the work of Michel Foucault who foresaw the 'death of man'. We are led to address similar time periods covered in previous chapters (ranging here again, from the sixteenth to the nineteenth centuries), a necessary overlap, illustrating how the different perspectives and critiques we describe are historically embedded. To compare the critique of our present found in Horkheimer and Adorno, for example, to the diagnosis offered by Foucault, it is necessary to understand the very different histories they construct.

To restate the case, modernity attempted to tear itself from a pre-modern mind-set where, according to Horkheimer, reason was not only 'a force' existing in 'the individual mind'. Reason also had an objective or cosmic dimension, upon which the great philosophical systems of pre-modernity, such as those of Plato and Aristotle, and scholasticism, were built.[1] These systems 'aimed at evolving a comprehensive system or hierarchy, of all beings, including man and his aims', where 'the degree of reasonableness of a man's life could be determined according to its harmony with this totality.' That greater cosmic or objective structure, 'and not just man and his purposes, was to be the measuring rod for individual thoughts and actions.' This pre-modern conception of reason, Horkheimer claims, 'never precluded subjective reason' as a force existing in the individual mind, but the latter was regarded 'as only a partial, limited expression of a universal rationality from which criteria for all things and beings were derived.'[2] In pre-modern societies the measuring rod for judging individual thoughts and actions remained, in other words, beyond the grasp, influence and control of man.

A rational existence in the modern sense is judged very differently. As we have seen it argued in the previous chapter, it prioritises calculative or instrumental reason. An institution is now considered rational if it has been designed according to a logic governed by the necessity of achieving an end that takes little or no account of wider considerations. The wider goals of the Enlightenment – the bringing about of a more moral, humane and just social being – can be 'parked'. In any case, they will be realised (so it is assumed) as economic efficiency is achieved. Oddly, we arrive at a situation where institutions, and individuals, can be rational even in an irrational context – one devoid of overall reason except the instrumental one of ensuring that the means for getting the job done are effective in their application – if they still manage to pursue immediate goals in a logical manner. Reason is considered to be operative, and can be pursued individually, so long as it demonstrates 'the ability to calculate probabilities and thereby to co-ordinate the right means with a given end'.[3]

Horkheimer recognises that other, less directly instrumental forms of reason persist in modernity, but they are shorn of cosmic significance. When the 'philosophers of the Enlightenment attacked religion in the name of reason; in the end what they killed was not the church' but the idea of a universal order, or measuring rod, to which we would submit all thought and action.[4] Reason hereby 'liquidated itself as an agency of ethical, moral, and religious insight'. Older ethical, moral and religious systems were still able to exist. And in some respects, the destruction of a universal order protected religion in modernity, allowing it to continue and to some extent thrive in an increasingly secular context. As Horkheimer argues, religion perhaps even 'profited from this development'. The reduction of universal reason to instrumental forms made religion 'safe from any serious attack'. Religion was to some extent neutralised, of course, becoming 'one cultural good among others', but this allowed it to linger on, and even prosper, fulfilling needs generated by modern societies, filling a vacuum in social life.[5]

One might extend Horkheimer's analysis regarding religion to the high-minded ideals that lie behind the modern liberal university (see Chapters 11–12). Accordingly, this university has not been entirely destroyed by managerialism, audit and instrumental reason. It lingers on because its liberal ideals can be instrumentalised to some extent, and rendered 'socially useful'. Instrumental reason will accommodate itself to anything and anyone, on the condition they be rendered calculable. Thus, religious institutions, and educational ones too, may continue to exist and continue to promote systems of belief within an instrumental order. And yet, though they survive, there is a 'wasting away' of what might be called their 'real spirit' before the instrumental reason that guarantees their afterlife.[6]

There is, according to its critics, something traumatic about modernisation. In Europe, its effects were spread over centuries, giving European cultures time to accommodate themselves to modernisation, time 'to soften its shattering impact ... through the formation of new social narratives and myths'.[7] But modernisation has impacted elsewhere too. The philosopher and cultural critic

Slavoj Žižek is not alone in claiming that modernisation, and the bewilderment it causes as it launches each society into a process of development without ultimate sanction or meaning, have been most brutally felt in non-European, non-Western societies, that have been exposed to its abrasiveness more abruptly, and in some instances more recently, 'without a protective screen or temporal delay'.[8] These developments have, he argues, contributed to the rise of fundamentalism, and the reassertion of religion and direct insight as a retreat from the distress of modernity. Which is not to argue that European modernisation came at the proper time, or that there is a 'normal' time for modernisation where some societies have come too late, without time to adapt. Modernisation 'never comes at its proper time, it always occurs "too fast", as a traumatic rupture'.[9] Nevertheless, traumas that were spread across a century and more, have been collapsed into decades for so-called developing countries.

New foundations, old attachments

Modernity might be associated with a newfound confidence in the powers of human ingenuity and productivity, but modernity is also, we would argue, associated with deep, though disavowed insecurities. This condition follows 'the death of God' – a Nietzschean argument introduced in the previous chapter – referring to the declining influence of Christianity in the West, where knowledge and human understanding are no longer subservient to Scripture, and where the ultimate purpose of human existence is no longer defined by reference to God, resulting in a profound sense of loss. Instead of confronting the nothingness suggested by a world without God, and considering how inconsequential human existence might look when confronted by the vast insensibility of the universe, modernity is defined by efforts to paper over, and perhaps overcome (or at least distract from), this loss of meaning. Here the figure of 'man' is elevated to the place formerly occupied by the idea of God; 'man' becomes himself a transcendental subject, a trans-historical source of value and meaning. This produces our distinctly modern humanism, which no longer places man above other creatures simply because he has a soul in addition to a body, or because he was cast in the image of God. Rather, the human figure becomes interesting and important in its own right, no longer deriving its status and significance from its attachment to God. Man replaces God as the master concept holding a belief system in place, the single unshakeable meaning that is beyond questioning or doubt and which gives meaning to our lives and purposes. Jacques Derrida argued that such a transcendental basis and legitimation lay at the heart of all systems of thought, all totalising analyses, and that this 'transcendental signified' is always an illusion, as open and vulnerable to questioning as any other belief.[10] Though the Enlightenment idea of man and his capacities has become fragile, it is still the idea that governs modern self-understanding with its faith in science, progress and self-improvement and its aim of the mastery of nature through knowledge. The fragility and inadequacy of this particular ruling idea are perhaps to be observed in the continuing attachment of large populations to traditional religions and to a range of superstitious or, what might be viewed as, irrational convictions. It may also be attested to by the ways in which the idea of man as a governing principle of being has fragmented into subaltern concepts that have come to occupy central positions in people's belief systems – the proletariat (Marxism), blood and race (Nazism), the market (liberal economics) and of course that ever-recurring foundation of modern selfhood, the nation. Perhaps the most poignant and exotic (considered against the ambitions of Enlightenment thinkers) variation on the transcendental subject is to be seen in that product of capitalism and its publicity arm (as Adorno and Horkheimer would have seen it), the self as a narcissistic project, the self shorn of societal commitments and historical loyalties, dedicated to the fulfilment of what it needs in order to be 'itself'.

However, thinkers who are unreservedly attached to the project of Enlightenment will deny that they suffer attachments to ideas such as these, and so also deny they are affected by a continued desire for quasi-divine or transcendental backing, a desire that is basically pre-modern in origin. They reject Adorno and Horkheimer's provocation, introduced in the previous chapter, that 'enlightenment reverts to mythology'.[11] They believe themselves detached from myth, and from the necessity of belief. Unencumbered by religion, human reason can finally be allowed free rein, leading to new, better and more rigorous ways of thinking about nature and society. The promise of reason is to base all understanding, all ideas and all values upon the careful, diligent work of thought cleansed of allegiance to anything other than the pursuit of scientific truth. All things can now be submitted to the scientific gaze, including man himself. Enlightened people were those who believed that the key to unlocking the mysteries of the universe lay in directly observing and studying the natural and the man-made world. The human past would be submitted to similar inspection, as its boundary walls and burial sites were exhumed, their artefacts taken, exported and reassembled elsewhere. But such paeans to reason are problematic. This passion to collect and catalogue, to organise all phenomena in vast taxonomies, was driven, some would say, by the urge to power driving the conquests and acquisitions of Western imperialism, as much as it was driven by a desire to make the world decipherable to human understanding. If Nietzsche, Heidegger, Adorno and Horkheimer are right, modernity achieves an unparalleled intensity in its quest to impose order on everything it surveys.

As modern man took up position where a divinity had once stood, he bore some resemblance to the figure he replaced. To return once more to Horkheimer and Adorno, it could be argued that 'in their mastery of nature, the creative God and the ordering mind are alike. Man's likeness to God consists in sovereignty over existence, in the lordly gaze, in the command'.[12] According to the *Dialectic* this likeness produces inevitable estrangement:

> Human beings purchase the increase in their power with estrangement from that over which it is exercised. Enlightenment stands in the same relationship to things as the dictator to human beings. He knows them to the extent that he can manipulate them.[13]

But when the thing to be manipulated is man himself, things get rather more complicated, and perhaps in ways Horkheimer and Adorno did not anticipate. As we explore later in this chapter, human beings are not simply manipulated in modernity – made calculable, and rendered subservient to instrumental reason. The modern man of science is not simply estranged from himself and his fellow beings. Rather, the scientific gaze leads to a kind of intimacy, a desire to find out what 'makes us tick' which is completely unlike the distant gaze of a dictator or divine overlord. This more intimate gaze mimics a different sort of divinity, a caring god, one that is constantly present and continually felt, a presence that leads the individual to introspect, to engage in endless enquiry, in an on-going attempt to make the self knowable and account for the soul.[14]

This quest for order, for ensuring everything has its place and measure, is not a straightforwardly totalitarian injunction. Rather it becomes embedded in thought as an indisputable way of approaching things, as a commonsense way of going about one's business, a way of understanding and dealing with phenomena. As such, the pursuit of order and reason is something that anyone can participate in. Anyone may take part in modernity; indeed, everyone should participate if they have reached its threshold. Modernity is defined by its openness in this respect, by its willingness to involve anyone who agrees to participate in its terms. One such term of engagement is the willingness of participants to submit themselves to the rules of reasoned, measured, ordered and orderly debate. According to the rules of such debate, in principle anyone with scientific training will always assent to the better argument. Personal preference and allegiance are to be put aside before the force of reason. Free of all prejudice, open to new ideas, rational people must set aside all superstition and even personal pride for the sake of truth. In polite society, 'reasonableness' is to become the connecting principle about which participants will gather and communicate. It becomes the universal glue that will bind them together as religion once did yet without that tendency to schism and conflict, if not blood-letting, that had once beset matters of religious conscience. Reasonable individuals, modern men and women, would work together, and apply themselves to endless debate and enquiry.

For education, the implications were ultimately global in reach, rendering thinkable the idea that a single, reason-led educational project might transcend all cultural and religious barriers. Yet all these attempts to replace a Christian order and rationale with an increasingly secular set of values and pursuits would eventually suffer from the precarious nature of their foundations. These foundations were problematic since they were located in the creature that was seeking to give substance to these efforts. They were located within 'man' himself. As Michel Foucault argues in

The Order of Things, man appears in modernity as 'a strange empirico-transcendental doublet'.[15] According to this analysis, our modern enquiry into the nature of man is an empirical investigation of the constitution of the object 'man' that bases itself on the hypothesis that such a creature exists. Man is not only an invention of modern thought but also the grounding, the foundation of that thought. Empirical study has to assume the prior and transcendent existence of 'man' in order to proceed in its enquiries. This has produced a rather baffling dynamic, where empirical study forever assumes and attempts to outline the nature of man, but never achieves its objective. As we explore below, in attempting to discover himself, man only enters in a game with his own finitude, with his own limits.

The Order of Things

In *The Order of Things* Foucault links the making of 'man' as a paradoxical being to the development in modernity of the human sciences. As a modern endeavour, initially including subject areas such as economics and human biology, these sciences expanded over the last two centuries into newly established fields of enquiry such as sociology, psychology, and eventually educational studies. What all these disciplinary fields share is that human beings in themselves have become the object of scientific interest. This endeavour was complicated by the fact that unlike other objects of scientific interest, such as animals or natural phenomena, human beings can be influenced by the understandings generated through science. Humans are, quite uniquely, also the *subjects* that are responsible for and are responding to the findings of those new regimes of knowledge that are concerned with human activity. Hence, modern attempts to understand and describe human behaviour were also, unavoidably, efforts to influence the behaviour described. This is the problem that is created when, as Foucault argues, man becomes both the object and the subject of his enquiries. The radical implication of this epistemic and ontological predicament is that ever since this modern interest in man took off, the foundations of modern understanding have been in a process of constant retreat. Modern man is constantly confronted, in other words, by his lack of objectively verifiable substance.

The complex situation modernity presents itself with can be observed in the field of education, which is not only tasked with understanding more about the education of human beings (how best to educate, and so on), and nor is it simply influenced by the knowledge produced (by educationalists and other social scientists). Education also more or less deliberately seeks to form (i.e. educate and cultivate) the very objects of study. This double bind is observable in the very deliberate link education establishes between modern fields of knowledge and the cultivation of a modern citizenry. Educational institutions such as schools often served here as conveniently placed laboratories in which the human sciences were able to carry out their investigations. As we explore in Chapter 11, these sciences benefited from the institutionalisation of increasing numbers of children and young adults, allowing the human subject to be investigated in the unique confines a school provides. Educational institutions acquired a new and distinct function in modernity. They brought under one roof the objects of research, providing a wealth of data for the development of educational psychologies, sociologies and so on. At the same time, they were uniquely and deliberately tasked with altering the human phenomena they described.

Renaissance thought

According to Foucault's argument, the rise of modern man was preceded by a very different approach to natural phenomena. In the Renaissance, the world was understood according to an overarching system of 'similitude', where affinities were sought between objects and words. Indeed, words were not treated as necessary labels that we improvise and attach to things. They were not treated as mere tools, as straightforward representations of things. Words were respected and approached as if they were things themselves. And so, when correspondences were observed between words, as between things, it was assumed that they were somehow related. Understanding was fundamentally interpretative in this sense, where it was a matter of divining the significance of resemblances between things and between words.

The task was to seek out a divine order that has left its signature everywhere, in traces and marks that are to be found imprinted on things and words. From this perspective, to discover that 'aconite [a poisonous plant] will cure our eye disease, or that ground walnut mixed with spirits of wine will ease a headache, there must of course be some mark that will make us aware of these things'.[16] According to Renaissance thought, these signatures, or visible marks, are all there to be deciphered, as one notices that the walnut resembles the brain, or that the seedpods of aconite resemble the eyes. This gives access to the nature of things that have been ordered for our benefit. The order of things is revealed in these surface traces, just as 'the lines of a hand or the furrows on a brow' are seen as 'tracing on a man's body the tendencies, accidents, or obstacles present in the whole vast fabric of his life'.[17] There is no need to look beyond the surface, or to investigate hidden depths. Rather what is required is the ability to pick out the significant traits from all the phenomena that surround us, and interpret their meaning. Because the signatures left over from the divine ordering of the cosmos never exactly replicate what they resemble (the walnut is not a perfect representation of the brain, the aconite seedpod does not perfectly resemble the eye, the furrows on a hand do not perfectly describe one's fate), interpretation is necessary.

Similarly, words are not arbitrary, nor are they transparent; their meaning must be deciphered. They are treated as if they were mysterious, magical even, and pregnant with meaning, as if they bear within themselves traces of a divine order that can be given over to interpretation. In this regard the texts handed down from antiquity are viewed as a treasure-trove, where there is 'no difference between the visible marks that God has stamped upon the surface of the earth, so that we may know its inner secrets, and the legible words that the Scriptures, or the sages of Antiquity, have set down in the books preserved for us by tradition'. In both cases, there are signs that must be discovered 'and then, little by little, be made to speak', be made to reveal the nature of the God that gave them existence.[18] Here Renaissance man was considered uniquely endowed amongst animals, being the only animal able to discover and interpret the divine order. But he was not able, thereby, to separate himself from it. He was free and powerful only on the condition, that 'by means of his wisdom, which is also his knowledge, he comes to resemble the order of the world, takes it back into himself and thus recreates in his inner firmament' that outer firmament which exists in 'the depths of the heavens and beyond'. This man will discover 'that he contains the stars within himself' and is thereby attached to, made in the image of, and confined by, everything he understands.[19]

The 'Classical Age'

In the period directly following the Renaissance – a period Foucault rather confusingly calls the 'Classical Age' (not to be confused with classical antiquity) – a new order of truth took hold. The classical age, according to Foucault's periodisation, lasts from the early seventeenth century until about the time of the French Revolution in 1789. Seeking to investigate what made thought possible in this period Foucault detects a transition in human understanding. The world was now presumed knowable in itself, as a set of external realities existing beyond language. Even as scientific instruments were required to uncover these realities (as a microscope, for instance, reveals what is hidden from the naked eye), the realities they revealed were considered already 'out there' existing independently, and available for discovery. Crucially, language no longer offered an opportunity for discovering the hidden nature of the world, as if language contained within itself a rich and necessary tapestry of hidden meaning. As Foucault puts it: 'The profound kinship of language and the world was thus dissolved'.[20] Things and words were now separated from one another, where writing and speaking were no longer to be understood as anything more than what was written or said. Words became tools; they did not hold within themselves secret meaning or give access to the divine order of the universe.

The epistemological challenge became one of measurement instead of interpretation. Rather than seek to discover the affinities between things (and between words), it would be better to order them in vast tables. The measurable variations between things became the point of interest, rather than the affinities or apparent resemblances between them. Signs for things, such as words, were now treated as entirely arbitrary, contingent and instrumental. They were, quite simply, tools for identifying things to be measured. Classical age thinkers would no longer treat signs as things in themselves, and hence did not seek the meanings of words in order to construct understanding. Rather, they were only interested in how accurately these arbitrary sign systems were able to represent the nature of the 'real' world.

According to Foucault's analysis, during this period knowledge was chiefly representational in form. Realities were treated as if they could be unproblematically represented through, for example, an accurate textual description, a map or a painting. These signs or sign systems were not considered to be interesting in their own right as if they held within themselves truths of their own. Maps or words were just tools used in representing something else. The act of representing the world was not viewed to be a problem or obstacle in coming to know it. Whilst some thinkers still maintain to this very day (perhaps the majority of scientists and some analytic philosophers, for example) that the world is directly knowable, and that we must simplify our representation of things so that we can cut through the veil of language, this philosophical position now has its critics. It has become seriously controversial to claim that, for example, words can accurately and straightforwardly represent the nature of things. In the classical age, by contrast, this controversy did not arise because representations were not yet viewed as potentially troublesome. Here a narrow empiricism held sway. It was sufficient merely to observe, measure and record the world, amassing data that could be tabulated and organised into great compendia of knowledge.

This kind of approach did not last long, however. The classical age would soon come to an end. The desired taxonomies (schemes of classification) proliferated, and recorded knowledge became increasingly unwieldy. The human sciences were also troubled by the fact that there was no ultimate 'third party' (a role formerly occupied by Gods, sacred texts and divinely inspired sages) to which they could appeal to verify or substantiate their conclusions. There was no third party that would confirm the findings of the human sciences as truthful, universally applicable statements about the human condition. Since the authority of religion had given way, the human sciences were compelled, rather impossibly, to resource a neutral and universal outlook from within themselves. And so, in a quest for truth, in an attempt to find the supports for understanding in something more substantial and foundational than human subjectivity, the human sciences became more and more interested in working out what was going on 'in a sort of behind-the-scenes world'.[21] They were, in other words, no longer satisfied with describing the surface features of measurable things.

Doubting the power of empirical description to reveal the 'truth' of the world, those working in the human sciences began to suspect the existence of submerged forces and influences that must themselves be investigated. With the death of God, in other words, 'man' eventually sought to justify his knowledge elsewhere, by claiming that it was built on foundations that exist beyond immediate perception. In so doing, he discovered a new depth in things, and new hidden depths in himself.

Modern understanding

In *The Order of Things*, Foucault outlines 'the threshold of a modernity that we have not yet left behind'. It was on this threshold, he argues, that the 'strange figure of knowledge called man first appeared', establishing 'a space proper to the human sciences'.[22] The assumption took hold that man has foundational characteristics, though they are always obscured. Roughly dating from the beginning of the nineteenth century, there was a transition away from classical thinking, as representations themselves became interesting, which is another way of saying that they became problematic. It could no longer be so easily assumed that representations of phenomena are themselves straightforward and transparent, that words directly and accurately relate those things they describe. It could no longer be assumed that they form 'an unquestioned, self-justifying starting point' for thought and understanding.[23] Rather, words intervene, mediating and complicating our understanding of those things they claim to label. The Cartesian phrase 'I think, therefore I am' does not make sense any more from this point of view, since the subject who thinks it is not viewed as being transparent to himself. Modern understanding does not rest here, of course, at this realisation. It does not simply problematise representation; it attempts to look beyond representation, assuming that something more fundamental lies beneath. Modern understanding hopes to look beyond representations, and seek in things 'an order that now belongs to things themselves and to their interior law'[24] – the laws of nature, of language, of economy, which are presumed to exist as things to be discovered. Hence the person who declares, 'I think, therefore I am', now believes he is the product of so much more than consciousness; he is produced by hidden laws that constitute the thinking subject, laws that the modern man of the human sciences will attempt to uncover.

Hidden depths were assumed, then, as modern thought descended into a submerged interiority that it attempted to describe. Psychoanalysis posited an unconscious that, all unawares to the subject, determined its thinking and action. Following Hegel and Marx, historiography was revolutionised as a study of the movement of largely hidden forces that drive history. Literary theory was constituted as an endeavour that could uncover meanings that the author was unaware of. Sociology was inaugurated as a science that claimed to detect truths about human social being that eluded empirical/positivist observation. Statistics was born as a discipline concerned with unearthing statistical regularities that could be observed in natural phenomena only after the application of algorithms developed by statistical science. And education was conceived as far more than a simple pedagogy of induction into prevailing social mores (as Locke might have conceived it), and far more than an introduction to the existing state of knowledge (an uncomplicated process of knowledge transmission). Education was now studied as an enterprise driven not simply by liberal ideology or administrative calculation but one haunted by schematics of power and control, by hidden curricula, concealed forms of social reproduction, and irreconcilable conflicts. The production of modern disciplinary knowledge across all these fields was now based on the quest to discover those hidden phenomena that make us what we are, but which, by definition, must remain hidden if they are to function.

These hidden laws are only given expression through the sovereign gaze of man who places himself as their last achievement. He 'unveils himself to his own eyes in the form of a being' who is already produced by those laws and hidden phenomena.[25] These laws are presumed to have produced that modern man of science who is, finally, able to give them at least approximate form in his consciousness. In this sense, they owe their conscious existence to his gaze. They only take form in, and are mediated through, that perception. This presumed sovereignty – the idea of the sovereign gaze – persists even as the modern quest for knowledge finds itself drawn into a period of discord and fragmentation. This fragmentation occurs once surface phenomena are suspected of being the mere epiphenomena, by-products, or surface effects of something more substantial operating at a submerged level. In the classical age, no equivalent discord existed, since it could be assumed that 'knowledge formed a homogeneous whole', with each domain of enquiry in principle connected to each other through measurable systems of difference.[26] It was a matter of measuring, labelling, and describing the distance between things, which could, it was presumed, be assembled in vast tables that expressed the overall order of things. In the nineteenth century, this confidence was gone and 'the epistemological field' (the field of knowledge) 'exploded in different directions'.[27] Modern research could no longer be understood 'as a linear series of enquiries employing the same basic method in different domains'.[28] Knowledge was now divided into different dimensions, where each area had its own accepted techniques and procedures. The human sciences proliferated in this context, claiming to discover foundational or hidden traits in human histories, languages, social phenomena, and individual and group psychologies. This revealed an 'inexhaustible treasure-hoard of experiences and concepts' that the newly founded sciences might investigate interminably.[29]

The growing suspicion of surface representations, of the ability of signs to adequately represent things, generated significant and ultimately intractable problems for the construction of knowledge. The treasure-hoard of experiences and concepts this interest in man's depths created, generated 'a perpetual principle of dissatisfaction, of calling into question, of criticism and contestation of what may seem, in other respects, to be established'.[30] So far, this has only helped perpetuate the human sciences (and other areas of enquiry), which advance towards their own limits 'only with their back to it' – waiting for human phenomena to unveil themselves as fast as they are analysed and represented in thought.[31] This multiplication of work for the human sciences did not help stabilise or bring to view what they attempted to investigate. The claim to investigate the hidden laws that give man his substance may have revealed his finitude or limits (showing that he is a natural phenomenon, an effect of hidden laws, rather than a free agent able to create the world unimpeded), but it did not give him security by describing those limits. This discovery of man's bounded nature, this 'primary discovery of finitude', which defines the modern era, is also an 'unstable one'. It leads only to the quest for more discovery, for a better understanding of those laws which are never fully understood.

This link between the discovery of finitude, and the 'monotony of a journey' of discovery that never ends, occurs because 'nothing allows' this discovery of finitude – of the fact that we are limited by so-called laws that are not immediately available to our understanding – 'to contemplate itself'.[32] With some notable exceptions (psychoanalysis would be one), the limits of human understanding, the nature of human finitude, are simply not accepted, though they are testified to by each failure of research to ground itself in the elusive figure of man, or the hidden laws of nature, or economy, or whatever. They are not accepted, in the sense that their acknowledged existence does not halt the endless quest to describe limits that must remain, by definition, always beyond description.

The death of Man

Foucault argues that the ground is 'once more stirring under our feet'.[33] It is indeed conceivable, Foucault speculates, that we are approaching another threshold in Western culture, one that will follow the death of God, with the death of Man. As Foucault famously concludes his book, 'one can certainly wager that man would be erased, like a face drawn in sand at the edge of the sea'.[34] That is to say, it is conceivable that a time will come when we no longer resource understanding in that modern humanism, in the assumption that man is or must be foundational, that he can build from himself and his own resources the necessary structures of civilisation, and that these can be justified and perfected in the self-discovery of foundational laws of nature, economy and human psychology.

Foucault is clearly at odds with Kant, who sought to base man's understanding in himself (see Chapter 7). Foucault argues that this way of thinking would eventually unravel, for it is based on an impossibility that would eventually become apparent. Here Foucault seems to look ahead to a new, post-foundational, post-humanist way of thinking, one that no longer assumes hidden depths, or insists that human activity be guided by its quest for deep understanding, by its search for as-yet hidden foundations or indisputable structures that would justify its existence. Foucault imagines a new way of thinking, one that would no longer have man as its ultimate referent, one that would not insist that all understanding must ultimately, and in principle, be filtered through that sovereign gaze. Foucault envisages the death of Man, not as the end of humanity, but as the end of a certain way of thinking about humanity, one that has led human being into decidedly narrow confines.[35]

Rootless and wandering

Modern faith in the idea that human understanding might have some justifiable, foundational basis, that will one day become apparent, is waning, as this basis forever retreats before each new analysis and discovery. This growing uncertainty has had a profound influence on education to the extent that it has become more and more difficult to agree upon the purpose of education, or to hope that educational aims could ever be achieved since the human phenomena they deal with are so complex and intractable. This lack of consensus concerning its nature, and diminishing hope concerning the realisation of its values (whatever they may be), has left education open to multiple interventions and assumptions concerning the aims and purposes of educational activity. Arguably, this lends education to a situation where it is largely emptied of commitment to a singular value system or divine sanction. It is filled up instead with a variety of techniques, each justified in their own idiosyncratic way.

This collapse – reducing the defence of education to the valorisation and perpetuation of educational technique – could be viewed as the product of a failure to account for the substance and superiority of modern humanist thought. It was hoped that modern humanism would be legitimated through appeal to some foundation or other that would give it grounding. This project never succeeded. And so, the desire to give our lives substance and meaning – and in our case, the desire to give education content and purpose – is now largely expressed through a dogged commitment to all that is left, where all that we have remaining is the activity of being modern, the endless quest for production and knowledge-seeking that modernity inaugurates.

When discussing education today, educators give little time to a discussion of its value, most often finding themselves preoccupied with improving its technique. We find ourselves seemingly surrounded by educators who discuss nothing but technical matters in Heidegger's sense (see Chapter 8). This is not a personal failure of the educators in question. The problem these educators share is of a more general nature: the empirical reality of education is given such high status now, precisely because the 'transcendental' justification for education has been lost. Reliant as it is on a modern humanism that can only justify itself by reference to its unplumbed depths, modern education is cast adrift, and hence left uncertain of its mission and purpose. It can only grasp on to the one thing it knows to be certain, which is itself, its own practices and procedures. Almost all that remains of education, then, is the reality of its existing techniques and methods. Consequently, these techniques and methods are held very close indeed. One might say, they are the 'heart and soul' of education today.

Education is not radically decentred, as one might expect, by growing uncertainty concerning its purpose, and the nature of its task. Arguably this is because we remain within the order of things, within the modern 'episteme' or era that Foucault describes. The end of Man which Foucault sees on the horizon is not yet completed. Though the positioning of man as subject and object of its own enquiries leads to its own impossibilities, this conception of man remains with us precisely because its impossibilities are never fully perceived. And so we still assume, for example, that lessons can be taught based on an increasingly sound understanding of human psychology, for instance. We still assume that educational curricula can coalesce in the increasingly independent, conscious and self-aware subjectivity of each pupil. We still teach as if each lesson could cohere, at its limit and objective, in the mind of each student. There may be multiple lessons in each lesson (multiple 'take-home messages'), but we still teach as if some aspect of each lesson will be taken home or stored whole for future use, given form and consistency by the meaning-giving agency (or sovereign understanding) of the student. Yet at the same time we teach in the realisation that each lesson remains imperfect, that it confronts insurmountable challenges, and that these are based in our incomplete knowledge of the subject matter of education, which includes an imperfect knowledge of the individual and group psychologies of those taught.

Still, education continues as if it could be perfected, as if one day a perfected educational science or practice could be realised. Educators remain trapped in a double bind. They teach as if each lesson, and education finally, might overcome the hidden forces that hinder it. But these hidden forces are also recognised as its basis, since they lie behind and condition the consciousness of those whom education seeks to teach. That education might be bound up with and bound to produce confusion, broken lessons, failed communications and fundamental impossibilities, is still relatively unthinkable.

At its limit, education still attempts to form the individual of modern humanism, however impossible subsequent theory might claim the existence of that individual to be. Though the idea of 'man' is replaced by a conception of the human being, an apparently genderless term, the figure of man described by Foucault remains in this 'ambiguous position as an object of knowledge and a subject who knows: enslaved sovereign, observed spectator'.[36] Students and teachers embody that impossibility, the ambiguity of this position. In modernity they became, and still remain, 'observed spectators'; studious and studied; active ('sovereign') and acted on ('enslaved'). Education participates both in the formation of human subjects, and in the production of knowledge about those subjects (or others like them), thereby contributing to a system where the ultimate nature of, and reason for forming the subject of, education is an ever-retreating formation. We are bound to it nonetheless, as one is 'bound to the back of a tiger',[37] unable to escape, out of control and tearing forward. If *The Order of Things* is to be believed, we are suffering the affects of an educational project operating without sanction, and a humanism gone feral. A rootless humanism, it is doomed to wander interminably. It remains forever obsessed with finding itself. Its thirst is only aggravated by the repeatedly discovered incompleteness of its self-understanding.

10

Critique, Emancipation and Education

What is critique?

As a concept and practice, the importance of critique is insisted on in higher education, where criticality is taken to be a defining requirement of academic life. It remains, nonetheless, a rather puzzling and less than straightforward business. Scarcely any university course will fail to assert that it values the development of critical thinking as a key aim. The student who embarks upon a course in a university humanities or social sciences department will find that course rubrics and module assessment criteria will exhort them to think and read critically, tutors will comment on the critical competence of their work and they will be encouraged to see their performance as a student of culture and society as an essentially critical activity. They will be expected to demonstrate other competences but they will be made very aware that their worth as a student will, apparently, be judged to a significant extent on their ability to critically analyse/reflect upon/engage with/ review the texts, data, arguments, ideas, views and findings they encounter in their studies. Critique and its cognates – criticism, criticality, critical thinking, critical awareness – are everywhere in the academy, like banners staking out the territory, signalling the distinct and unique nature of the field the student has entered. That field, that territory is, of course, the domain of Western thought and, in particular, that shrinking corner of the academic field in which 'man' thinks about himself, about his nature, his place in the world, his capacities and his limitations, his thoughts and feelings and his destiny. The protocols of critique, its proponents suggest, are what distinguish Western thought from the kinds of knowledge and modes of enquiry that have been developed in other cultures, in other civilisations. Critique, it might also be said, is what polices Western thought, what keeps it honest and faithful to its authentic purposes.

This account of Western exceptionalism trails a certain racism, as if Western scholarship discovered a master code that eluded other traditions, a code whose discovery renders the achievements of non-Western thought questionable, if not obsolete. The assumption can too easily be made that outside the West it never occurred to anyone to question why they were required to think or act in certain ways, let alone express views that conflicted with established understandings. Critique has certainly been practised in cultures beyond Europe, but it is indisputably the case that nowhere else has so much been made of it. It is true that students from other cultures are sometimes concerned as to what criticality might be, what they will have to do in order to pass muster as a critically functioning student. In fact, this is an anxiety shared by many students from indigenous Western backgrounds who are similarly taken aback by the insistence at every turn in the academy that they be critical.

Yet what is meant by critical thinking, by critical practice, varies widely. If one considers the research output of university humanities or social science departments, critical practice can denote the ability to adjudicate between conflicting arguments, to assess the quality of evidence presented, or to problematise ideas and issues on the basis of some normative framework. Criticality can be applied to the matter of rendering a truthful account of reality as it is – for example, to an analysis of the successes and failures of different methods for encouraging mathematical learning in the early years of schooling – or it can be applied to an argument for how things should be. And that 'should be' might simply amount to a recommendation as to how some educational goal might best be achieved because of available evidence, or it might involve the questioning of an educational policy on grounds of principle. For example, committing one cohort of school pupils to a heavily vocational curriculum and another to a broader, more 'academic' programme invites the accusation that foundational educational values are being transgressed – in this case the educational values of equality of opportunity for all pupils and the right to an education that will develop their full human potential. In other words, critique can operate at the level of empirical enquiry or at the level of socio-moral theory.

As such, critique can work comfortably within its institutional setting, accepting the boundaries, the established directions and methods of the field within which it operates, but working always towards the refinement of its procedures for producing knowledge; or it can seek the transformation of the academic field in which it is located, the radical redirection of its aims, purposes and self-understanding. Critique can be acquiescent in what might be seen as the dominant values of society or it can commit itself, however implausible such a project might seem, to the subversion of existing relations of power and their replacement by some other organisation of those relations.

These two divergent options show the breadth of activity the word 'critique' can be used to signify, ranging from acquiescence to revolt. In fact, the picture is much more nuanced and complicated than this depiction of the situation suggests. Critique operates on a spectrum. Critical practices can be more or less committed to change within their fields of research or in the social or human domains they investigate; they can aim at the reaffirmation of existing understandings, at their modification, at their substantial renewal or at a radical transformation that falls short of the overthrow of a system of thought or social organisation. Empiricisms can put critical thinking at the service of gathering aspirationally value-free, objective information about the world, but empirical research can also serve pronounced social–political analyses which are framed within a different order of critique.

In the university criticality is regularly practised within specific bounded contexts. For the student, critical aptitude is to be shaped within the constraints of the academic essay or dissertation and university academics are subject to similar disciplinary pressures. Academic critique has its conventional forms, such as the professional journal article, and occasions of critical performance which are regulated by established protocols, such as the university seminar. Intellectual critique may abound and proliferate within these contexts, and yet, despite its elevated status as the objective which all good (that is to say, all enlightened) educational institutions must encourage, criticality is subject to definite restrictions. Academics are, it can be argued, largely compliant in their everyday navigation of the system they serve; better at surviving within the system than subverting it or refusing the power plays it imposes. Of course, most academics would vigorously reject the suggestion they lack criticality or the courage to speak truthfully to power, cleaving as they do to modern ideals of free thought, debate and intellectual exchange. Academic freedom is held up by those working in the university as the freedom that defines the institution, a freedom that we lose at our peril. However, it seems clear that academic freedom, the freedom to indulge critique wherever it may take you, is only realised in a restricted context.

To some extent this follows the longstanding separation of philosophy from everyday life (see Chapter 2), where philosophy can now be approached as an intellectual concern that has little or no relation to how one chooses to live. In modernity, this decoupling of intellectual and practical concerns allowed intellectual activity to operate free of certain kinds of dogmatism. It allowed for the existence of academic freedom within clear limits. But it is a split that comes at a cost, making things difficult for those seeking to practise what they argue, for those hoping to align intellectual commitments with everyday existence. And so, while modern educational institutions may encourage their members to 'think freely', they are relatively intolerant of those who follow through on their ideas by putting them into action.[1] The academy, or indeed the school, is uncomfortable with those who not only have ideas and opinions that differ from the dominant institutional view, but who also insert them into practice, thereby turning those ideas back on the institution and its policies through direct action or through public critique of institutional decisions. The teacher who writes to a local newspaper expressing disagreement with their school's decision to become an academy or the academic who publicly criticises the educational validity of a university course is likely to be putting her career in a degree of jeopardy. As those who resist and fall foul of this system might argue, their crime was to 'embody a certain consistency between acts and thought' – something that is 'rarely treated with leniency'.[2] In this chapter we explore this dual legacy of the Enlightenment, where systems designed to encourage free thought are attached to mechanisms of constraint. We argue that in addition to the problematic relation between critical thinking and everyday practice, in its own realm, the realm of disembodied thought, critical-ity is subject to additional problems. We will go on to argue that within today's avowed commitments to criticality an uncritical dimension persists. This problem takes in much more than the cynicism of an educational system that increasingly rewards compliance and discourages dissent. As we will go on to argue, there is a more basic problem at issue here, a problem with criticality itself.

A brief consideration of the origins and history of the concept will, we suggest, cast some light on the contradictions inherent in the practice of critique and in the project of enlightenment it has served.

Critique – etymology and history[3]

The words critique and crisis have a common derivation from the Ancient Greek *krinein* (decide) which referred to the actions of separating, judging and deciding as they were applied in three distinct spheres: in the administration of justice *krisis* (decision) referred to the action of restoring order in a dispute through a judicial decision; in medicine it came to refer to the crucial turning point in an illness (hence the current medical term 'in a critical condition'); in the later Hellenistic period *kritikos* (able to judge, skilled in judgement) referred to the study of literary texts. This later meaning came to a measure of dominance during the Renaissance – a critic was someone who engaged in the philological exegesis or reconstruction of ancient texts in order to restore them to their original condition. As we saw in Chapter 5, the philologist sought to combat the textual corruption brought about over time, through a critical reading of the text and its history of decay, aiming to bring into being the text's truth, the authentic meaning that had been obscured or distorted by erroneous versions of the original manuscript.

We would suggest that awareness of what Connerton calls the 'overlapping con-notations' informing the notion of critique is helpful to an understanding of what critique/criticism/criticality has become during the modern period.[4] Particularly useful to keep in mind as we sort through the varied ways in which critique has been understood, applied and argued over are the ideas of (i) the critic as judge, as adjudicator of the true state of affairs, (ii) the idea of truth as in need of rescuing or uncovering from sedimented misrepresentation, and (iii) the idea of the critic as the bearer of justice.

We begin our exploration of what critique has signified in the modern period by turning once again to Immanuel Kant's canonical statement concerning the relation between critique and power.

The age of criticism

According to Kant the eighteenth century was to be 'the age of criticism'.[5] It was during this period that critique, the exercise of critical judgement, acquired its modern senses. Kant was perhaps the greatest, certainly the most acclaimed, figure in the intellectual and cultural moment that is referred to as the Enlightenment. Thinkers like Kant, Rousseau and Voltaire identified freedom as the essential destiny of humanity. They saw servitude to traditional authorities – above all, the established church and the superstition and ignorance it imposed upon the bulk of humanity – as the barrier preventing human beings from achieving full maturity and independence. Servitude to tradition prevented human beings from achieving, as individuals and collectively, a society governed by reason and organised on the core principle of freedom.

It is important to note that along with the rise of modernity described in the preceding chapters, these ideas came to fruition in the period of the absolutist states (see Chapter 8). This form of government had been instituted to put an end to the religious wars that had spread slaughter across Europe during the sixteenth and seventeenth centuries. In 1648 The Peace of Westphalia, a series of treaties that marked the end of more than a century of conflicts, established that it was the sovereign nation state to which the subjects of different countries owed their allegiance and whose laws and dictates they should obey rather than any religious authority. These newly territorialised states, it has been argued, were concerned to guard against and constrain religious zealotry by imposing a separation of morality and politics, and to govern in ways that were guided by reason rather than revelation. Many of the features of modern democratic nation states find their origin in the institutions of government invented in this period, the most notable example perhaps being the establishment of an administrative bureaucracy whose brief was to find ways of organising, policing and taxing the state's population in the interests of national order and prosperity.

Under the conditions of absolutist rule, therefore, it was thus not too risky a business to inveigh against the power of the opposed religious denominations that had licensed the division and bloodshed. Nevertheless, the absolutist states, as the name indicates, were also politically authoritarian governments headed by divinely ordained monarchs. There would have been good reason for Enlightenment thinkers to tread carefully when it came to criticising the political powers of the day, however cultivated and enlightened those powers might profess to be. Connerton argues that 'a systematic network of hypocrisy' operated amongst Enlightenment thinkers,[6] a self-denying ordinance that allowed them to develop the political implications of enlightened thought without directly questioning the authority of their despotic rulers or proposing alternative forms of government. It must, however, be said that many of these thinkers were not of a revolutionary cast of mind. In 1784, Immanuel Kant, for one, was happy to accept the supreme authority of Frederick II of Prussia, as is reflected in his famous, approving statement that the licence offered by his 'Prince' is to: '*Argue, as much as you want and about what ever you want; but obey!*'[7]

The frameworks of thought established under these conditions were very influential. Kant argued for a separation between what he described as a 'public' use of reason and its 'private' use.[8] In effect, he suggested a social order in which one is expected to be obedient in private, that is, when performing the duties one has been assigned – as, for example, a government official. But this is matched by the expectation that one can raise questions in public, participating in open and free debate. His claim was that freedom of the first variety could be 'very narrowly restricted without the progress of enlightenment being particularly hindered'.[9] Despite its origins in a system of despotic rule, this division is still endorsed today as a potentially worthwhile separation of thought and action, as a means of allowing dissent within an established social order.

More radical critics than Kant may nevertheless object that the operations of critique are unacceptably compromised by such an arbitrary division between the free public use of reason and its domesticated private forms. Such critics generally see themselves as representatives of its greater public use. In so doing, they seek to extend the territories of critique so that in principle nothing is beyond censure. But one might argue in response that this critique of the restraints imposed on critique fails to appreciate that the private use of reason was itself a 'remarkable human invention'.[10] This is the argument made by Ian Hunter, who claims that the idea of detaching practical and procedural (or private) reason from its more idealist and abstract (public) counterpart, built the 'capacity to detach governmental decision from personal loyalties and religious passions'. Indeed, 'far from representing a split in a formerly unified moral personality or public life', this separation 'was a positive organisational and ethical acquisition'. It allowed the modern state to develop organisational forms of a purely bureaucratic nature. These relatively autonomous zones of bureaucratic calculation raised the modern state above the 'principled blood-letting' that had beset religiously inspired government.[11] Critique was restrained, yes, but only so that it might avoid descent into old forms of unthinking conformity to fundamentalist doctrine. Such a defence of the limitations imposed on critique suggests, indeed, that modern critics be more grateful to those hypocrisies that made the position of the morally elevated critic a liveable, and relatively comfortable, occupation. However, Hunter's argument is not one that is popular with critical theorists.[12] For Hunter effectively argues that critique was only allowed to exist and thrive, in its own limited way, on the condition that it knew its place.

It would be a mistake to dismiss Kant for wishing to have his cake and eat it. It would be too easy to impugn him for dividing reason into its public (free) and private (enslaved) forms, or for favouring argument for its own sake, so long as those arguing remained otherwise obedient in their official posts. While this antinomy between 'free' thought and obedient conduct both precedes Kant and most certainly outlives him, with Kant we find initiated something far more problematic. Following Kant, it became apparent that, if Enlightenment was to be philosophically justifiable, the very frameworks of free thought would themselves need to be carefully regulated. From a philosophical perspective, rational thought should only be developed within a clearly defined structure that would determine the form and content of debate.

For Kant, the quest to become free is to be based on a critique of how we were enslaved, how we were denied the free use of reason, becoming yoked instead to the unthinking conventions of tradition. In this respect, as we have seen, Enlightenment reason attempts to free us from constraint and yet at the same time this critical and philosophical project is designed to establish those foundations upon which (and within which) a free use of reason will operate. Hence Enlightenment philosophy inaugurates a critical enterprise in which the primary mission of rational thought is to legitimate itself. Its purpose is to establish the foundations that will allow it to operate. Or, to put it slightly differently, Enlightenment philosophy attempts to establish a platform from which it can judge all other systems of thought. It attempts to authenticate itself and establish its own foundations, whilst at the same time offering an account of our enslavement to previous 'less rational' foundations that we must, accordingly, destroy. Having no initial foundations of its own, Enlightenment reason is forced to begin mid-sentence.

In response to the question: 'Do we now live in an *enlightened* age?' Kant would say, 'No, but we do live in an age of *enlightenment*'.[13] The philosophical project of Enlightenment was very much open; it was just beginning. As his *Critique of Pure Reason* suggests by its very title, Kant offers a model for the self-critique of enlightenment itself. This distinctly abstract, theoretical mode of critique is not only attentive to those authorities that declare themselves in opposition to Enlightenment; it is also suspicious of those authorities that claim to support it. In an attempt to discover the conditions out of which enlightened thinking might grow, Kant triggers a tradition of thought that attempts to discover with ever-greater precision the extent to which our thoughts and actions are predetermined, whatever our conscious intentions. This is coupled to a parallel project that seeks to build from first principles those foundations out of which a more rationally ordered society might emerge.

The process of working towards enlightenment is necessarily destructive, since new foundations can only be properly constructed once the old foundations have been removed. In its most radical and purest form Enlightenment reason recognises no limitations on its destructive activity. It sees superstition and mythology everywhere, even in its own structures of thought. Hence within the self-critique of Enlightenment was the potential for it to become 'ruthless toward itself' as it eradicates 'anything which does not conform to the standard of calculability and utility'. Indeed, as we saw in Chapter 8, this is the case made against enlightenment by Horkheimer and Adorno in the *Dialectic of Enlightenment*.[14] Of course Kant envisaged the process of Enlightenment in more conservative terms, arguing that 'a public can achieve enlightenment only gradually'. Hasty attempts to bring about an enlightened age, including revolutionary ones, are to be deplored. A revolution, Kant argues, may:

> bring about the fall of an autocratic despotism ... but it can never bring about the true form of a way of thinking. Rather, new prejudices will serve, like the old, as the leading strings of the thoughtless masses.[15]

The progress of Enlightenment will be slow, Kant argues, requiring a gradual transformation through which the old constraints are lifted. This transformation can only be achieved through the tireless work of reason, and will only be realised in the population as a whole through its careful education.

Thus, despite its potential radicalism, according to Kant the project of Enlightenment demands considerable patience, since old traditions die hard and new foundations take time to establish. The situation is hardly helped by the fact that these foundations must be legitimated by a use of reason that is attempting to authenticate itself *through reason*. If this sounds painfully abstract and suspiciously circular, you are getting the point. In attempting to uncover the conditions that would give a legitimate basis for all human understanding, Enlightenment critique gave way to a form of speculative thinking that was abstracted from daily life.

Critique and its critics

It is not universally agreed that critique, the critical attitude, is an uncomplicatedly good thing. Modern forms of critique can be subjected to a Nietzschean analysis, for example. According to Nietzsche's genealogy or history of morality, modern forms of judgement and critique are derived from a flawed moral order. Contemporary religious and liberal moralities are descended from a slave morality, Nietzsche argues.[16] These moral systems were produced from a position of weakness, as the slave classes of antiquity suffered under aristocratic rule. Their moral understanding, which was to form the basis of Christian morality, was a product of their curdled resentment, as they faced a ruling order that lived by distinctly unchristian heroic values. Within this history, critique figures as a procedure for reducing human possibility to a mean level, for reining in the aristocratic affirmation of life and the unboundaried expression of its energies. Why bother with this grudging, self-inflated version of complaint when you could be 'driving, willing, acting', Nietzsche argues?[17] Critique, as a 'mode of evaluation',[18] is born at the moment when *ressentiment*, the vengeful, purely negative bitterness of the plebeian mind, invests itself with a morality.

Turning aside from Nietzsche's imaginative prehistory to more mundane perceptions, it may be noted that this depiction of critique as a negative, carping activity chimes with the popular suspicion of criticism as a destructive force and with the time-worn complaint of entrenched authorities that critical voices have nothing positive to offer by way of alternatives to current policy. At a more philosophical level, the Nietzschean sense of critique as an attempt to impose a restrictive organisation, a rationing, of human thought and behaviour in accordance with a miserably impoverished and sceptical reading of the world, is to be found in comments like these of the philosopher and sociologist Bruno Latour, which strikingly evoke the delightedly self-righteous judgementalism that he and others detect in the critical attitude:

> Do you see now why it feels so good to be a critical mind? Why critique, this most ambiguous *pharmakon*[19] has become such a potent, euphoric drug? You are always right! When naïve believers are clinging forcefully to their objects ... their gods, their poetry, their cherished objects, you can turn all of those attachments into so many fetishes and humiliate all the believers by showing that it is nothing but their own projection, that you alone ... can see. [Then] ... you strike them ... and humiliate them again, this time by showing that, whatever they think, their behaviour is entirely determined by the action of powerful causalities coming from an objective reality they don't see, but that you, the never sleeping critic, alone can see. Isn't this fabulous? Isn't it really worth going to graduate school to study critique?[20]

However, revulsion at the critical impulse, as it has developed within the humanities, is perhaps met with most dramatically in the work of Nietzsche's heirs, Gilles Deleuze and Michel Foucault. Deleuze saw the dominant tendency of philosophical thought as an attempt to impose transcendent values upon the human capacity for desiring, so that reality is dematerialised into a metaphysics designed to corral and ration human possibility.[21] The invention of the notion of man was one such attempt, as was the Freudian notion of the Oedipus complex.[22] For Deleuze, rather than being inescapable, essential truths about the human condition, such conceptualisations were historically constructed and authoritarian interdictions on becoming, based in a morality of negativity. To the contrary, philosophy's task, and the key to living, is to affirm and to create, in defiance of the injunction to judge and thereby limit in advance the operations and outcomes of desire. Similarly, Foucault saw 'the curious activity of critique' as 'an instrument, a means for a future that it will not know ... a gaze on a domain it very much wants to police'.[23]

Suspicious though it may be of critique, the work of Foucault, Deleuze and Nietzsche still operates in a critical idiom. The Enlightenment leaves us with a rather peculiar inheritance. It is difficult to take a position either for or against enlightenment (or indeed critique) because it is, in itself, decidedly ambiguous (we will recall Adorno and Horkheimer's analysis of the dual nature of Enlightenment: social freedom *and* domination). For this reason, critics of Enlightenment reason may still recognise its influence upon their thought, indeed recognise their necessary immersion in its consequences. This is clearly the case with Michel Foucault. Hardly your typical Enlightenment thinker, Foucault spent his life exploring its promises and their problematic effects. Foucault was nevertheless prepared to place himself within the project of Enlightenment, recognising its commitment to questioning those forces of 'religion, law and knowledge' that maintain humankind in what Kant described as a state of immaturity.[24]

However, in a lecture of 1978 Foucault combines an attack on what he sees as a mistaken direction taken by critique since the eighteenth century and an argument for a critical attitude that is less concerned with schemes for the perfection of human understanding and more engaged with a practical insubordination directed at questioning and refusing the regulatory, governmentalising effects of power. He was concerned to identify how, in its attempts to establish the conditions out of which true knowledge could be created, Enlightenment critique was diverted into a whole series of abstract attempts to uncover the transcendental limits and foundations of knowledge. It was assumed that universal Reason must exist, and that basic moral laws could be derived from it. The object of philosophy became the object of critique, which was to discover and outline these laws and principles so that we might build our human existence upon them. As it dedicated itself to tracing the origins of error and illusion, attempting to seal itself off from the corrupting effects of power, critique confined itself to a realm of generality. Critique was forced, or forced itself, into a theoretically rarefied position from which it could not effectively engage with the strategic and technical particularities of those systems it questioned. It was unable to engage with them as fields of interaction and possibility, and thereby disqualified itself as a source of modification and change.

Foucault argued against the abstraction of critique, for a turning away from this kind of transcendental enquiry, and towards an analysis of events or 'singularities' that obey no 'necessitating principle' and hence are irreducible to a single cause.[25] The abstractions of post-Kantian philosophy are far too inflexible to deal with such complex, ever-changing realities. Hence Foucault gives up the habit of the philosopher who seeks to authenticate, to legitimate his use of reason before all else. Instead, he is interested in how legitimacy is established in the first place (i.e. not from the better argument, but out of a particular dispensation of power). He attempts to free us from a kind of philosophy that is obsessed with establishing foundations. Foucault hopes thereby to revive critique, remove its self-imposed boundaries, and render it actual, so that it might play a role in the transformation of everyday life. In so doing, he seeks to overcome philosophy's obsession with itself, placing critique once again on the offensive, opening it up, rendering it less abstract and less inflexible, so that it is able to engage with the 'perpetual mobility' of events. [26] Critique ceases to be a principle or alchemical substance capable of translating the base matter of mundane reality to a higher, purer condition – it becomes, once again according to Foucault, a tool that can be put to work on the problems of the present.

In practice, however, although the relationship between its foundational principles and their practical implementation had not been decisively established, enlightenment became an unstoppable, 'blindly pragmatised'[27] force. As we have seen argued, philosophers and critics were, then, in many respects, left high and dry by an age of Enlightenment in which the old (pre-modern) powers were undermined by the activities of industry and science, rather than by the work of the philosopher and critic.

In this context, an endeavour such as Foucault's, one that hopes to revive critique, to wake it from its abstract slumber, may be worthwhile. It could, in the case of education, open critique to new possibilities and new insights, since critique would no longer be restrained by assumptions that dictate its appropriate form and object. It would no longer be tied to what, in the context of education, becomes its single most important constraint; a desire to authenticate education itself, to assume something about this thing we call education which is foundational, and which is to be protected at all costs by the educational critic. Yet any attempt to reanimate critique will encounter difficulty. It risks underestimating the extent to which critique remains, perhaps despite itself, attached to those very things it is supposed to question. The question presents itself as to what exactly is foundational and in need of protection.

Critical pedagogies

In contradiction of the argument that critique has withdrawn from a debased and imperfect reality in order to consider and thence pronounce upon the true and ideal forms of human social and moral being, it can be pointed out there is within the field of education a strong tradition of emancipatory praxis that sees itself as very much involved in practical interventions intended to charge teaching and learning with liberatory purpose. Emancipatory praxis within education has taken two obvious forms. Liberal or progressive pedagogy has been particularly influential at the level of primary and secondary education. It adopts what is very much an Enlightenment view that the subject of education – the schoolchild – possesses innate capacities that must be released from the bonds of ignorance, convention and prejudice that inhibit their full human development, their progress to a full humanity. It wants to free the learner's intellectual and creative (a key word for the progressive educator) potential by removing the effects upon their development of a disfiguring and restrictive authority. This authority is conceived in terms of oppressive forms of schooling that inhibit the learner's growth (another key term) and those elements in their background that have similarly distorted or frustrated the fulfilment of their innate capacities. Some versions of progressive practice allow for an exploration of that 'background', but generally the emphasis is on compensating for its deficiencies and mending the damages it has inflicted. The child is the site of an intervention whose primary focus is on their emotional and psychological growth rather than their intellectual development, although progressive educators would no doubt claim that they are laying the necessary foundations for learning within the disciplines.

The second form of emancipatory educational praxis, frequently referred to as critical or radical pedagogy, is to one degree or another related to Marxist theory and has been especially influential at the tertiary – higher education – level of education, although versions of critical pedagogy address themselves to the primary and secondary school context.[28] The social analyses of Frankfurt School critical theory have fed into critical pedagogy, but arguably the most vigorous form of educational praxis has been that which has drawn on the work of the Brazilian educator Paulo Freire.[29] Freire argued that education is always a political practice and that its pedagogy, usually sustaining conformity with a society's dominant ideology and thus acting as an oppressive force, could be a 'practice of freedom' which enabled the oppressed to understand the true circumstances of their condition and equipped them with the critical awareness that might guide action in overturning their subjection. Such a pedagogy involves the teacher – who, in a state system, is always the representative and agent of oppression – in a constant re-appraisal of their beliefs and practices in order to fulfil a commitment to 'the people' (a key term in Freirean and other radical pedagogies) and the transformation of their social being. Critical pedagogues aim to interrupt existing forms of socialisation by which students are unknowingly co-opted to a dominant order, and to replace these unthinking conventions with more self-conscious, self-actualising and democratic modes of participation and self-formation. This is to be achieved by giving students the means to challenge the educational and social order that conditions them. Hence critical pedagogues seek to anchor themselves in the contexts they dispute. And by so doing, they appear to collapse the distinction between educated critic and local practitioner. In this critical tradition, it is considered axiomatic that only contextually embedded critiques will deliver their participants to emancipation. Emancipation cannot be passed down from above. It can only be achieved through practices of empowerment and self-emancipation, that is, through local and situated struggle.

It will be immediately apparent that critical pedagogues are more self-consciously 'political' than progressive educators. They seek social transformation, a radical re-ordering of power relations. Progressives, in contrast, largely neglect social critique – at least they appear to do so in primary and secondary school classrooms. At the tertiary level, the emancipatory pedagogue would argue, the liberal academic is content to work within the parameters of the existing social dispensation, accepting that the system of liberal democracy is essentially benign in its intentions, although its performance needs vigilant scrutiny and, where it falls short in the enactment of its democratic commitments, robust criticism. Those last two sentences could be taken as a summary of what radical critique takes to be wrong with liberal, progressive praxis: its caution about change in fact amounts to collusion with an unjust, democratically deficient system. Yet liberal educational theory, valorising the democratic right of individuals and communities to exercise free choice in their own self-formation, shares with its more radical counterpart a distrust of authority, in the form of state power which encroaches upon and diminishes that freedom. The task of the liberal educator is to reconcile the obvious fact that it is the educational machinery of state education that equips young people with the capacities necessary for them to participate in a democracy and that educator's commitment to an idea of the autonomous moral individual who controls their own development.

Both liberal and radical critics justify their judgements concerning social and educational practice by reference to an authority which legitimates their prescriptions. For the progressive the legitimating authority is that of the sovereign moral agent, the self who authors their own destiny, whose autonomy is not to be violated by governmental power. The emancipatory or critical theorist bases their legitimacy in the authority of the people as an oppressed class who are denied their completion as human beings.

It will be clear that progressive and critical pedagogies share a certain Kantianism. These emancipatory pedagogies engage in a struggle for common humanity against systems that would deny it, becoming framed by an Enlightenment worldview which posits definitive conceptions of what it means to become 'fully human'. Both versions see education as the agent of liberation from a state of ignorance and dependence imposed by dominatory power; they view the same prospect of advancement to full humanity once men and women are set free from their servitude; they share a deep wariness about the concentration of power in a state or governmental form, conceiving of power as a resource that in the wrong hands threatens human freedom; they are both concerned to shape individual subjectivities and society in accordance with norms derived from their critical reflections on ideal forms of the self and social being. The criticism has been made that they thus impose a tribunal, or a system of judgement, upon the management of human affairs, its governmental decision-making, that – ironically – is intended to shape, regulate and confine human development within the boundaries defined by its critical investigation into the essential nature and *telos* of human existence. Critique, viewing a domain that it would like to police, thus becomes just another system of control, another attempt at exercising dominatory power.

A further criticism of emancipatory education, radical and progressive, lies in the fact that its practitioners are everywhere obliged to transgress their commitments in that however steadfast their intent to liberate their charges from the shackles and blindfolds of illegitimate and oppressive power, they are agents of a governmental system who cannot escape the coercive entailments of their role. Short of relinquishing their positions within the system, they are inevitably caught up in the exercise of unequally distributed power – for instance, in preparing their students for systems of assessment that, by the lights of the emancipatory educator, are saturated by realities of social injustice. Unless they engage in a relentless and undeviating disavowal of their professional responsibilities, a total disobedience which would have to somehow avoid the gaze of those who have authority over them, emancipatory educators are in practice obliged to dilute the purity of their commitments when encountering certain other realities of the places in which they work – in the person of students who seem resistant to education's promise of full development (who fail to perceive that education, critical or otherwise, has any relevance to their future lives or who just want qualifications that will get them a job) and in a surrounding educational environment which is structured according to the requirements of power (what authority wants from its schools and universities). Perhaps the most telling point against emancipatory pedagogy is that its suspicion of power and government and its apotheosising of freedom amount to a disavowal of power, an irresponsible and unrealistic refusal to accept that reason can never be detached from the workings of power.[30]

The endurance of critique

Though the role of critique is still asserted as necessary in democratic society, in practice it often remains a marginal activity. In education, as in other fields, its effective functioning as a determinant of policy is diminished. Here principled critique is overtaken by more pragmatic ways of problematising society and its needs. Indeed, government regards principled critical analysis as an irritant operating on the sidelines of the arena of public policy. Nonetheless, critical reason's account of the free individual whose composition mirrors the wholeness that reason had discerned in the universe (its ideal of human completion) continues to exert a hold on educational discourse and practice. It is paid lip service by politicians and educators whose policies and practices are devised and conducted without paying real attention to the goal of complete development. It survives in governmental discourse in the language of 'equality of opportunity', the education of 'the whole child', 'personal development', 'empowerment' and 'voice' – a lexicon that government resorts to when it wants to lend a more humane glow to its utilitarian pronouncements.

Even when critique frees itself of such cynical attachments we are left with a situation where, as MacIntyre argues, both individuals and groups debate with one another from incommensurable, that is to say irreconcilable, moral positions.[31] We scarcely have 'enough agreement to be able to arrive at a common mind about what it is that we should be quarrelling about'.[32] The moral fragmentations of modernity pose real dilemmas for today's educational establishments that seek to 'civilise' their students according to the norms of a society whose moral frameworks are uncertain. It is here that the teaching profession perhaps comes to represent, in MacIntyre's words, the 'forlorn hope of the culture of Western modernity'.[33] As James Donald argues, modern teachers were 'charged with a mission that is both essential and impossible', to simultaneously make people free and to make them obedient, with educational thinking forever oscillating 'between utopianism and despair'. We find that education 'repeatedly promises to liberate the creative human talents of all people and then fails to do so'.[34]

A common but rather problematic solution adopted by many contemporary educators is to stick to some weakened version of enlightenment, and claim to be developing free thinking individuals of a more pragmatic kind, able to act with some degree of independence. This commitment will help reduce an unthinking conformity to authority, and allow people to engage in educated debate. Education, according to this view, must continue to help us learn new things, counter misunderstanding, and occasionally – and where appropriate – contest obvious abuses of power. It must assist individuals to position themselves as they choose within a pluralistic moral order. Universities are still supported by this weakened enlightenment philosophy as contributing to the common stock of human knowledge, and thereby towards a more prosperous social order. These watered-down commitments, as MacIntyre put it, have become the 'undeniable platitudes of the age'.[35] In this weakened form they remain in place as a 'set of no longer quite held, not to be completely articulated, background presuppositions, a set of almost but not quite believed propositions'.[36] An enlightenment narrative of sorts still constitutes the self-understanding of the profession. This narrative is in a fragile state, not so much because the arguments of philosophers have fatally undermined it. Rather, the enlightenment narrative and the emancipatory educational projects emanating from it are rendered fragile because they never found lodging within a communally accepted understanding of the educational good. This was the price paid for the profound social transformations which led to the freeing of western thought from the limits and boundaries of the medieval worldview. Set against the fragmentation of communal life, and against the irreconcilable moral conflicts and disputes which define our present, the reforming, rationalising critiques, the prescriptive formulations, of modernist thought, appear as forlorn attempts to impose an abstract and idealised conceptualisation of moral order upon irrevocably divided social and cultural forms. While medieval critique worked towards a better understanding and a better synthesis of tradition, modern critique is consigned to a negative role, anatomising and seeking to correct the misconstruals and the wrong directions taken by a society where thought, reason itself, has gone into error and the great rationalising project of Enlightenment has been betrayed.

The plight of today's educational critic, who measures education against impossible and increasingly weakened ideals, is summed up well by the following image: when educational critics view the modern school system, it has:

the appearance of a humble church built out of stones intended for a great cathedral. It is mocked by the scale of its unrealised potential, by the grandeur of the edifice that it might have been, if only its builders had not lost faith and gone into moral and political bankruptcy.

Educational critics typically view the contemporary school, and the contemporary university for that matter, as 'the flawed realisation of an ideal form'.[37] In so doing, they position themselves outside social reality, expressing disappointment at the untidy, messy improvisations and compromises that constitute today's educational institutions. They refuse to engage with the ambivalent consequences of enlightenment, insisting instead on measuring realities against lofty ideals that are no longer quite believed. The critic has nothing to offer but a point of view that measures educational realities against distant ideals; against them education must always fall short. Unsurprisingly, then, critique has become associated in popular usage with negativity; in a time-worn complaint, entrenched authorities attack critical voices for having nothing positive to offer, which is to say, nothing which can be realistically rolled out. Critics are attacked for their self-righteous judgementalism, for refusing to reduce their expectations to what can be practically achieved.

There is something admirable, nonetheless, in the critic's determination to remain uncowed by practical, concrete demands, which threaten to reduce what can be thought to what can be achieved in a given situation. The increasingly common insistence that educational establishments should offer only practically useful knowledge, which is to say, knowledge that fits the demands of society as they are presently configured, is surely to be resisted. The difficulty, however, is that in Western societies the practice of critique has been 'deformed into a professional activity'.[38] It has become a specialist pursuit of a kind that is, by definition, largely unavailable to a wider public. This marginal position – one that confines the refinements of critique to academic periodicals, the more serious forms of literature and high-brow journals – gives those occupying these positions moral status as commentators and spokespeople for the common good. Indeed, as moral notables, critical intellectuals often occupy distinguished university positions. Yet despite their eminence, they are unable to mobilise a strong alternative, because there is no established moral authority to which they might appeal.

Education is confronted by a bottom-line ultimatum: if an educational institution is to survive it must show that it is useful. It must serve 'as the reflex of an unquestioned society'.[39] In this context, it would seem as though critique has relatively little to offer. It cannot speak to this educational reality if it insists upon discussing that reality in negative, moralistic and abstract theoretical terms. The story of modernity is indeed the story of the disconnection of moral discourse from the realm of social decision-making. It is the story of the disembodiment of knowledge, of its separation from a cultural consensus. In this context, the high aims of Enlightenment reason provide a kind of decorative finish to the instrumental activities of today's education. They offer a kind of nobility and moral seriousness that is tolerated, even welcomed, so long as it does not undermine the reputational and, increasingly, commercial success of the institution it is associated with. Here, perhaps, the critic retains some usefulness. They lend education a status it would otherwise lose if it were entirely reduced to a bureaucratic rationale. They help us believe that education might still become the cathedral they say it has the potential to be. From this perspective, education seems to be always worth more than what it is.

But the critic might still attempt to evade a situation where the activity of critique is marginalised, and only called upon for the prestige and moral seriousness it still confers. That is, critique might still resist a game of power where it is welcomed and incorporated so long as it furthers the notion that society still orients itself to a higher good. Critique might resist its recruitment to the idea that despite all confusions and competing systems of value, despite ongoing exploitation and growing inequality, despite all conflict and disagreement, against all vested interests and systemic violences, society is still driven by shared principles of democratic sociality, national pride and universal humanism. Against all this, which would co-opt the critic into conformity with the status quo, it is still conceivable that they might work to enact forms of dissatisfaction that are productive, that inspire action and experiment. They might still engage in activities that are driven by the belief that education can be something other than what it has become.

11

Education and Government

Moral formation

Philosophy was once linked intimately to education. Each philosophy entailed a way of life and a set of spiritual practices that might be taught or acquired in the presence of a teacher who was also a philosopher. With the decline of ancient philosophy, the medieval priest replaced the philosopher as spiritual guide and the study of philosophy became subordinate to scripture. In modernity, the marginalisation of philosophy continued, as philosophy became a university specialism most educators could safely avoid. This does not mean contemporary educational establishments have no bearing on life as it is lived from day to day, only that their moral purpose is more often than not implicit, rather than overt and directly reflected in their curricula. Modern teaching in particular remains committed to moral formation, having extended, modified and multiplied ancient and medieval spiritual practices. It does so, however, without an overarching philosophical rationale.

If in the remaining chapters we appear to concern ourselves more with education than we do with what more recently counts as 'philosophy', this is because we are acutely aware that the separation of education and philosophy in modernity is systemic, and not due to a mere lack of interest amongst educators (which might be tackled by reasserting the importance of philosophy in general, or the philosophy of education in particular). To the extent that we as practitioners of education remain attached to philosophy, we also remain committed to its capacity to disturb current practices, through forms of counter-conduct (other ways of life) and rival conceptions of existence, which place present ways of life and prevailing discourse in question. As we do this, we continue to consider education as a species of moral formation, as a more or less deliberate mode of induction into a way of life. Judged by ancient standards, what education now lacks is the coherence an accompanying philosophy might give. This does not mean contemporary education operates without direction or purpose, though its overt aims are generally more immediate, tied increasingly to the perceived needs of present-day society.

In a society where traditional structures are under attack, both from the kind of theoretical critiques we have considered, and from the everyday forces of capital and industry, the problem of government rises to prominence. Following Foucault, we define government here very broadly, ranging from the government of states, to the government of families and individual lives.[1] These questions of government, of defining the rules of conduct for both oneself and others, are hardly new. Ancient philosophers were quite obviously preoccupied with the issue of self-government, exploring how a form of self-mastery could be perfected. This concern with self-mastery was then linked to the ability to govern the lives of others. When the philosopher addressed a wider, lay audience of aristocrats, administrators and rulers, it was quite common to assert that in order to govern others, a ruler must first learn to govern himself. This was, in large part, how philosophy justified its mission to the powerful.

We explore in what follows how themes of self-government and the government of others were revived and adapted to the purposes of a modern, liberal social elite. In this context, a task once considered to be the defining assignment of the ancient philosopher was given over on the one hand to what has been termed the cultural virtuoso, and on the other to a different kind of intellectual, the administrative bureaucrat.[2] Free of the philosopher's grasp, fresh connections were established between the government of others, and the government of the self. These themes were given prominence during the nineteenth century at a time when society was experiencing turbulence and upheaval associated with the expansion of industry and a growing, potentially volatile urban population. With the migration from country to town old social structures, ties, systems of subjugation and deference – the social relations obtaining between the squire or lord of the manor, the priest and the common people – were increasingly irrelevant and inoperable. In this context, new systems of government were required, ones that would form the populace in conformity with the needs of a technological revolution. This would be achieved not simply through coercion, but through the use of educational techniques that would attune and re-tune rather than silence the desires and hopes of individuals so that they came into better alignment with political objectives. We consider this dual mission below focusing in particular on the context of nineteenth-century England. We explore how the modern government of populations combines the moral example of a liberal elite with the bureaucratic pragmatism of mass education.

Government

The transition, in the seventeenth and eighteenth centuries, from theocratic to absolutist states across continental Europe brought to prominence a new administrative sphere increasingly separate from existing economic, cultural and moral realms. It was to become the realm of government, ruled by its own form of reason, a *raison d'état* (reason of state) that rendered all administrative decisions subordinate to the question of to what extent does this advance or hinder the welfare of the state?

The German historian Reinhart Koselleck argued that this separation of government from all other spheres was one of the great achievements of modernity.[3] Koselleck takes his cue from Thomas Hobbes, a seventeenth-century English philosopher who claimed that the alternative to an absolute state is a 'war of all against all'. This claim is obviously disputable, but for Hobbes it makes sense, since it is based upon the individualistic anthropology he develops. As Koselleck argues, 'Hobbes' individualism is the premise for a well-ordered State and at the same time the premise for the uninhibited development of the individual'.[4]

Hobbes set the foundation for modern liberal thought, defending the state from the interference of individuals who, since the Reformation and the subsequent split in religious authority, were thrown back on the authority of their own conscience, making each man judge and jury in social matters (Hobbes sought to protect the state, in other words, from the 'authority of conscience in its subjective plurality'[5]). Hobbes argued that 'the public interest ... no longer lies in the jurisdiction of conscience' but should be assumed by the state and its sovereign.[6] Hobbes also argued that within the severe juridical restrictions of a strong state, a civil society should be permitted in which men could go about their daily business governed by their own conscience. They should be allowed to do so as long as their aims do not conflict with those of the state. This was an achievement, Koselleck argues, because it prevented a return to the religious civil war that decimated much of Europe during the seventeenth century. The separation of civil society from politics was also, Koselleck argues, a precondition for enlightenment. It allowed educated people to be at liberty (within the limits imposed by the state) to pursue their own moral or spiritual interests without hindrance.

Building very much on Koselleck's analysis, the Australian theorist of government Ian Hunter attacks those who critique the administrative state, or the state of bureaucratic reason, for failing to base itself on absolute principles of moral perfection, universal humanity and justice. Indeed, for Hunter, as for Koselleck, the 'administrative state was born as part of a sustained movement to banish such principles from the sphere of government'.[7] That was its moral and political achievement. It was able thereby to detach itself from 'spiritual' politics, and occupy itself with more mundane administrative issues. The 'authority of conscience' that had once led to so much division, civil war and carnage, was replaced by a more reasoned politics that treated the survival and security of the state as an end in itself. The moral education of the citizenry would still be pursued, but this pursuit was now subordinate to the welfare of the state. Moral education was needed to produce a well-governed and productive citizenry rather than a morally perfect people. Unity of faith might still be desired, but it would never again be more important than the survival of the state.

There were, however, some unintended effects. The separation of morality and politics implemented by the state was later used against it. In Koselleck's words, the state was subsequently 'forced into standing a moral trial for having achieved something, i.e. to have created a space in which it was possible (for the individual) to survive'.[8] The 'authority of conscience' had been put to one side (and given its own non-political authority) by a political order seeking to pacify areas devastated by religious war. But this realm of conscience nonetheless remained as an 'unconquered remnant' within the new political order.[9] Eventually becoming revived as a politics of conscience, it would return with vengeance in secular form. As Hunter puts it:

> It was in this manner that the absolute principles of the 'politics of conscience', grown heavy with the blood of those who fought for them, gradually sank from sight in the manuals of European statecraft, even if they were to resurface - bloated with enlightenment and critique - as the ideals of moral and political philosophy.[10]

The structure of absolutism was a precondition for enlightenment, Koselleck argues, as it established a difference between public policy and private morality, protecting one from the other. Once private morality had its own permitted realm, this realm could support a pursuit of knowledge and reason that would otherwise have been unthinkable in a theocratic order. The disadvantage of this division, Koselleck argues, is that in isolation from politics, Enlightenment thinkers allowed themselves to develop unrealisable ideals, ideals that were never tested in the day-to-day life of political decision-making.

According to Koselleck, John Locke was a pioneer, developing a social contract theory that allowed the private domain to 'expand on its own into a public one'.[11] It was for this reason that his *Essay Concerning Human Understanding* would, in the following eighteenth century, 'rank among the Holy Scriptures of the modern bourgeoisie'.[12] With Hobbes, bourgeois morality was only allowed a secret and tacit existence within the moral authority of the state. Its scope was limited. With Locke, the scope of bourgeois morality was substantially increased. It was now permitted to take form in 'society', that is in the 'clubs' in which philosophers and educated people came together to discuss moral issues. Locke was nonetheless cautious, and emphasised that citizens should still 'as a rule obey the commandments of God and the laws of nature'. Crucially, however, these laws now 'received legal validity only from the consent or rejection of bourgeois society'.[13]

Koselleck's rather provocative claim is that this chain of thought (one that was taken up, extended and radicalised by later thinkers) not only subjected the state to the possibility of moral condemnation, it also 'prepared the way for the Terror [of the French revolution] and for dictatorship', and eventually led to twentieth century forms of totalitarianism.[14] In its separation from politics, from the new kind of politics that demanded negotiation and compromise, Enlightenment thought became dogmatic, with devastating consequences. In Koselleck's terms, it gave rise to a bourgeois intelligentsia that embraced the whole world, speaking on its behalf, confidently submitting all to its tribunal of reason. At this point, Hunter modifies Koselleck's argument, claiming, as we shall see, that the idealism of modern thinkers and modern educators has its place, helping shape the moral attributes of a citizenry. However, it characteristically over-reaches itself, attempting to comment on and often denounce the wider administrative and bureaucratic order that made it possible.

Both Hunter and Koselleck emphasise what they see to be the key achievement of the modern state – its removal of decision-making to a separate administrative realm not governed by conscience. The role of critical intellectuals in holding state reason to account (and giving it higher purpose) is thereby diminished in a way that may strike some as problematic if not dangerous. Hunter views liberal democracies as the ultimate beneficiaries of this division, and the freedoms allowed in these societies as necessarily dependent on the rise of administration and bureaucracy. Overall, it is worth noting that Hunter is perhaps more satisfied than Koselleck with these achievements. Writing in 1959 Koselleck remained disturbed by the 'state of permanent crisis'[15] that he associated with the cold war; he hoped too to highlight 'more persistent structures of the modern age ... the sense that we are being sucked into an open and unknown future, the pace of which has kept us in a constant state of breathlessness', as well as the 'pressure on our post-theological age to justify politics and morals without us being able to reconcile the two.'[16]

Hunter's insistence that bureaucracy and conscience should remain divided, an insistence which amounts to a celebration of bureaucratic reason, sets him too against his other main influence, Michel Foucault, who also took a more ambiguous position with regard to the achievements of government. Foucault was equally struck by the rise of government as a separate sphere, with a rationality of its own (he dubbed this rationality, 'governmentality'[17]). Foucault charts the massive expansion of administrative technologies concerned with governing the conduct of daily life. He notes too how questions of government are reduced in modernity to questions of welfare, to calculations of the extent to which government interventions advance or hinder the welfare of a population. But Foucault also notes that government is not straightforwardly benevolent in this new age (though it would like to appear so, neutralising debate by reducing political decisions to administrative questions, paving the way for what Koselleck calls the 'innocence of power'[18]). Administrative government is not straightforwardly good, or innocent, Foucault argues, because it actively defines those principles upon which its decision-making depends. And so, for example, government and associated agencies set about defining what constitutes welfare, what constitutes worthwhile life and social well-being, and hence what must be promoted in a modern society.[19] This necessarily involves systems of exclusion; systems that deny certain forms of life (or norms of existence) that contradict current definitions of welfare and notions of a healthy citizenry. Rather dangerously, perhaps, this places the basic aims of government beyond dispute: once welfare is defined it becomes a self-evident good. There is a disturbing logic at work in the argument that the aim of government is to promote the overall well-being and health of its population, when government (or governmental reason) is defining what constitutes well-being and health in the first place. We return to these issues towards the end of this chapter. First, we consider the more self-consciously principled end of modern education, that which is concerned with the education of a liberal elite.

A liberal elite

In our era of mass education, the education of elites is often treated as if it were a throwback from the past, a relic that will in time be overcome. But the hegemonic class, with its networks of power and influence, is strikingly persistent. Its members still have a disproportionate influence on social affairs. In a society where merit and not patronage is supposed to rule, established power still manages to use its wealth and influence to secure its interests, in part through a network of fee-paying 'public' schools whose graduates still disproportionately populate our professional and governing elites. For left-wing critics, these are straightforward abuses of power; they are easy to target though hard to dislodge. Less detectable, however, are the deeply persistent educational assumptions that were produced as part of the formation of this social group. They are much harder to detect, since no single group now has exclusive hold over them. Attuned to the needs of a nineteenth-century elite education, these liberal, humanist assumptions have since been extended to apply to education more broadly. We have come to depend upon them to justify the value of education, of education for its own sake, whenever education is felt to be under threat from instrumental and commercial forces.

Our modern, high-minded rationale for education was developed in the nineteenth century. Geared towards the formation of an elite governing class, it was designed to produce a special breed of 'educated man'. This was an attempt to generate the kind of 'self-reflecting and self-realising moral person'[20] modernity required. The educated man would be made to cohere as a moral being in a context of fragmentation and uncertainty. This endeavour coincided with the birth of the modern episteme Foucault identifies at the beginning of the nineteenth century, an era which would, of course, make the possibility of building that subject increasingly remote (see Chapter 9).

The assumed privilege of the educated man was not simply that he had received a privileged education. His education conferred a deeper distinction upon him, for he was credited with the authority to speak on behalf of others. This cultured individual could expect to speak and be listened to when addressing matters of cultural and social importance. Here what it meant to 'be educated' was narrowly defined; it was limited to a certain kind of learning, designed for those destined to provide the social order with its moral compass. In today's common parlance, someone is 'well educated' if they have risen up the institutional and educational hierarchy, if they have been to university. But to be well educated is not just about attending the right institutions and accumulating the right qualifications, since assumptions concerning what it means to be well educated today are built on older ideas of what it meant to be an educated person in a modern liberal society. These ideas, coming to fruition in the nineteenth century, were embodied in the person (or figure) of the gentleman.

The term 'liberal' when placed in conjunction with 'education' implies some kind of association between education and freedom. In its nineteenth-century sense, the word 'liberal' also implied that to become educated one would need to be free from necessity. Only those free of material distractions would be at liberty to become educated. And so a liberal education depends on a number of material givens, where economic constraints in particular must be loosened. In effect a liberal education is intended only for those who can afford it, or those who are connected with wealthy individuals or organisations who can afford it on their behalf. Liberal understandings are developed only by those able to avoid the constraints of necessity and the distractions of a working life. This includes the constraints imposed by domestic labour, and hence a liberal education tradition-ally excluded women in a patriarchal society.

In addition to economic freedom, a liberal education also requires free-dom from threatening pressures that may arise within the self. Not everyone is capable of this kind of self-restraint, or so it is assumed. As the nineteenth-century English poet and philosopher Samuel Coleridge put it, a gentleman is distinguished by the fact that he 'knows himself and walks in the light of his own consciousness'.[21] In other words, a liberal education demands a certain kind of self-mastery. This requirement provides the incidental satisfaction for those claiming to have achieved a liberal understanding, of being able to place themselves at the end of a long and noble lineage, going back to attempts at self-mastery attributed to ancient Greek philosophers.

Self-mastery and culture

As Ben Knights argues in his study, *The Idea of the Clerisy in the Nineteenth Century*, self-mastery is not considered to be an exclusively individual or narcissistic concern. In the nineteenth century it was, indeed, viewed as a prerequisite for positions of influence. As Coleridge put it, 'He alone is entitled to share in the government of all who has learned to govern himself'.[22]

Even though the idea of liberal education as a kind of self-mastery could boast an ancient pedigree (and this was part of its attraction), in its modern form it was devised to meet the problems posed by an increasingly secular order.

Indeed, the liberal education that became popular in the nineteenth century would secularise older Christian ideas of purity. It drew a sharp distinction between a transcendent realm of order, and the chaotic, impure and sensual disorder that was thought to reign below, in the decidedly impure realm of lived experience. In this scheme of thought, the latter (and lower) phenomena were denigrated. These material distractions, this unwelcome enmiring in a compromised mundanity, was to be overcome by the man of good character, by the man who had received a liberal education. Guided by a literary elite, which promulgated and adapted high humanist ideals to the needs of the nineteenth century, such a man knew about culture, and exuded its refined qualities. Indeed, he would invest culture with many of the attributes once associated with religion, where his greatest cultural achievements aspired to a transcendent realm once occupied by God.

Marginalised and oppressed groups, such as the labouring classes, the colonised and women, have typically been associated with a sensuous worldly realm and hence have been implicitly or explicitly denigrated along with it. In this context, it is held to be the duty of the liberal (male) elite to see through the disorder that surrounds them and those on whose behalf they presume to speak. Indeed, it is assumed that some ideas, particularly moral truths, need to be protected from an often hostile and debased reality.

In this secular order (in a world in which priests no longer occupy the guiding position, and thus hold the moral authority they once did) the educated man is elevated to become a member of an elite group, or 'clerisy', as Coleridge coined the term. This learned class would be responsible for preserving and disseminating a common cultural heritage. It would be revered for its ability to see through the untrustworthy seductions of immediate worldly phenomena; it would provide stability in times of change, offering intellectual and spiritual leadership to those masses who, cast adrift in a modern society, were judged to be in need of their guidance.

Overall, as Knights argues, this elite perspective 'emphasises a normative order and a hierarchy of values which is seen as beyond historical alteration', and which it becomes the job of the educated to protect. According to its advocates, the importance of this decidedly intellectual and spiritual project of the literary and philosophical elite could not be over-stated. This is because the 'affairs of the mind' are here related directly to 'the social health – the morality indeed – of the nation'.[23] In preserving and reproducing themselves, a literary elite would be caring for the social health of the country (and perhaps empire) they claim to serve. They would not necessarily be its rulers (as would Plato's philosopher–king), but they would have the ear of those who are in charge.

Despite its obvious elitism, the idea of a liberal education has certain attractions. It seeks to offset the dangers posed by the fragmentation of culture and society that necessarily occurs when a dominant structure of value (in this case, the Christian moral order) comes into doubt. It draws attention to the dangers of academic specialisation and intellectual fragmentation, a casualty of which has been a separation of moral questions from highly specialised academic enquiries (see Chapter 2). A liberal education does not abandon this moral dimension and is able to make connections across what have become distinctly disconnected fields of enquiry. It nevertheless perpetuates an assumption that moral judgements can only be made by those who have been appropriately educated. It develops an 'ideology of the intelligentsia'[24] that allows intellectuals to stand apart from society, positioning themselves above its preoccupations, believing that this kind of separation, this kind of privilege, is essential for intellectual activities that serve the well-being of society. This outlook allows the intellectual to maintain a benevolent vision of themselves, as a social benefactor who can only contribute to the common weal by abstracting themselves from involvement in worldly affairs. It is a notably self-serving, some might say delusional outlook. Of greater concern, perhaps, is that this kindly, rather self-gratifying vision betrays a palpable fear of losing control, of succumbing to the chaotic and sensual forces it associates with worldly affairs. This fear becomes expressed as a commitment to order that 'easily turns into a legitimation of the existing order on the grounds that at least it *is* an order'.[25]

Admittedly, as educational commitments go, these ideas seem more appropriate to the nineteenth century context where we might presume they were largely confined. They represent 'a constellation of notions about the way in which the universe is ordered and the conditions under which it becomes intelligible',[26] that seems to be found today only amongst the most conservative representatives of an ailing aristocratic class. However, these ideals were also those of a bourgeois intelligentsia, and are still in circulation today. They are not confined to reactionary conservatives. Well-meaning defenders of education for its own sake continue to serve and uphold the commitments of a liberal education, shorn of its more obvious elitism perhaps, but heavily laden with social conservatism. In order to further elaborate on this highly influential way of thinking about education, one that pictures it 'at its best', we move now to a consideration of *Bildung*, the German equivalent of liberal education.

The concept of Bildung

The German concept of *Bildung* like that of a liberal education is still used today to express a more cultured commitment to education. It is retained and revived by those who fear that the virtues of education are being lost through successive interventions that reduce education to a mere instrument for the conveyance of skills and certificates. These critics believe that a return to the educational philosophy of Bildung, with its emphasis on nurturing the human person in their entirety, might save education from the dangerous instrumentalism that besets it today, and perhaps save society too.

Bildung has theological roots. These predate the term's adoption in the late eighteenth and early nineteenth centuries by a post-revolutionary bourgeoisie. In its medieval usage, *bilden* means to create, mould or form in a practical but also spiritual sense. *Bild* refers to the Christian God, where God created human beings in his image (*Bilde*). Hence it designates both a point of origin and a destination. This gives Bildung its transcendental, but nonetheless applied and practical nature. As Koselleck argues, it is associated with the redemption of man through his efforts to 'imagine (*einbilden*) God in oneself, to reform (*umbilden*) oneself through Christ in order to share in God while a human being' and perhaps even 'transform God into a human being'.[27]

This religious connotation can still be seen in the work of Johann Gottfried Herder, a German Enlightenment philosopher who wrote 'Every man has an image (*ein Bild*) of himself, of what he shall be and become; as long as he is not yet that, in his bones he is still unsatisfied'.[28] Wilhelm von Humboldt, perhaps the most famous nineteenth-century advocate of moral self-formation, outlined something similar, claiming 'all *Bildung* has its origin in the interior of the soul alone, and can only be induced by outer events, never produced.' The moral man forms himself (*bildet sich*) 'in the image (*im Bilde*) of divinity through the intuition of the highest idealistic perfection.'[29]

The theological underpinnings of Bildung are thus fairly clear to see as it comes into modern use. It is transformed by thinkers such as Humboldt into a form of educated piety, one that refers to the cultivation of a person's humanity. The Christian hope of redemption is transformed into the increasingly secular, educational mission of Bildung. Here Bildung develops the humanist conviction that man becomes human only through education. This process involves the production of man as an individual, as a self-realising subject. His becoming is linked to the achievement of a certain form of self-awareness that education facilitates but does not guarantee. Bildung is framed by the Enlightenment worldview that places 'man' upon a pedestal, which burdens educational institutions with the realisation of his world-historical potential. It is the product of a belief in man's ability to drive his own development, to undergo a mission of self-determination according to his unique capacity for reason. What Bildung achieves is a synthesis between a more computational or functional understanding of reason, and the idea that reasoning individuals must also be men of good character and conscience. It gives Enlightenment its continued theological and moral dimension.

Bildung developed a culture of the self that persists to the present day. It still shapes our vision of the cultured and cosmopolitan individual, the person of good taste and character, whose poise and self-control, whose way of living and interacting, demonstrate both an individual achievement and a social ideal. In its nineteenth-century context, Bildung refers to a type of self-formation or self-cultivation that extends beyond the formal limits of education to encompass the entire soul of the person pursuing it. It relates not to a condition, but to an active behaviour or process. It is not self-absorbed, but leads instead to the production of exemplary men. The ambition of Bildung is considerable, as it is a kind of civilising process, one that links the self-formation of the individual to the overall and ongoing self-formation of society. Indeed, as Kant's contemporary Moses Mendelssohn put it, 'I consider the *Bildung* of humans to include the endeavour to arrange both convictions and actions such that they are in consonance with happiness; to rear and govern human beings'.[30]

In many respects, Bildung can be viewed as a response to the challenge of modernity, to the fear that 'man' has lost his way and requires new direction. In an industrial age, Bildung is looked to for redemption. As an educational philosophy and cultural ideal, it is embraced by an ailing aristocratic class and later by the rising bourgeoisie. Each group, in its own way, seeks reassurance, but will not let go of its commitment to the individual, and to the individual's capacity for art, innovation and industry. Bildung is embraced by those who can no longer authenticate themselves by reference to tradition. Instead its advocates must find reassurance in their own endless capacity for creation, for building things anew out of the present. Developed by their aristocratic predecessors, it became the educational ideal of a rising middle class, made prosperous and powerful by capital and industry. Bildung reassures its practitioners and followers that they are culturally superior, and that their superiority resides in their capacity for morally driven self-renewal. Bildung promises to give humanity direction and purpose through the personage of the cultured man.

Bildung and the university

As a modern educational philosophy Bildung can be traced to the decades around 1800, when the German empire found itself in confrontation with Revolutionary and later Napoleonic France. This confrontation sparked a debate about the reform of higher education and its role in holding together the political structures of empire. It was here that Bildung, or self-cultivation, was held up as a solution (or dangerous fantasy, as Koselleck's analysis would have it[31]), through which higher education could supply the national unity that was felt to be under threat.[32]

If this vision of higher education claimed that education would serve as a great unifier, charging the university with a new and ambitious set of demands, it also contained a plea for academic freedom. It was claimed that the university could only serve the state, and the wider interests of humankind, if it was funded by, but otherwise separate from, the narrow everyday demands that the state might make of it. True moral–spiritual guidance must, in other words, be free from the instrumental demands of everyday politics. Naturally, in defending academic freedom in this way, this philosophy of education became popular with academics. The educational philosophy of Bildung conferred upon the academic a cultural role of great importance.

The concept of freedom associated with Bildung helped justify the separation of the university intellectual from society. It stipulated that the academic in question should be free from the immediate demands of society, which are viewed as potentially ill-formed, short-sighted and intellectually impoverished. Again, we have a rationale for elite culture which insists that the intelligentsia perform best when freed from social constraints. One such constraint would be the insistent demand, understandable from a different point of view, that the intelligentsia have an obligation to help solve the social problems of the day. Those who make such demands have little patience for the cultured refinements of the intellectual who insists that they are only of use to society on the condition that they are given the time and privileged space to pursue their intellectual work, and the space to refine their sensibilities unperturbed.

In a very real sense, of course, the academic does need time to think (and discuss and write) and needs an acceptance that they must inhabit a 'space', a position, that is not always immersed in the practicalities they study. Even the most deeply immersed researcher needs to withdraw from the material realities they engage with in order to reflect on and organise their thoughts and write their research. There is a kind of philistinism, an anti-intellectual closed-mindedness, to many critiques of academic detachment. And in that sense, we too resist the insistent demand to respond with urgency, relating to the needs of the present as they are presently defined. We would also add that the freedom granted to withdraw from direct engagement with the world, to take stock of the evidence collected and to come to conclusions, is in increasingly short supply in the modern university. We nevertheless note how this space, the university space we occupy, has been constructed for a type of intellectual activity which is on the whole socially conservative, which constantly and complacently reaffirms itself and its cultural importance. In present-day circumstances within which academics are increasingly pressured to generate funds for the university and work in collaboration with other institutions and communities, the old university vision of an elite Bildung is recalled by some with a kind of painful nostalgia. If only the academic and intellectual was valued again as they once were – as the guardian of high culture and refined human understanding, granted time and space in order to cultivate themselves and hence fulfil their social duties. The problem with this lament, of course, is that the reactionary nature and social conservatism of this academic ideal are quietly forgotten. It functions before all else as an attempt to preserve an older elitist order by holding back the tide of events.

The German philosopher Johann Gottlieb Fichte argued that the scholar must achieve a state of inner harmony and moral integrity if he was to undertake such an important task. He has to become the *'ethically best* man of his time'.[33] Having achieved this exalted state, the scholar would along with his peers, take upon himself the education of mankind, seeking to enlighten society about its 'real needs' and how they could be met. This commitment to overall moral advancement helped replace 'the Christian narrative of salvation with a vision of permanent progress' that it would be the scholar's job to superintend.[34] If this sounds incredibly immodest and not a little paternalistic, it is worth noting that academics are still encouraged to occupy similarly immodest positions albeit cloaked in the democratic guise of entrepreneurialism, as they write bids for research funding explaining how through their work they will answer society's grand challenges. Indeed, it is in the financial interest of today's university to portray itself as essential to our collective salvation, as it claims to offer solutions to the social, environmental and economic problems of our time.

As with a liberal education, an education in Bildung placed specialist knowledge in relation to a necessary all-round character formation. It was designed to develop a disposition towards learning that would enable the student to become self-directed and flexible to a range of social problems. Again, students and aspiring scholars had to be freed from any concerns regarding their livelihood, so that they could separate themselves from worldly distractions. Students should live, according to Fichte, in small communities where their needs are catered for by the university, thus 'minimising their commercial exchange with the rest of society'. They would be distinguished, moreover, by special uniforms, which would be their 'dress of honour'.[35]

Fichte's uniforms symbolise the student's membership of a larger body, one dedicated to the pursuit of learning and self-cultivation. They symbolise the disciplinary character these students were expected to develop. They represent the moral seriousness required of those who, through their membership of the university and involvement with it, were to become members of an increasingly secular cultural elite. The quest for knowledge in which each student was expected to participate had the highest aims. Students would indeed be encouraged to view it as a calling – where the prosperity of society depends on the devout commitments of the university scholar. As Fichte put it:

> All our enquiries must aim at mankind's supreme goal, which is the improvement of the species to which we belong, and students of the [modern university] must, as it were, constitute that centre from which humanity in the highest sense of the word radiates.[36]

Overall, it was hoped that universities would become a template for the renewal of society, producing individuals who, because of their carefully devised character formation, would go on to exhibit in their very being the values considered to be those required of modern civilised life. Indeed, it was hoped that they would generate through their selfless activities the cultural unity that a nation under threat so needed. These aspirations were pitched high. Informing the developing Germanic university system, they had significant influence elsewhere, feeding into the Anglo-American idea of the university and the function of a liberal education.

As we will now see, other segments of the population were the recipients of a less liberal educational programme, one that has had social and political significances that endure to the present day.

Mass schooling, popular education

Attempts to redefine elite education would never satisfy all the needs of industrial society. The education of the rest of the population would have to be addressed. In the nineteenth century, it was feared that an increasingly democratic society threatened the highest cultural achievements to date, presumably because 'it enshrined the values of the ordinary, the mediocre, because its wants were of the moment, unadvised by history and heedless of the future'. This was the context within which a new liberal elite hoped to defend high culture, and keep society healthy, maintaining a realm 'in which literature and history made sense'.[37] Its representatives hoped to secure a cultural stronghold from which the highest human values and commitments were preserved for the benefit of humankind. And yet, in nineteenth-century Britain, as well as in other newly democratic nations, it was clear to some that as the vote was slowly extended downwards – initially to comparatively wealthy male landowners, then to men of more modest means, then to all men, and finally to all men and women – that the education of all would become an increasing priority. The foundation and composition of a system of mass education became a real concern. An elevated humanist educational philosophy was brought into alliance with a bureaucratic pragmatism, in order to produce an educational system that would secure social order and the maximisation of human resources.

While proponents of liberal education were asking themselves 'what happens to high culture in a democratic society?',[38] a diverse group of intellectuals, bureaucrats and social reformers focused their attention on the potentially formative influence of mass education. The construction and eventual entrenchment of mass education in this era could be viewed as the function of an elite conspiracy, a straightforward attempt to keep the poor in their place and maintain the structures of a deeply hierarchical society, one that has been built on the capitalist exploitation of the labouring classes. After all, the overt rationale for mass education was that it would train all members of society so that they would occupy without dissent the roles designated for them within the social order. There is some justice in this assessment of the drive for popular education, but it is also the case that it was motivated by more 'democratic' and kindly intentions, such as the wish to use education as a tool for raising the cultural levels of the poor, drawing on the findings of science regarding child health and development – a kind of modest enlightenment – and for education to chime with other schemes for serving social betterment, pre-eminently perhaps the construction of modern systems of sanitation, but also initiatives to improve conditions in the workplace and in health care. Equally, there was the concern that through education the enfranchised should be taught to cast their votes as reasoning, and reasonable, citizens. They should be taught to 'think for themselves' as democratic citizens. They were not, of course, encouraged to pursue thought wherever it might take them, rather they were to be socialised through mass education to think and act in conformity with the dominant political rationality. They would be educated to live within established political structures. These structures were not simply the malign artifices of capitalist exploitation. They were 'positively' designed to assist the poor to a greater state of health and productivity. Indeed, this 'positivity' of mass education is what assisted it in becoming a deeply formative force in modern society.

Disciplinary origins of mass schooling

In England, driven by the need to produce a citizenry that could contribute to economic growth and compete with Germany and the US, the state slowly became involved in the education of working-class children, at first providing limited funds in the form of government grants from 1830, and later setting up its own 'board schools' from 1870, intended at first only to 'fill the gaps' in existing school provision. By 1870, the techniques, institutions and procedures of mass education had been largely set in place by a range of religious and philanthropic organisations. Despite a reluctance by government to get involved, the possibility of state-sanctioned mass education had been long discussed. In 1807 it was debated in the House of Commons, where the MP Davies Giddy gave a notorious speech in which he argued that:

> giving education to the labouring classes of the poor [would] teach them to despise their lot in life, instead of making them good servants in agriculture, and other laborious employments to which their rank in society had destined them; instead of teaching them subordination, it would render them factious ... it would enable them to read seditious pamphlets, vicious books, and publications against Christianity.[39]

Against this position, other commentators felt that education could achieve the exact opposite. As the London magistrate and founder of one of the first police forces in England, Patrick Colquhoun, argued it would be an agent in 'preventing those calamities which led to idleness and crime ... by giving a right bias' to the minds of labouring people. Education should not seek to 'elevate their minds above the rank they are destined to fill in society', but it could be used to teach labouring people better, more industrious habits, that would serve the state well.[40]

At the beginning of the nineteenth century, the first mass schools – called monitorial schools – were organised rather like factories, bringing together vast numbers of poor children and imposing upon them a common regimen. These schools were also laboratories of a kind. They were places in which the children of the labouring poor could be observed and scrutinised. They combined architectural design with intimate record keeping in such a way that pupils were at all times available for inspection. In *Discipline and Punish* – now, we would suggest, an essential text for those studying education – Michel Foucault links the development of such systems to a much broader shift in operations of power.[41]

It was once the privilege of the powerful and famous to be visible and known, Foucault argues. Those further down the social order did not merit that distinction and lived in comparative obscurity. But at the turn of the nineteenth century those at the bottom of the social order became interesting to power through forms of inspection that increasingly over the last two centuries have made almost all aspects of daily life visible to others – and hence governable. This visibility extends far beyond one's immediate environment, as processes of record keeping capture those inspected according to the traces they leave, and allow this knowledge to be amalgamated, transported and shared. In this way, the everyday banalities of life have become the focus of processes of inspection, description and ordering. This led to the rapid growth of the human sciences in the nineteenth century, establishing an intimate nexus between knowledge and power. Effectively, disciplinary institutions produced knowledge that could then be reapplied to inform the development of future disciplinary practices, framing indeed what it meant to be a pupil, or child, or patient in disciplinary–institutional terms. In principle, this gives everything we consider self-evident about ourselves an arbitrary institutional origin. According to the logic of this modern disciplinary regimen, citizens would not obey power because they had observed how on occasion those who disobeyed could be very publicly and brutally punished (on the gallows for example). Rather, a modern citizenry would learn to govern itself in every detail because it felt the constant gaze of a form of inspection for which no aspect of one's life was too trivial to be of interest. Citizen-subjects would learn to live and act as if constantly observed. Arguably, the paradigmatic institution in which they acquired this habit was the modern school.

Pastoral care

Early in the nineteenth century, the factory or monitorial school embodied the exemplary arrangement of educational space. Nevertheless, during that century another form of schooling was developed for the children of the poor labouring classes, with this latter form eventually becoming educationally dominant. It would gradually infiltrate and complement the regimen of diligent record keeping and constant inspection which defined the monitorial school. This early nineteenth-century disciplinary institution was eventually superseded by the mid-nineteenth-century moral training school where decidedly more intimate systems of government were pioneered.[42] Moral training schools developed and applied a form of 'pastoral power' deriving from earlier Christian institutions.[43] It was here that the educational influence typical of the priest in rural, pre-urban communities continued, though in an increasingly secular context, where the teacher adopted and increasingly monopolised a social role once reserved for the local pastor. This earlier 'educational' role demanded a spirit of self-sacrifice, in which the Christian pastor was expected to connect his salvation to the salvation of those under his care. It set in motion a mode of inspection in which the pastor was to guide the congregation through his intimate knowledge of those in his care. This knowledge was produced as individual members of the congregation were encouraged to confess their innermost thoughts, actively seeking the guidance of their pastor.

Transported to the towns of the Industrial Revolution, the priest's responsibility for the souls of his congregation was taken over by the schoolteacher and, with this duty of care, the techniques for governing the shepherd's flock were introduced into education. The logic of pastoral care contributed to the idea that teaching should be considered a form of professional sacrifice for the present and future moral, social and educational well-being of the pupil. The pastoral teacher of the moral training school based their professional identity and judged the success of their work on the strength of those connections they established with their pupils. This is a relationship model that endures to this day. However, what characterises today's school is, we argue, that the moral mission of education is underplayed. Hence the moral techniques remain, but the legitimating moral discourse has fallen away.

In the nineteenth century, the moral mission of education was still candidly acknowledged. For this reason alone, it is worth returning to the context of nineteenth-century education to remind ourselves that education must always have a moral dimension, even if it is not much invoked. It is often assumed, however, that nineteenth-century education received its moral impetus from cultural grandees such as Matthew Arnold, Thomas Carlyle and John Ruskin. Such figures are either then credited by liberal commentators for their humanising influence in an age of capitalist expansion – prioritising the importance of moral development, resisting the reductive demands of business, healing the rift between culture and society and so on – or they are attacked by left-wing critics for providing a legitimating ideology which gave the ruling class a favourable vision of itself (allowing that class to believe that, as it enjoyed the fruits of an exploited labouring class, it was serving a higher purpose). These liberal and neo-Marxist accounts nevertheless tend to agree that Arnold and his fellow cultural missionaries were the principal moral agents of the time.

A rival account can be found in the work of post-Foucauldian scholars like Ian Hunter and James Donald who claim that the main architects of popular education were those bureaucrats who were more directly responsible for its implementation.[44] These agents developed a moral technology of schooling shorn of the high aims of liberal education, designed instead to develop habits that would make a labouring population more amenable to the needs of the nineteenth-century nation state. This was no small achievement in the political context of the early nineteenth century where state involvement in schooling was highly controversial, viewed by some as a potentially dangerous extension of state power to areas that would be better governed by religious conscience. In this domain, the influence of the church, fragmented as it had become, was still strong. To successfully introduce state actors in this context was the achievement, Hunter argues, of a particular form of bureaucratic reason. In this view, bureaucratic reason is distinctly advantageous for sustaining and developing social harmony in that it reduces social, political and religious matters to questions of administration. It detaches decision-making as far as possible from 'personal' loyalties and moral principles, and provides the 'organisational *habitus* for the intellectual technologies of statistical survey and procedural analysis'.[45] As Hunter puts it:

> These were the circumstantial imperatives that gave rise to what Weber identifies as the central features of bureaucracy: formal division of jurisdictional areas; an office hierarchy; a system of 'files' or information inscription and processing; expert personnel; strict procedural management of office routines; tenure and pensions. Such are the material and spiritual conditions for separating political administration from the personal will of those in power, and for routinely transforming the exigencies of government into technical problems open to technical solutions. Instead of taking the bureau for granted, or contemptuously dismissing its 'technicism' we must learn, by exercising our historical imaginations, to appreciate it as a remarkable human invention. The capacity to detach governmental decision from personal loyalties and religious passions, far from representing a split in a formally unified moral personality or public life, was a positive organisational and ethical acquisition, involving an important augmentation of our technologies for living.[46]

There is no pathos here for other modes of life, or forms of education, that existed free of bureaucratic reason. Rather, Hunter views the bureaucratic domain as a key area of modern life that allows social problems to be addressed without a subsequent descent into conflict. The bureaucrat has moral practices of their own, and these should be admired for their restraint and measure. Crucially, for our purposes, Hunter argues that bureaucratic reason allowed the state to separate education from vested interests. It achieved this aim by recasting education, by dividing its processes into a whole series of mundane governmental tasks. Hunter argues that the great achievement of modern mass education, of the introduction of secular and universal schooling, was not down to the idealism of social reformers, or the political pressure of disenfranchised groups. It was the product of a more basic shift that placed 'the school system next to the sewerage system' as just another necessary component in a well-governed, well-administered society.[47]

The instrumental reduction of education to measurable outputs, its conversion to a mere sequence of technical activities requiring managerial, administrative oversight, is a feature of modern education that many educators and critics still bemoan. Modern education is instrumentalised, they claim, and thereby debased. There are too many managers, these critics continue, there are too many bureaucrats, wielding too great an influence over something that is basically not their concern. What makes Hunter so challenging to contemporary educational thinkers, to critics such as these, what constitutes his radicalism as a thinker, is that he completely upsets the premise of this argument. According to Hunter such commentators fail to see that this 'reduction of education' to instrumental concerns was the necessary first step leading to its universal provision. In this instrumental form, education could finally emancipate itself from religious segregation, vested interests, political infighting and tradition. Principled educators still had a role within such a system, as prestigious moral eminences, exemplary moral figures. They were still employed for those qualities. Yet they were not cultural grandees of the stature of Arnold, Carlyle or Ruskin (Arnold was, of course, also a schools' inspector – a grandee working at the technical–administrative level). Moral educators were integrated into mass schooling on a very different basis, not as spokespeople for a common humanity, but as moral functionaries working within a larger governmental system over which they had no jurisdiction. Principled educators overreach themselves today, Hunter argues, when they attack the bureaucratic order that made universal education possible. They appeal to higher ideals that simply have no purchase or wider relevance in an educational system that was built on very different, governmental principles.

The most significant figure in this transformation of education was James Kay-Shuttleworth who, as secretary of the Committee of Education from 1839, was responsible for determining the character and organisation of the mass school. He, like many of his contemporaries, was still motivated by religious belief, arguing that the schoolteacher would require 'no small support from Christian faith' to reverse 'the mental darkness, the stubborn tempers, the hopeless spirits, and the vicious habits' of common children. But Kay-Shuttleworth would place this moral mission within the bureaucratic structures of state provision. Within that structure morally guided teachers would still be required. Teaching still demanded a 'spirit of self-sacrifice and tender concern for well-being'. But such teaching would be based on a sober understanding of just 'how degenerate these children are'.[48] Statistical surveys and psychological reports would thereby augment more overtly religious diagnoses. Recognising along with Christian pastoral educators such as David Stow, that in the crowded interior of industrial cities such as Glasgow, the old pastoral system of Christian care was no longer able to operate, Kay-Shuttleworth hoped to develop a system of moral formation appropriate to the needs of the massive urban conurbations of the nineteenth century. This was a period in which workers, amassed in great numbers to serve the needs of industry, threatened to become an insurrectional force. Their moral training was a priority.

The moral training school was designed specifically to counteract what were viewed as the malign influences of urban living. It was designed to lay hold of the 'power of the Sympathy of Numbers' – which was Stow's term for the effects of peer pressure – and put it to use in the moral presence of the schoolteacher.[49] Pupils were observed at play – during which they were expected to reveal their natural tendencies – and then called into the school hall for lessons in, amongst other things, moral conduct. The entire school would be recruited to an investigation that would conclude by 'applauding the good deed, or condemning the misdemeanour'.[50] Grouped as an assembly, the mode of punishment would be discussed and negotiated. In this way, all pupils would participate in moral correction, where an abstract case was first considered, before the real case that it represented was punished.

In the moral environment of the mass school, the pastoral teacher signified the moral template to which all would aspire. He would embody norms 'whose very inaccessibility' would inspire a 'relationship of constant emulation'.[51] But his presence would not be an austere one, indeed the pastoral schoolteacher was expected to place himself, as Stow put it, 'on such terms with his pupils so they can, without fear, make him their confidant, unburden their minds, and tell him of any little mischief they may have done'.[52] The overall objective, here, was to develop the child's capacity to reflect on and govern the self, internalising a process of moral supervision, so much so that it became automatic. The ultimate objective was to work towards a governable, self-regulating citizenry that would police its own conduct and act in accordance with established norms, thus obviating the need for coercion.

Despite the heavy moral discourse through which it was expressed, the morally steeped practices of nineteenth-century education are not as distant as we might perhaps like to think. Indeed, we can already see within the moral training school the origins of more recent ideas, such as those of a '"child-centred" pedagogy, overseen by an unobtrusive yet vigilant teacher'.[53] More recent pedagogies that pay attention to the natural environment and dispositions of the child may be designed in a similar fashion to bring attention to a child's existing dispositions so that these natural tendencies may become the object of intervention and self-government. Our present education is perhaps more subtle, or at least not a little coy about its moralising effects, but it is no less extensively imbued with techniques of moral formation – though these techniques no longer obey a clear, explicitly stated moral purpose, but are enacted instead as a mixed inheritance of governing forms. As such, it could be argued that a system which functions by lavishing attention in various ways on the individual formation of educational subjects, so that they may become productive within a wider social space, is only more intensively pursued today. This is, in Hunter's words, the result of an 'intimate and reciprocating relationship between the intensification of the personal sphere and the expansion of the sphere of public administration'.[54] This analysis should prompt thought about the claims of child-centred or progressive education (Chapter 10), about the idea that theirs are liberatory practices that evade the constraining effects of power. Modern education is defined by the connection it maintains between the formation of individual subjectivities and the administration of society.

A humble church

The promises of a liberal elite were tied to systems designed to secure and shore up the position of a privileged group that would presume to speak on behalf of others. To the extent that liberal principles were applied elsewhere, even in the lowly context of the mass school, they were only implemented because they could be adapted to serve practical, governmental ends. Effectively, 'culture' was allowed entrance into the space of popular education, not, as cultural intellectuals imagine, as the bearer of, and means of fulfilling, the promise of man's full cultural development, but because there was a need to mass-produce the cultural exemplar. The teacher became the representative of a moral order pupils were expected to respect and orient themselves towards.

This way of understanding schooling is significant, Hunter argues, because it serves to 'reverse the usual priority between culture and education',[55] where education is conventionally attacked for its failure to realise the promises of culture. Instead, we might pay attention to how modern education mobilises culture and high ideals on its own terms to serve more mundane ends. From this point of view, we would no longer express disappointment at the untidy, messy improvisations and compromises that constitute today's educational institutions. Instead of viewing education as a 'humble church built out of stones intended for a great cathedral', instead of approaching educational institutions as if they were the 'flawed realisation of an ideal form',[56] we might consider education from the perspective of its achievements, some of which have been dangerously effective. In modernity, its institutions have achieved a kind of dominion over social and political life that would, from a pre-modern perspective, be simply unimaginable.

Nonetheless there are, in our view, problems with Koselleck's analysis, and more so with Hunter's – despite the unsettling effects of the latter's analysis, which are eminently useful insofar as they disturb educational pieties, in particular the cries of betrayal that come continually from progressive educators and critics, and despite Koselleck's affirmative account of the development of modern government and bureaucracy as distinctly valuable spheres of thought and calculation – both lines of argument lead to the exclusion of moral critique, for Hunter in particular – from the educational and political systems they describe. Moral critique becomes a potentially dangerous interference in the smooth running of state and educational machinery that would otherwise be torn apart by a politics of conscience. This line of argument also results in Hunter's remarkable, wilful blindness to the enduring presence of social class as an agent of reproduction, control and domination within the system. Whilst we would argue that the formation of liberal and mass education was not the simple effect of class conspiracy, inevitably class feeling amongst politicians and intellectuals did inform the shape it took. The modern university and modern school were formed as a rather more complex and conflicted system. It was produced as a strange mix of oppression, cultural enhancement and containment that unavoidably – however the ruling elite might have regretted it – produced some sort of conscientisation, a raising of cultural and social understanding.

12

Confined to the Present

A state of crisis

From the perspective of government there is no educational crisis, no real educational crisis, despite its regular announcements of the inadequacies of the nation's schools in comparison with those of our international competitors. These are merely problems that need to be resolved if education is to function more efficiently in the interests of the economy. Educational systems are today well established, making their contribution to the formation of a citizenry that remains largely within and subservient to the socio-economic order which it has been educated largely to accept. There is widespread feeling nonetheless that education is in a state of crisis. This sense of crisis is generated in part by the rise of an educational 'improvement' agenda.[1] This positions educational establishments as being always deficient in some respect, or likely to become so in the near future. Today's schools are overwhelmed by the insistent demands of relentless target setting and the perpetual fear of being labelled inadequate by the schools' inspectorate. Today's universities are obsessed with improving their status, reputation and market share. As institutions, it is as if schools and universities can never do enough; their position is never assured, improvements are always possible. But this sense of crisis is still more deeply felt. Educators, both teachers and lecturers, have a strong sense that older, and in their eyes more meaningful, educational ideals are losing traction in the face of an apparently relentless drive to have education satisfy the latest economic and utilitarian demands. Many educators are mourning the gradual attrition of progressive ideals in particular, lamenting an educational project that achieved a high watermark in the 1960s but has been in decline ever since. Surrounded by so much expressed regret, we suggest that it is worth taking a more sober view. Otherwise we risk falling into an easy mindset that contrasts our fallen educational present to a fabled golden age that preceded it. Against this simplistic, but undeniably seductive point of view, it is perhaps more instructive to view the educational present as being as much the outcome of adapted (some would say adulterated) progressive educational techniques as it is the victim of reductive target-setting and over-testing. We will begin by considering perhaps the most successful argument – successful in terms of the wide adoption of its ideas – for progressive education of the twentieth century, Deweyan educational philosophy. Our contention, as we consider the unique pragmatism of this approach to education, is that it paved the way for its replacement by focusing on the immediate contexts of educational practice. In this chapter we also review the history of the modern university, coming to similar conclusions. Since its inauguration in the nineteenth century this institution has operated to limit educational thought and research activity to engagement with the facts of social existence as it is currently configured by technocratic rationality, to a consideration of what needs to be done to satisfy present objectives that are presented as irrefutably reasonable goals. In school and university we detect a similar process, one that recruits educational thought and activity to servicing the needs of a tyrannical present which is posited as an unquestionable historical necessity.

Dewey and progressive education

The North American philosopher and educational reformer, John Dewey, played a prominent role in the development of twentieth-century progressive education. Indeed, there was a time when students of education could not expect to graduate without having Dewey's *Democracy and Education* recommended as a core text.[2] Today, by contrast, it is quite possible to graduate without ever studying Dewey.

Dewey's educational philosophy was informed in part by the evolutionary worldview of Charles Darwin, whose landmark book *On the Origin of Species* was published the year Dewey was born. From an evolutionary perspective, Dewey views education as a process through which society reproduces itself by transmitting knowledge and conventions from one generation to the next. In previous 'simpler societies' the education of the vast majority of initiates could take place informally through experiences gained while growing up. In the vastly more complex societies that characterise more recent history, however, Dewey decides that the education of all must be taken care of in specialist institutions. The task of initiating a citizenry into social mores has become too complex for an educational process based only on informal interaction. Thus we find that for Dewey, mass education is an expedient, devised in response to the social circumstances of societies that had simply become more complex and culturally differentiated.

But Dewey's philosophy, like that of many progressive educators of his day, has a more troubling aspect. The evolutionary metaphors used to interpret social development were also used to understand child development. Typically this posited mankind in the form of 'white', European and, perhaps, North American societies, 'as the developmental end point of human history' where the goal of progressive education was to take the child through stages of development that mirrored the stages by which it was presumed such societies had themselves formerly developed.[3] The child would accordingly pass through earlier developmental stages of savagery and barbarism, eventually reaching the civilised condition best represented by contemporary European and North American educated, intellectual elites. This developmental sequence encouraged educators to allow younger children to engage in 'savage' learning activities, where appropriate, and supported the idea that children's impulses and instinctual curiosity should be nourished rather than ignored or suppressed in an environment where they could 'grow naturally'. Children who displayed 'arrested' development were understood as though they had become trapped in an earlier stage of history. They were placed alongside racially marginalised social groups, who were thought to represent an arrested, earlier stage of human social development.[4] Apart from the obvious racism inherent in this way of thinking, it placed progressive education in an interesting if not contentious position. Progressive education is seen as representing in itself the culmination of human history, and the method for its further improvement.

The racist associations of early child-centred pedagogy should not lead us to presume guilt by association when confronting current day child-centred pedagogies. What is significant, for us, is how such arguments were employed to make a case in favour of a less prescriptive education of the young child, one that recognises the value of play and exploration. This was an argument for less directive forms of teaching, approaches that are not modelled on later stages of development, forms of teaching that do not insist, earlier than is necessary, that children sit still, for example, and devote themselves to more recognisably scholarly activities. But as the overt racism of this scheme suggests, these arguments were ideologically driven. The 'savage' in the young child was not to be celebrated as such. Children's impulses and instinctual curiosity were to be nourished so as to better incorporate the child into an educational environment designed to produce a certain kind of citizenry. This set of associations makes it difficult to take at face value more recent arguments in favour of 'play for its own sake', since one suspects such arguments for being already subservient to a particular technology of person-formation and a particular rendering of the political.

According to Dewey's educational philosophy, the pupil is to be treated as a social being, and schools should cultivate an environment in which social intelligence, that kind of intelligence presumed necessary for modern civilised living, can be acquired. In other words, we find education here defined as the process which prepares citizens for life in the society in which Dewey finds himself, a liberal democracy. Dewey formulated his philosophy at the turn of the twentieth century as the United States faced a rapid influx of migrants of multiple nationalities, cultures and religions. The challenge facing those working in schools was to bring these increasingly diverse communities into alignment with the aims and values of the receiving country. The aim was to create harmony between diverse groups and socialise them into a liberal way of life. In this context, the so-called 'traditional' educational approaches of the time were viewed by figures such as Dewey as ineffective. These traditional approaches attempted to transmit knowledge from teacher to learner without due regard for the varied backgrounds, interests and experiences of the pupils concerned. Here the 'progressive' or liberal approach set real challenges to a system based on a more didactic and direct transmission model of education. For according to Dewey's educational philosophy, the entire school curriculum would be better off if it were based more firmly on questions and enquiries initiated by the learners themselves. This would make the curriculum meaningful, and enable lessons to connect with learners because they were constructed in their terms. Indeed, the entire school would become an extension of the home and the community, building on already existing knowledge and experience, even feeding back through the learners themselves to the communities from which they came.

Each school would become a society in microcosm, modelling the civil order for which it prepared its occupants. For Dewey, democracy is about far more than just voting. Learning to live in a democratic society is about learning to live in association with a diverse range of people, making decisions together about collective issues. For this reason, it is important that the diversity of the school's intake matches the diversity of wider society. Members of the school community would be encouraged to focus on what they had in common, rather than what might divide them.

Modelled in school, democratic processes might well involve shared decision-making, collective deliberation and open debate. What this taught, however, was the importance of subordinating personal interest to a particular vision of democratic procedure. It was, moreover, not configured as a challenge to authority in favour of the collective voice of the student body. Indeed, while knowledge would be treated as contingent, contextual and constructed, the teacher would still fulfil an essential role mediating between learners, and teaching them how to associate with one another.

In an early essay, Dewey expressed his commitment to the idea 'that every teacher should realise the dignity of his calling' where the teacher operates as 'the prophet of the true God and the usherer in of the true kingdom of God'.[5] This statement is somewhat surprising at first sight, given the materialist bent of Dewey's philosophy. But it is borne out in his later work, which reconceptualises religion as a secular activity. Education, in turn, is given primary responsibility for establishing the basis of social harmony and modern spiritual life. It is given responsibility for establishing a secular 'Kingdom of God' on earth.[6]

This suggests a line of descent connecting progressive educational practices to their Christian precursors, something we noted in our consideration of the nineteenth-century moral school's debt to Christian pastoralism, which was also a shaping influence on modern child-centred education (see Chapter 11). In a secular context, the teacher continues to concern themselves with the moral formation of a citizenry, with its perfection and harmony, and in doing so comes to embody some of the virtues to which students are expected to aspire. To the extent that today's teachers still present themselves as facilitators rather than directors of learning, an aspect of the progressive tradition is retained. Progressivism has nevertheless lost its more strongly prophetic point of view, which looked beyond the immediate scenario of the classroom, seeking to model society in microcosm across the structures of the school. Progressive methods such as learner-initiated enquiry have been largely absorbed into a wider armoury of pedagogic techniques that are collected together in the absence of a guiding educational philosophy. The moral formation of a citizenry continues, and the teacher still adopts an exemplary role. But the teaching profession now largely operates without appeal to a substantive, collectively agreed vision of a better society.

The rise and fall of progressive education

Progressive education steadily gained influence throughout the first half of the twentieth century. Many educationalists developed an ideological commitment to the idea that students should be allowed a greater role in their learning, that teaching should be responsive to their interests and experiences, that schools should foster tolerance and integration, and that pupils should be prepared to become productive, self-directing members of society. Traditional knowledge and its transmission through didactic teaching were viewed as conservative if not reactionary. In return, the progressive educational philosophy associated with Dewey was roundly attacked in a parodied form for 'dumbing down' teaching. Indeed it has been blamed ever since for an overall loss of authority in the classroom. Dewey has been accused of having 'infected schools with epistemological and moral relativism', for substituting socialisation for 'true education', and so on.[7] What such ideological disputes forget, of course, are the intellectual and political foundations of progressive education. Rather ironically, considering the zeal with which conservative critics attacked it, progressive education was rooted in an educational philosophy designed to paper over the social rifts that often most trouble conservatives. Through giving greater attention to the individual learner, the teacher would encourage the student to become more fully involved in and hence committed to their education. At the same time, they would be inducted into the social mores of a liberal society, learning to live as an active, productive and responsible citizen attending to the needs of their community as much as to their own.

In Britain, the high point of progressivism lay in the 1960s and 70s with initiatives including the organisation of curricula into student-led enquiry-based modules, and the founding of community schools.[8] Since then progressivism has been on the defensive, facing an insistent emphasis at the level of government on what had for some time been referred to as getting 'back-to-basics', which involves the inculcation of core skills and knowledge and accountability through testing. Schools now compete with one another for their pupils, and wealthier parents compete in the housing market to live within the catchment areas of the best-performing schools. The result is an educational landscape where pedagogies are increasingly constrained by the pursuit of examination results, and schools are becoming once again less and less diverse in their intakes. While progressives continue to survive and practise their craft in schools and university education departments, they feel their professional identities and their progressive convictions to be under threat of extinction from the reductive demands of contemporary educational policy. And yet, though progressivism is on the back foot, it remains as the assumed alternative to more utilitarian contemporary trends in schooling. Critics of increasing instrumentalism in education still rely on some vision of a progressive alternative that defines for them – in however indistinct a form – the educational utopia of our times. As such, and despite the best efforts of reactionary critics to extinguish it, progressivism remains unassailably with us.

Dewey and pragmatism

Progressive education has pragmatic roots. John Dewey was indeed a key thinker in the development of a philosophical movement known as 'pragmatism', along with contemporaries such as William James, and more recent philosophers like Richard Rorty. This philosophical tradition operates in a context where the foundational claims of tradition, religion and metaphysical philosophy have been largely abandoned. Originating in the United States in the latter half of the nineteenth century, pragmatism was designed to meet the needs of pluralistic, modern industrial societies. Giving up on the idea that the ends of human activity can be pre-defined or known absolutely, pragmatism decides whether something is worthwhile by testing its effects in a specific context. Applied to education, pragmatism asserts that the purpose and nature of education are to be defined locally. This adjusted focus allowed progressive educators to continue operating in a context where the ultimate ends of education (such as emancipation, enlightenment, the exercise of reason in human affairs, wisdom, human flourishing, etc.) are in doubt, poorly defined, or in dispute. It allowed educators to gain meaning and direction by focusing on a specific educational context, drawing purpose from that context rather than from moral absolutes that define the value of education 'from the outside'.

It should come as no surprise that pragmatism will be rejected by those who cannot forgive it for abandoning foundational claims. It is open to attack from those who refuse to confront the consequences of what Nietzsche called the 'death of God' (see Chapter 8). But there is another criticism of pragmatism one might adopt. This critique follows through with the implications of pragmatism and investigates where that pragmatism might lead. As an educational philosophy, it favours problem-based enquiries, rather than the imposition of externally set curricula. It prefers situated thinking to abstract contemplation. Teaching is reconceptualised as a modern craft activity, as a profession involving skilled work applying practical know-how to specific contexts. Pragmatic teaching focuses resolutely on the practical needs of specific educational settings, developing context-specific responses, rather than global recommendations that ignore the peculiarities of each teaching scenario. It produces 'concrete answers to concrete questions, as posed by the interests of individuals, groups, or the community'. It addresses itself to 'the problems and interests of society as it is'.[9] It has contempt for 'mere theory' and for abstract thinking in general, believing that knowledge is useless unless it is applied. At this point the reader might well be wondering what the problem is with pragmatism. Max Horkheimer makes the case against.

For Horkheimer, pragmatism threatens to reduce truth to 'nothing but the successfulness of the idea'. Theory, in turn, becomes 'nothing but a scheme or plan of action' and philosophy becomes an applied science.[10] Admittedly this represents pragmatism at its most radical. But Horkheimer views Dewey's philosophy, so influential on education, as representing 'the most radical and consistent form of pragmatism'.[11] Horkheimer's claim is that by judging an idea according to its usefulness, that is according to its effects, the logic of probability begins to dominate: 'For if a concept or an idea is significant only by virtue of its consequences, any statement expresses an expectation with a higher or lower degree of probability'. This makes prediction 'the essence not only of calculation but of all thinking as such ... Probability or, better, calculability replaces truth'.[12]

Such claims may sound rather alien to those traditions of progressive education that are designed to foster schools as communities of practice, that privilege the child's learning above externally imposed demands, that make curricula relevant to the needs and experiences of the learner, and that build lessons out of questions and enquires initiated by the learners themselves. Surely the pragmatism of progressive education must be of a different type, being less about calculation, more about nurture and individual care? But to the extent progressive traditions remain focused on educational conduct, to the extent that all teaching problems are understood as problems of practice solvable only through practice, to the extent that thought abstracted from the immediate situation is attacked, and the teacher as practitioner or craftsperson is promoted, progressive education risks becoming just another expression of 'the triumph of the means over the end', which is after all the hallmark of modern instrumental reason (Chapter 8).[13] Education consequently becomes a matter of improving the means by which we are educated, rather than serving (and interrogating) the ends that education might pursue. From this perspective, the fact that progressive education is being replaced by an educational orthodoxy that favours testing, prediction, retesting, and incessant measurement and evaluation, is less surprising than it otherwise might be. The very pragmatism of progressive education – by which it gives up on the pursuit of ends, or at least transforms means into ends, focusing resolutely on the processes by which we are educated and the needs that arise in the course of everyday educational scenarios – seems to prepare the way for the test-informed instrumentalism that progressives rail against. Progressive education might view itself as the most evolved form of education to date, but it could also be viewed as a necessary step towards the somewhat pinched and blindly pragmatic idea of education that holds sway today.

The modern university

There is a sense amongst those working in higher education that universities are under attack. Like schools, universities are increasingly organised around fickle metrics and performative criteria. As means triumph over ends, as educational relationships are instrumentalised, education is justified according to its more or less immediate effects. The university, subject department, degree programme, or individual teaching session is justified by the extent to which it manages to 'inspire', lead to better results and outputs, attract students, perhaps widen participation, answer a pressing social problem, or contribute to economic prosperity. Whether judged by institutional metrics and ranking, or by claims to be having a social or economic impact, the purposes of university education are reduced to the immediate needs of society.

This was not always so. As we explored in Chapter 11, university life was once diligently separated from the distractions of 'worldly concerns'. Such distractions were felt to include the corrupting effects of commercial society, the short-sighted demands of the political classes and an intellectually impoverished and overly impatient population. The necessity of a cultured elite was asserted, as we saw in the previous chapter. This intelligentsia would operate far better and be of greater benefit to the population if not directly answerable to that population. Only under these conditions would the highly educated few be able to generate the refined sensibilities that would enable them to see beyond the more immediate present. Only then would they come to a full understanding of our finest human ideals, achieve self-mastery, suppress the passions, cultivate reason, and thereby raise the moral tone of society.

Notions such as these have not been forgotten. They are still mobilised, however shyly, by today's academics. But they are lived out alongside more immediate demands to become cost-effective and relevant, to secure funds for the university, and gain the support and interest of an expectant public whose needs and desires are increasingly expected to inform the scope, design and dissemination of research. In a peculiar twist, academics are now encouraged to believe that it is precisely through these channels, through engagement rather than withdrawal, that the civic mission of the university will be fulfilled, as it works – or so it tells us – towards a better and more prosperous society.

The conception of the modern research university

There is a shared unease amongst the academic community that the university is in a state of crisis. The contemporary university is certainly undergoing signifi- cant, if not revolutionary, internal adjustment as it responds to changes in how it is funded and audited, as well as to the threat posed by other organisations claiming to offer teaching and research more efficiently and at reduced cost. But it remains in place as an imposing edifice. As a secular institution it can draw on its long heritage. The university still prospers as a global organisation with significant cultural, economic, social and political interests. Or to put it in terms academics still disavow, the contemporary university is 'big business', bigger than ever. To say that this institution is in crisis is then slightly misleading. Perhaps it would be more accurate to say that although the corporate university prospers, a certain vision of the university is under threat. For many, this would be some version of that old ideal, the ideal of the modern research university, which can be traced back to the foundation by Wilhelm von Humboldt of the University of Berlin in 1810. Universities of this older kind had a certain purity of intent that many today feel they have lost.

The nineteenth-century research university established the basic moral and epistemological framework of our own contemporary university system, with most universities founded since 1810. The basic architecture of the modern research university was set in place alongside efforts to embed Bildung and lib- eral education (see Chapter 11). If we wish to understand the problems of the contemporary university then, we must see how they are rooted not only in argu- ments for Bildung, but also in a set of institutional structures and procedures that were developed in the nineteenth century. Here the research university was itself born out of crisis, out of an attempt to bring coherence, meaning and unity of purpose to a fragmented reality. As Chad Wellmon argues, the modern university was established in response to the epistemic and moral crisis brought about by eighteenth-century Enlightenment.[14] The modern university sought to organise and give coherence to what was perceived as an increasingly incoherent intel- lectual and moral landscape.

The modern university achieved this aim by establishing itself as the home of knowledge production. This was an unprecedented achievement. The pursuit of science, for example, had formerly been the domain of learned society and the independent man of fortune. Now it was the product and preserve of university life. The university would become the ultimate giver of epistemic authority – it would authenticate all forms of official knowledge. Each domain would have its associated expert, housed in a university alongside other experts. Leaders in each field and subfield would then be accompanied by their respective under-labourers and students, operating together as tribunal and testing house, endorsing some knowledge claims, dismissing others. This epistemic achievement was matched by the ability of the modern university to establish a research ethos where students and academics disciplined themselves to the pursuit of knowledge (rather than divine understanding), each committed by an act of faith to the overall project the university represented.

As we saw in Chapter 5, Renaissance humanists operated in a very different context, drawing from a common intellectual culture that still had some intrinsic coherence. It demanded mastery of rhetoric, as well as Latin canon and scripture. Detailed knowledge of this established core of humanist learning was favoured above intellectual specialisation. Renaissance scholars were polymaths by training. Like the scholastics before them, they were able to comment on and participate in the development of a shared culture of learning. The unity of knowledge these scholars took themselves to represent could be presumed because it was sanctioned by their confidence in the natural or divine order that lay behind it.

The twin demands of eighteenth-century Enlightenment – the pursuit of knowledge without restriction and the transmission of that knowledge to a wider populace – sounded the end of the humanist ideal that men of learning could be men of diverse intellectual accomplishment. It also increasingly tested their confidence in the natural or divine order that their accumulated knowledge and learning sought to reflect. The humanist concern with preserving ancient texts, with accumulating learning under the protection of each scholar, placing it in a shared institutional and cultural depository so that it would never again be lost, gave way to the gradual expansion of print, until books and other texts were simply too numerous to assemble and absorb. Eighteenth-century scholars, those preceding the establishment of the modern university, nonetheless attempted, with increasing futility, to record all that had been and was being written in extended bibliographies, or *lexica*, as well as in periodicals designed to assist the general man of learning. These periodicals attempted to digest and organise books, and recommend which texts in this expanding list were worth reading above others (where no single lifetime would be even remotely sufficient to read them all).

The hope lingered on that individual scholars might still survey the entirety of learning. These textual aids, these lexica and periodicals, these books on books, were intended to help them achieve or at least work towards that objective. By accumulating all that had been written in condensed, organised lists, these lexica gave the impression that the eighteenth-century 'empire of erudition', as it was known, still had some coherence and unity. These were, after all, the last years of the 'Classical Age' Foucault describes in *The Order of Things* (see Chapter 9 in this book), where knowledge was accumulated and catalogued, guided by the assumption that it was sufficient for science to measure and record. As Wellmon argues, the textual devices scholars employed during this period provided a sense of security. They 'flattened the history of knowledge' into a 'single, seemingly timeless world of print'.[15] But these diligent records and lexica only gave an impression of unity. They only 'stood in' for the 'desire to control and organise knowledge'.[16] The reality that was becoming harder and harder to deny was one of an expanding and fragmenting universe of print.

At the same time as scholars attempted to account for all that had been committed to print, advocates of enlightenment were exhorting one another to engage with the reading public, and make this accumulated culture and learning 'available to all'. An increasingly literate public required a 'popular philosophy', as it was called, one that would do battle with the foes of Enlightenment – these being ignorance, prejudice, superstition and unreasoning adherence to tradition.[17] Enlightened scholars were hence to become educators, in the popular sense. They could no longer 'just' accumulate, preserve and exude learning. It was felt they must use that learning to facilitate the perfection of a citizenry. Their assigned task was an exacting one, however, as the Renaissance humanist synthesis of canon and scripture no longer existed. The fragmentation of knowledge was also a feared ethical fragmentation of the individual who was no longer able to situate themselves within a coherent view of the world in which they were to function as an ethical subject.

A modern research ethos

The research university was presented as a solution to this self-made crisis of Enlightenment. It coped with the fragmentation of knowledge by giving up on the old expectation that men of learning achieve mastery in fields as diverse as philosophy, mathematics, theology and the natural sciences. In some cases, it even legislated against professors giving lectures across multiple fields of learning, though this was once common practice. Academics would now largely remain and lecture within their specialism, where each specialism was itself lodged within an academic discipline or subject. This new conception of research encouraged the scholar to pursue each respective specialism ever further, with the assurance that the university could contain such divergent interests, and thereby provide the necessary coherence within its unitary structure. Knowledge would no longer be produced in fragmented form, culminating in an incoherent mass of books, in a proliferating field of print against which it was impossible to measure the quality of each contribution. Organised into respective disciplinary subfields that were also institutional categories, each containing their own disciplinary expertise, new additions to knowledge would find their place and measure.

The individual scholar no longer wrote for a general audience of learned men, displaying all-round accomplishment as he did so, measuring his 'worth and value' according to his 'individual apprehension of some metaphysical, God-like view of the relationship of all knowledge'.[18] Rather, he defined himself and his worth according to his degree of specialisation. His devotion to that specialism was his nourishment. His worth was measured by his selfless commitment to the never-ending development (and possible further subdivision) of knowledge over time. He worked in an institution that supported others who, like him, were performing a similar function in their own subject areas according to similar rules of scholarly engagement. He participated as a member of a group that was working as a whole towards the furtherment of science (where science was at this point an all-encompassing term, referring to knowledge in general).

As a general pursuit, science itself was reconceptualised. It became a self-referential project that did not point back to some 'divine or natural order', but rather 'to its own operations and [internal] history'. If classical conceptions of science 'sought to harmonise the individual with the cosmos', the modern research university 'sought to harmonise the individual with science as a distinct social sphere'.[19] This social group would be made up of those content to pursue science as a good in itself.

The effects of the self-referential nature of the modern research university on scholarly practice need to be emphasised. The educational function of the research university would be justified if it produced more researchers, who would produce more knowledge. The older vocational function of the university, namely to pre-pare lawyers, doctors and priests, continued, but this vocational aspect no longer defined the overarching purpose of the university as an institution. The modern university began to dispense with an older hierarchy, where the vocational cat-egories of law, medicine and theology had once been the supreme subjects of study, the highest faculties in the university. Research in any subject justified the university, to the extent that it embodied the modern research ethos of endless enquiry. As a social group, modern researchers would be indefatigable. Committed to the same ethos of industrious, disciplined investigation, their consolation was the fact that intellectual progress no longer depended on the isolated polymath and genius. Rather, it was the inevitable product of the collective, organised indus-try of the university.

It is argued that 'early modern cultures' had 'no conception of research' since they were still grounded in the authority of canonical texts.[20] Modern research, by contrast, is only grounded in the authority of existing texts to the extent that they have not yet been superseded, or because they are about to be superseded by a new discovery or revised point of view. In a complete reversal of the early mod-ern mindset, for the research university the *older* a text becomes the *less* it is able to function in the progress of science. As a text ages, its 'authority' diminishes. Antiquated texts may be subjected themselves to research enquiry, but they no longer play a role in current debate. In this sense, the modern pursuit of research was entirely new. It would operate according to a shared, implicit set of rules gov-erning how the academic should frame enquiries and eventually communicate findings to other specialists. These findings would be reported in the established organs, or journals of each subfield, using shared systems of citation or mutual acknowledgement, as well as shared modes of address, that related each new dis-covery to the latest research in the area of enquiry it advanced.

With the academic now fully absorbed in the disciplined, disciplinary activ-ity of modern research, the feared fragmentation of knowledge is free to become the defining feature of the modern university. As we have seen the individual scholar was no longer expected to absorb diverse forms of knowledge. There was too much to learn. There was too much simply to list in general bibliographies, let alone master. Academics and their students would have to be trained to work very differently, guided by a different set of hopes. They would be trained to imagine themselves as contributors to the development of overall human understanding, even if no individual could ever fully apprehend that unity. Here the impression of unity, of collective enquiry, where each academic and student views themselves to be contributors to a larger intellectual project, was more important, it might be said, than its actuality. And this impression was given by the very fact that so many academic researchers were working in concert according to similar disciplinary procedures that governed how knowledge was best produced and recorded in each respective subfield.

The unity of modern science is not to be found, then, in the completeness of its findings, or in the unity of its subject matter (where science was once intended to reflect the divine order, or the order of nature). Rather this unity derives, following Kant, from faith in the unifying potential of human reason. Here human reason is not configured as a distinct mental capacity, as if it were something a single individual could master. Rather, human reason is viewed as a transcendental object, a pursuit of human agents working with one another, communicating and testing their ideas through mutual critical enquiry. In practice, the unity of science derives from its 'commitment to method' and its ability to form a troupe of researchers and students who share that commitment.[21] The modern research university is driven by, and finds security in, its methodological procedures.

The research university responded to the self-made crisis of Enlightenment in a second sense, Wellmon argues, by giving up on the idea that scholars should be both experts and popular philosophers. It would cultivate the moral prestige of nineteenth-century men of culture such as those discussed in the previous chapter, but these men of culture would not dilute themselves or their learning by making it accessible to a wider populace. At best, they would be moral exemplars for those pedagogues introduced in Chapter 11 – the writer of popular literature and the moral schoolteacher – whose educational mission and institutional context fitted them far better to that role. The status of the learned man was no longer dependent on his wide accomplishment or synthetic overview. It was increasingly given by the narrowness of his pursuits, by his membership of a group whose ethos and mood were one of dedicated, narrow-gauged seriousness. It was a disposition that could exist alongside, but would eventually outlive, accompanying nineteenth-century notions of liberal education and Bildung.

If the modern research university had any overall moral message, it was this: if we are disciplined and self-controlled, if we are governed by procedure and common protocol placing ourselves in the service of perpetually unfolding science, if we give up on the idea of a synthetic overview of all human understanding and concern ourselves instead with the quality (or at least doggedness) of each individual research project, we will contribute to the collective endeavour of human enquiry and industry that can only result in further cultural and material progress.

The modern university in question

Lyotard and performativity

The modern university established a research ethos that would become the basis of its replacement. The diligent single-mindedness of the modern research scholar gave way to the performative hyperactivity of today's academic, who may work across disciplines as much as within them. Anticipated, to some extent, by Jean-François Lyotard in *The Postmodern Condition* first published in 1979, this new regime has risen to prominence as older discourses have fallen from favour. It follows a gradual loss of faith in the high ideals of Enlightenment and a loss of faith in the promise of the modern research university. It also follows a loss of conviction whose endpoint Lyotard famously characterised as 'incredulity toward metanarratives'.[22] This growing incredulity (or disbelief) generates a crisis for educational institutions, since they are no longer so readily legitimated according to universal categories, such as universal reason or morality, or the pursuit of independent truth. Instead, they are legitimated according to more immediate and lowly objectives, such as their operating efficiency, rather than their ability to realise transcendental, higher goals. The performance efficiency, or 'performativity', of educational establishments has increasingly become their primary objective. Great emphasis is now placed on their ability to meet desired outputs, rather than their capacity to enquire into the nature of and question the desirability of those outputs themselves. Hence the question now asked of higher education and the knowledge it produces is not 'Is it true?' but 'What use is it?', which generally means 'Is it saleable?' and 'Is it efficient?'.[23] As Lyotard recognised, the general effect has been to 'subordinate the institutions of higher learning to the existing powers'.[24] The loss of an independent, legitimating rationale has led to a situation where the university is more and more vulnerable to objectives that are not of its making.

Previously, Lyotard argues, the task faced by academics 'entailed the formation and dissemination of a general model of life',[25] legitimated by a moralistic and sometimes emancipatory narrative. In a 'context of delegitimation' however (where there is a loss of faith in modern ideals), universities 'are called upon to create skills, and no longer ideals – so many doctors, so many teachers in a given discipline, so many engineers, so many administrators, etc.'[26] There is a return to vocational categories, though they are no longer crowned by theology and the formation of a priesthood. Consequently, there is nothing left that distinguishes the university from potential competitors. Indeed, if other institutions can be shown to fulfil these tasks more efficiently, the university is expected to give them up.

A recent example of this contraction of role is that schools rather than universities in England are now expected to take responsibility for the training of teachers. Formerly, this might have been resisted by a rationale that universities offer something 'higher' – some kind of access to greater learning and expertise – that schools on their own are unable to offer. Where once it could be argued that universities offered an independent point of view from which to approach the profession of school teaching, a 'view from the outside' that would be invaluable when developing a critical view of the teacher's professional practice, today the intellectual and moral independence of higher educational institutions is no longer valued or trusted. Hence, the knowledge universities now promise to transmit, deemed necessary for the training of future workers and professionals is, as Lyotard argues, 'no longer designed to train an elite capable of guiding the nation towards its emancipation [or towards its moral betterment], but to supply the system with players capable of acceptably fulfilling their roles at the pragmatic posts required by its institutions'.[27] The university defends itself today by showing that it can and will do what has been asked of it.

In order to adapt to circumstances that are not of its making, it is felt necessary to 'break down barriers' within the university itself. The old nineteenth-century model of the university, where each disciplinary subfield has its own place within the system, its own methods and its own recognised experts, is now seen as outmoded. Traditional academics of this kind are dismissed for remaining within their 'disciplinary silos', for working in splendid but useless isolation. Against this work habit from which they are presumed to suffer, such academics are invited (rather insistently at times) to become interdisciplinary, to adopt an approach to knowledge production that, for Lyotard, is 'specific' to this 'age of delegitimation and its hurried empiricism'.[28] In effect, it is believed that once interdisciplinary research sheds the old boundaries of disciplinary enquiry, it will better relate to a complex reality, which is to say, it will be more amenable. The problem with isolated academic disciplines is that each adopts a specific point of view, and hence, is not always so easily adapted to shifting needs. By forcing academics to communicate across traditions, and across worldviews, these old disciplinary barriers to becoming operationally efficient and responsive are weakened. In a performative culture, the critical and pre-ordained gaze of a disciplinary worldview is regarded as an increasingly useless affectation.

It is perhaps remarkable that academics still work within older discourses – of criticality for example – however superficially they may be enacted. It seems that as one educational age follows another, select educational notions from preceding ages are retained (though not without adjustment). Hence the ideal of a liberal education lives on in the university, just like the ideal of a progressive education lives on in the context of schooling. Indeed, once it becomes an impossible ideal (impossible to realise in an age of performativity), the notion of a liberal education is held onto rather desperately. For this reason, it is important that we examine how these older educational philosophies are kept in play, and explore how they operate in new contexts. It is worth remembering that in the history of education each historical transition point is not absolute. To take an immediate example, Lyotard claims at the end of his account of education, of its delegitimation, and then 're-legitimation' through performativity, that this new performative age sounds 'the knell of the age of the Professor'.[29] But the end of something is often only its transformation into something else. In this case, the figure of the Professor is not about to go extinct. To the critical gaze, it might seem that the Professor has been transformed from a person with recognised expertise – who can profess on a specific topic like few others – to a person who is expert in institutional conformity, who knows how to work the system, and advises others how to do so too. Though many professors still present themselves as defenders of a liberal education, or more occasionally, as proponents of a more dissident politics, most will not have succeeded in their posts on that account. Many will have reached the top of their profession because they have learned to give the system what it needs.

The rise of the entrepreneurial university

The self-evident prestige of the modern university as bastion of progress, Enlightenment and truth, is now under threat. We live in the age of the 'entrepreneurial university', which relates to the world on very different terms. Conforming to the postmodern condition Lyotard described, the entrepreneurial university no longer seeks to guide us towards a better future through its privileged understanding of the processes that underlie our existence (though for now at least, remnants of the predecessor university are tolerated). Instead, time collapses into an entrepreneurial concern with the present, a concern to maximise existing resources. The experience of finitude noted by Foucault (Chapter 9) is thereby adjusted. Our experience of human finitude is less the product of a modern drive to understand and master anonymous historical processes, an endeavour which engages in endless enquiry at the ever-retreating limits of human understanding. Rather, finitude is experienced in the entrepreneurial condition of 'being permanently in a condition of limited resources' that must be maximised at all costs. Guiding modern ideals, such as progress and the formation of a rational citizenry, are replaced by objectives that are more closely focused on the contingencies of the present. Hence words such as 'innovation' or 'excellence' are given prominence now, where innovation in particular is a decidedly ahistorical concept with 'no point of orientation beyond what is needed or available in a competitive environment'.[30]

Pedagogic practice in the entrepreneurial university is driven by an obsession with the pace of technological change. Students, it is claimed, no longer learn as they once did; they have very different needs. Today's student – awkwardly dubbed 'Thumbelina' by one recent philosopher, presumably because she relates to the world via touchscreen and thumb[31] – finds herself, it is said, more or less permanently connected to online media, relating to the world through this virtual space. The consequences for education are assumed to be monumental, and few expect the pace of change to abate. Educational institutions are positioned as playing a game of constant catch-up where anything traditional is almost considered outmoded by default. New approaches, new pedagogies, must constantly be constructed in a breathless attempt to keep up with the next generation of digital innovation. This feeds into a performative culture where education is always in response mode.

Though the modern university pursued aims that were problematic to say the least, the entrepreneurial university comes with its own associated dangers, including the danger of its dissolution. As already noted, in an entrepreneurial age it is sensible to ask 'Why do we still need universities when it is possible that each of its functions (research, teaching, service/innovation) is being performed more efficiently (more excellently) by other monofunctional institutions?'.[32] This question can be posed because the shared sense of purpose that pervaded the modern university is in doubt.

A more likely prospect, however, is that the university will further absorb the practices of its competitors in an attempt to stay ahead of the game. As a result, the distinctiveness of university life is likely to be further lost, with its traditions of independent and critical enquiry being the first casualties. The university will become less and less distinct from other large corporations, and less able (and willing) to sustain points of view and forms of enquiry that are at odds with prevailing norms. It is our view that, for all the inadequacies and problems of the modern university as it existed until some point in the second half of the twentieth century, this university at least retained the potential to support those who wrote and taught against the prevailing attitudes of the day. The great danger of the entrepreneurial university is that its foreshortened outlook risks generating its own form of detachment. This detachment would be of a very different kind from that enjoyed by the modern university academic, because the entrepreneurial academic is required to engage with the public that the university is said to serve. It is no longer considered acceptable for the entrepreneurial academic to stand aloof and removed, coolly anatomising and pronouncing on the mundane reality that lies beneath. Rather, today's academic must get 'engaged' with reality, and 'reach out' to the public. What this risks generating is a university sector occupied by individuals who share little 'except for their permanent attempt to face the needs of an outside environment'.[33] The danger is that academics become detached from *everything but* the immediate needs of their environment, and are left marooned in a present that they are unable to distance themselves from.

Today's university workers are expected to devote themselves to the enhancement of their own institutions, through the pursuit of institutional innovation, excellence, ranking, student satisfaction, research funding, and so on. Most academics today no longer give consideration to a new research idea without first asking if the proposed research is fundable and if it will result in publications that will enhance personal prospects and institutional prestige. Work that is likely to be at odds with the fashions of the day, that may not as a result secure funding and could well lead to writing that will struggle to gain acceptance by one's peers in the most prestigious journals, may not, for those reasons, be pursued. Or such research will be adapted to make it palatable, and thereby fundable and liable to be published. The overall effect is insidious – the basic research question, 'Is it true?', has been almost entirely replaced by its impoverished cousin, 'What use is it?'. As academics find themselves constrained by the insistent demand to respond to matters of need, they are governed by a performative culture that is obsessed with capitalising on everything they produce. As a result, academics risk losing a point of view that is perhaps not one of 'free thought', but is at the very least able to take a position which allows those working in a university to reflect on, and perhaps contest, how we are compelled to act and think in certain ways.

A crisis of its own making

Education *is* in crisis. Established institutional practices and forms of self-understanding are in a state of flux. But as this chapter has argued, this crisis of education is not the product of various malevolent forces trespassing on a core set of values and commitments that are basically good. Rather, the crisis of education is to some extent a crisis of its own making, as institutional attempts to face up to the challenges of modernity result in educational practices that pave the way for their own replacement. Hence progressive education, with its focus on the immediate context of each educational scenario, gave way to those highly reductive and instrumental forms of educational pragmatism that are today equally obsessed (though in a different way) with the 'improvement' of each educational moment. In a similar fashion, the self-absorbed research ethos of the modern university prepared the ground for the entrepreneurial university, which is left marooned in the present, but is nonetheless able to depend on the continued industry of its well-disciplined workforce. Another way of putting this is to say that the crisis of education is the logical, though not inevitable, outcome of the unfolding crisis of modernity. It may be seen as symptomatic of the wider loss of value and direction that characterises our epoch.

13

Epilogue

The idea of a university

In 1950 the political philosopher Michael Oakeshott wrote an essay, 'The idea of a university'. It is essentially a defence of liberal education at a time when it was under increasing threat from the utilitarian or instrumentalist ideas of education we have met with in previous chapters – ideas which are based on the assumption that education's primary purpose is to serve the national economy. Oakeshott presents a picture of the university as a moment in time in which the undergraduate (generally assumed to be male) can experience a 'break in the tyrannical course of irreparable events ... a moment in which to taste the mystery [of the world] without the necessity of at once seeking a solution'.[1] He will be surrounded 'by all the inherited learning and literature and experience of our civilisation ... in the company of kindred spirits'. A university offers 'the gift of an interval'. It is a place offering the opportunity of education as a conversation 'with his teachers, his fellows and himself', a place where he will learn that education is not to be confused 'with training for a profession, with learning the tricks of a trade' or with vocational preparation or 'a kind of moral and intellectual outfit to see him through life'. When ulterior purposes such as these intrude, 'education (which is concerned with persons, not functions) steals out of the back door with noiseless steps'.[2] A university should have no truck with learning that aims at power, at what he calls 'the exploitation of the world'.[3] A university's teaching should interest itself 'in the pupil himself, in what he is thinking, in the quality of his mind, in his immortal soul, and not in what sort of a schoolmaster or administrator he can be made into'.[4] Oakeshott laments the fact that the idea of a university has become 'mixed up with notions such as "higher education", "advanced training", "refresher courses for adults"',[5] enterprises that are admirable but which have nothing to do with a university:

For these ideas belong to a world of power and utility, of exploitation, of social and individual egoism, and of activity, whose meaning lies outside itself in some trivial result or achievement – and this is not the world to which a university belongs; it is not the world to which education in the true sense belongs.[6]

This world of power mistakes itself for the whole world, dismissing what does not contribute to its purposes as misconceived. Universities should be wary of the patronage of this world, lest it finds that it has 'sold its birthright for a mess of pottage', that instead of studying literature, science and history for the intrinsic value of these disciplines, they become engaged in something other than education – training men and women 'to fill some niche in society'. A university's 'first business is with the pursuit of learning' and not with some 'ulterior' social purpose, and its second concern is with 'the sort of education that has been found to spring up in the course of this activity'.[7] Such a university will not fit out a graduate with 'an armoury of arguments to prove the truth of what he believes' but with 'some knowledge, and, more important, a certain discipline of mind, a grasp of consequences, a greater command over his own powers'. He 'will have had the opportunity to extend the range of his moral sensibility' and 'to look for some meaning in the things that have greatly moved mankind'.[8] A university will have no claim on the title when 'its learning has degenerated into what is now called research' and teaching has become instruction, when undergraduates come with no sense of finding their 'intellectual fortune' and desire only to be equipped with a moral and intellectual veneer and a qualification or certificate that will 'let them in on the exploitation of the world'.[9]

It will be apparent that, as a statement of the nature and concerns of the university, Oakeshott's essay is seriously out of kilter with the state of actually existing universities. Modern university education, as is the case with primary and secondary education, is precisely structured according to an 'ulterior social purpose', to the formation of a citizenry that will be equipped with the skills, attitudes and competences believed necessary to the flourishing of the national economy. This is an idea of the university, and of education, that is generally shared by the population at large, by parents who expend energy, ingenuity and financial resources in order to secure places for their children at 'good' schools and by young adults weighing up which university course will offer them the best prospect of access to a financially rewarding career. Both the parents of schoolchildren and, at some stage in the educational process, the subjects of education – schoolchildren – accept the necessity of acquiring the qualifications and certificates that will offer occupation of a safe and profitable niche in society.

What characterises educational institutions at every level is a drive for results, for success measured according to some set of criteria that have nothing to do with education as Oakeshott understood it: nothing to do with the slow nurture in the student of disciplined thinking, a moral sensibility and the sense of a relation to a civilisation's traditions of thought. Instead schools and universities will be judged as effective or not according to externally devised and imposed metrics. They are subjected to pitiless, unrelenting competition, through public listings of 'top' institutions and ranking across league tables. The integrity and independence of education as a professional practice governed by its own ethos are routinely violated as a matter of necessity. Our rulers and their servants – and, by and large, the general population – seem incapable of seeing anything wrong in their co-option of the educational realm.

Oakeshott pictures a community of scholars engaged not just in their own particular endeavours but also in a conversation with each other, 'a body of scholars' sharing in a mutually supportive and beneficial intercourse, an exchange which is a vital part of civilised being.[10] They do not interact as if participating in 'a race in which the competitors jockey for the best place'.[11] Oakeshott envisages entry into a university as a period of escape. Presumably drawing on his own experience, he says that:

> a world of ungracious fact had melted into infinite possibility; we who belonged to no 'leisured class', had been freed for a moment from the curse of Adam, the burdensome distinction between work and play. What opened before us was not a road but a boundless sea; it was enough to stretch one's sails to the wind.[12]

This imagining of the university as offering access to an unbounded world of intellectual possibility has its attractions. What university teacher would not welcome a student who sees themselves as embarking on a course of open-ended enquiry, an open-minded exploration of knowledge? Unfortunately, as we have tried to make clear, this is not the world that today's student enters, nor the actuality that the university teacher–researcher inhabits. Nor is it likely that every student will see the environment of the university with quite the rapt excitement that Oakeshott describes. It is doubtful that such a university ever existed save in the idealisations of scholars like Oakeshott, and in the exceptional experience of a minority of students who have been happy to engage in learning 'which has no immediate use' and no particular end-point in terms of qualifications and career destination.[13] Today's scholars or (as we must with due accuracy refer to them) researchers have, all of them, to argue the social – which is to say economic – utility of their studies if they are to survive in post. The survival of whole tranches of the education system – the arts and humanities – is threatened by the difficulty they have in making a plausible case for their immediate usefulness. Their attempts to do so often find them attempting to satisfy criteria which serve distinctly extrinsic social purposes and justifications – for example, the surprisingly good employment possibilities a humanities education offers its graduates or the contribution of the arts to the national economy. Oakeshott would rightly have seen such clumsy attempts at the appeasement of power as evidence of the successful pollution of the pursuit of learning by the world of utility and exploitation.

Oakeshott was right about two things. He saw that appeals to what he saw as the realm of power in terms other than those validated by the discourse of power would be ignored as irrelevant and mistaken. For this world of necessity 'whatever does not contribute to its own purposes is somehow errant'.[14] What we might call the representatives of the prevailing socio-economic hegemony are not susceptible to arguments from a moral or philosophically critical position. He was correct too in his distinction between scholarship and research, insofar as the former has as its end the pursuit of learning as an endeavour that is ever-provisional and unfailingly self-critical whilst the latter all too often aims at prompt answers and solutions to problems set by authorities who are external to the university. In all other respects, Oakeshott's 'The idea of a university' is an insubstantial and unconvincing document. It posits an educational realm which is untouched by the schemes and effects of power when, as we have made clear in this book, it is and always has been concerned with shaping individuals in conformity with the intentions and purposes of the powerful. The manipulation and direction of individual conduct are built into the practice of education. Oakeshott says in his essay:

> For about 400 years in England the education of the would-be scholar and of the man of the world has been the same, and this tradition belongs to the idea of a university.[15]

What he speaks of here is the formation of a particular persona; the cultured gentleman we met with in Locke's musings on education – the disciplined induction of an individual into a particular social niche, his shaping by figures of authority into the sort of person fit to occupy a particular station in life, as a scholar, an intellectual, or as a man of the world. His education has been an exercise of power just as much as the schooling of the feared phantasm of the nineteenth-century moral school, the semi-feral urban child, and just as much as the recipient of a Renaissance humanist education. Oakeshott is also apparently blind to the social meaning of the idea of 'the man of the world'. It perpetuates a narrow conception of 'the world', one that confines itself to the higher affairs of power and culture. This ignores and denies recognisable existence to the many other worlds people inhabit. People of these 'worlds' must also learn how to manage themselves in the various social groupings they inhabit – at work, within the family, in their local communities, in any trade organisations they might belong to, in their recreational activities or in relation to the world at large. Of course, the 'man of the world' occupies and conducts himself within a differently articulated space, that of the man who knows how society is and should be run, who sees how his actions – in his adopted profession, within his family, within the social networks he belongs to, within any professional group of which he might be a member or in his recreational or cultural pursuits – sustain and perhaps improve the existing structures of society. The man of the world has been educated to play his part in governing the world, possibly directly in his professional activity or indirectly through his engagements in that discursive space where men of the world discuss and come to conclusions about how the world is and should be ordered. The world this figure inhabits is what Oakeshott would have called the world of power. The man of the world is thus subjected to power through the particular class-specific education he undergoes and he is, courtesy of that education, qualified to act as an agent of power, as a representative of the governing classes. The foregoing is not intended as a quasi-Marxist critique of mid-twentieth-century class society, although it almost inevitably veers off in that direction. On its own terms, as an attempt to give representation to and speak for a way of life, Oakeshott's view is entirely inadequate and curiously irresponsible in the manner of its conception. He either fails to see or refuses to acknowledge that education is other than a hallowed ground undefiled by a concern with 'social purpose', 'utility' or 'activity'. His essay describes very well the beginnings of the usurpation of the university by instrumental rationality but his response to its challenge seems to be to accompany education as it 'steals out of the back door with noiseless steps'. One might ask where it is stealing off to, in what place the 'idea' of a university might find its home once the actual university is abandoned to barbarism.

Professors of Education and the state of the discipline

It is worth dwelling upon the distinct place occupied by education departments, and educational studies, in today's university. One way of doing this is to examine the history of that ceremonial event, the inaugural address, which commemorates the arrival or making of a new professor in the university. Taking form as a public lecture, it gives the incepting professor an opportunity to reflect on the state of the discipline, and, somewhat inevitably, on their contribution to it.

'For most Englishmen, education is at best a boring subject, unless their own children are involved. Then they become bores themselves'.[16] With these words Harry Armytage began his inaugural address in 1954, at the University of Sheffield. The jocular implication seems to be that the incepting professor, Harry Armytage, might turn out to be just as boring as most Englishmen on the topic of education. His candour is perhaps a little put-on, but shows confidence in the intrinsic and unquestionable necessity Armytage claims for a Professor of Education in 1954. Indeed, he declares that the 'very existence of a chair of education would appear, to any right-thinking person, a serious reflection on the character of the University which created and sustained it'.[17] By investing in Professors of Education, universities demonstrate the seriousness of their commitment to education as a distinct area of enquiry.

As a historian, Armytage offers a brief history of his predecessors. Given the relative youth of education as an academic discipline, Armytage does not have to reach back much more than a century, where one of the earliest proposals for a Chair of Education in England was issued in 1833 for the University of London:

The Professor of Education should possess a knowledge of more than the general principles of all the sciences; but he would, of course, be inferior to the other professors in their respective departments. It would be his province to combine all their different objects; to point out the relative importance of each science; their mutual dependence; and so to consolidate them in the mind as to give consistency and strength to the character ... To him it would belong to render all acquisitions of the pupil tributary to his happiness; so that whether he was distinguished in the Classics, in Natural Philosophy or in Mathematics, he would possess comprehensiveness of mind and expanded feeling of benevolence.[18]

Clearly a version of liberal education is operating here, one designed to accompany the rise of the modern research university. By offering 'one common ground upon which all can meet', the Professor of Education would maintain the unity of purpose and civilising intent of fragmented disciplinary pursuits. This professor would mediate the specialisms and ensure that the pursuit of knowledge retains its commitment to a form of progressive enlightenment that is civilising in its effects. This proposal was at once an argument for the importance of education as a distinct area of academic study and a reassurance that this position would be one that 'invades no vested interests; offends no prejudice' and 'conciliates sects and parties'.[19] The Professor of Education would effectively guarantee the success of the modern research university by bringing all departments into alignment with their basic mission, to civilise and humanise. The 1833 proposal floundered, however. One is tempted to speculate that the existing professors had no appetite for a professor of everything and nothing, a professor inferior to all others in expertise, but superior in benevolence and synoptic view.

The first established Chair of Education would have to wait until 1876. It would be a less ambitious appointment.[20] Indeed, according to the combined evidence of British inaugural lectures over the next century, subsequent chairs in education only led to greater specialism. There was an overall shift away from the 'wide sweep of learning' and 'cultivated prose style' of the first appointments.[21] Armytage viewed this in 1954 as a missed opportunity, and argued once more for education as a 'discipline of reconciliation'.[22] Having teachers especially in mind, Armytage believed the education departments of his day were ideally placed to produce such reconcilers: 'Where better can one sift and apprehend ideas than a postgraduate year where arts and science graduates are gathered together in one department?'[23] Echoing the words of Michael Oakeshott, Armytage argues that the role of an education department:

is to afford a little breathing space of one year to all intending teachers, in which we try and help them put together something that has, in many cases, been progressively taken apart and broken down to its constituent elements. We hope in this year that students can learn something about their knowledge, and its relationships to other kinds of knowledge, and, in doing so, become the kind of teacher needed in the twentieth century.[24]

His hope is that future educators may obtain 'a synoptic vision' by which they could 'appreciate, if not assimilate, the vital ideas of the times'. Even though like 'Moses on [Mount] Pisgah, they might not enter on the promised land, they might at least see what is before them'.[25]

Armytage has been remembered as 'the last of the great liberal historians of education'. His outlook 'involved optimism, idealism and a faith in gradual progress'. His work 'constituted a reminder of liberal values that came in the context of the late twentieth century to appear all too fragile'.[26] In his inaugural address, Armytage seemingly attempts to revive the liberal tradition he represented by placing the professor of education at its core. This would be a project of selfless professorial devotion and would involve some humility, since the professor of this conception can pretend to no greater expertise than his professorial colleagues because his subject (education) has no independent content. His consolation, and claim to honour, is his pre-eminence in the art of reconciliation. The professor of education, Armytage argues, gives unity of purpose to a knowledge project that otherwise risks fragmentation. Armytage was of course giving his address towards the end of an era in which professors of education could still deliver their inaugural lectures against a cultural backdrop which presumed that 'the purpose of education', as Wilfred Carr writes, 'was to bring about a progressive improvement of the human condition by developing the emancipatory power of autonomous human reason.'[27] This era has now passed.

'It has been my misfortune to become a professor at precisely that moment in history when to do so has been rendered meaningless'.[28] Thus began Wilfred Carr's inaugural address in 1995, as he took a chair in the Philosophy of Education once again at the University of Sheffield. The inception of a new professor in today's university remains a fairly grand event, with the incepting professor wearing the traditional medieval gown even if the university was founded in the period of modernity. Beyond the occasional gown and mortarboard, no other vestiges of the medieval university remain. As material (or even imagined) objects ceremonial chairs no longer exist, since so many professors are incepting today that the idea of having a chair that can only be filled once it is vacated would unduly hinder the proliferation of professors and titles. In the medieval university, the chair, or *cathedra*, bore resemblance to the bishop's chair, where 'the ability to sit lawfully in this chair entailed the ability to speak with recognised authority on orthodox and canonical doctrines'.[29] In late modernity the professorial chair signifies a wage differential. As Carr reflects, there is no longer 'widespread allegiance to uncontested and impersonal standards of rationality and truth'.[30] Any suggestion that the conclusions of an inaugural lecture 'can be upheld by universal standards of objectivity will immediately be disparaged as credulous and naïve.' For his predecessors, Carr continues:

> the inaugural lecture afforded the opportunity to elaborate authoritative answers to questions about educational principles and ideals. For me, the inaugural lecture

can be nothing other than a mode of academic presentation designed to mask the extent to which claims to professorial authority are always distorted expressions of the will to power.[31]

Though few would confront the plight of the inaugural address with such direct-ness, it remains the case that faith in enlightenment is no longer easily presumed. The professor can no longer profess in the tradition of a liberal academia. The potential boredom of an audience can no longer be justified by the intrinsic value of the subject matter. Of course liberal education remains entrenched – it's just that it exists in an atrophied, twilight form. It is not the envisioned nineteenth-century education of the gentleman who, as Samuel Coleridge put it, 'knows himself and walks in the light of his own consciousness'.[32] It is not built on the overtly stated necessity of self-government, deemed a prerequisite for governing others. Nor is it explicitly based on the refinement of the soul, following Wilhelm von Humboldt's vision of Bildung. Rather, as introduced in Chapter 12, it has become embedded as a research ethos of the disciplinary self. An attenuated form of liberal education has become entrenched as the serious minded and diligent (if not always productive) pursuit of the academic, of the master practitioner in the performative arts of research. Born into this era, professors of education would attempt to claim expertise like any other; labouring in the diminished faith that specialism leads to progress.

Confronting education

For a moment in the twentieth century, at places such as the University of Vincennes in Paris, militants were openly confronting the professoriate and the educational establishment more widely, accusing it and the university machine of basic complicity with a capitalist order. Writing in 1978, Jean-François Lyotard recalls how:

> Just two years ago, this or that leftist commando was bursting in, denouncing the magisterial function, the star-system, alienation, apathy, cutting the electricity, rais-ing his clubs, locking up the teacher awhile, and abusing the students. In their eyes, our palaver, our readings, our reffinements [sic] are gimmicks at best, and at worse treasons.[33]

But the profession endured. In the end, the modern university was more per-turbed by its own growing dependence on managerialism and performativity than by the militant outsider.[34] Here the research ethos of the modern university would eventually become the basis of its replacement. The diligent single-mindedness of the modern research scholar gave way to the performative hyperactivity of today's academic researcher, who may work across disciplines as much as within them.

What ties the late or post-modern university together, once its basic telos falls away, are the simple habits of teaching and research (including the basic format of the lecture, or academic paper) that were established by its predecessor. In this context, the successful academic and the successful educator best fulfils these habits as a calculative being, spending so much, too much time as one puts it, 'looking over our shoulders before we act'.[35]

The professional educator is today 'living in the permanent crossfire of objectifying processes', trapped in the interstices of a system that seems beyond adjustment. For such teachers and academics, it is often the case that 'before the deed is the thought of recording it'.[36] In other words, there is still much willing participation in a system so many lament as inevitable. Brute instrumentalism reigns but only against bad conscience. The educational order still requires the consent of those who willingly fulfil its impulses. As such, it relies upon a broad array of residual attachments to education. For so few of us can say 'when it comes to neglecting fundamentals, I think I have nothing to learn'.[37] These fundamentals, and fundamental commitments, linger on as a set of never quite believed but nonetheless persistent ideas (as commitments to emancipation, enlightenment, the exercise of reason in human affairs, wisdom, human flourishing, etc.).

Our view is that 'education' and its practitioners should be decidedly noisier about the transformation, some would say hijacking, of the realm in which they practise. In doing so, however, they should give due attention to their complicity in the challenging circumstances they confront. To be clear, we are not arguing for a stance of inflexible refusal of every governmental injunction. Nor are we de-schoolers or advocates of any schemes for setting up and withdrawing to 'alternative' sites of education. For good measure, we are also sceptical of the claims made that digital technologies can create virtual alternative sites of learning which might make school and university redundant in their present forms. We are stuck now and for the foreseeable future with the present educational dispensation and it is to that that we direct our arguments.

At the same time, we remain cautiously attached to an intellectual project, such as that represented by this book, which seeks to offer a measure of conceptual clarification which might be of use to those many actors working and studying within education. There are clear advantages to this kind of project, one that mobilises philosophy in education. It helps us see that there are no meanings that can be taken for granted in terms such as 'moral formation', 'intellectual endowment', 'acculturation', 'social solidarity' and even 'learning'. They are all problematic, which is to say in need of critical elaboration. And we hope that we have provided some sense of the contested nature of such terms. But education remains a site of struggle beyond the grasp of academic philosophy. It is often best understood through a troubling of education, a perpetual confrontation with systems of power that reveals the limits within which we operate. Here it is not only a question of picking the moments and points where you think you can bring pressure for change to bear, but also of knowing when we must proceed through less direct tactics involving 'silence, exile and cunning'.[38]

Philosophy remains useful, for it allows us to see how thinking (and hence acting) might remain 'pre-censored', determined in accordance with dominant norms and forms of understanding. It allows us to see how, at their extreme, the possibilities for individual identity might be heavily circumscribed. This prompts consideration of other ways of being, forms of life that cannot be reduced to, or formed in accord with, the indices required for scientific-rational manipulation. The benchmarks of professionalism and competence in education become a little uncertain if not entirely doubtful as a result, as do negative evaluations claiming to identify and drive out incompetence and poor conduct from educational institutions. It becomes possible, from this point of view, to argue for different forms of conduct, for educational activities that are all too easily frowned upon and driven out of education for being unproductive, insufficiently active, unmeasurable, or unreadable according to dominant norms and understandings that dictate what it means to be a 'good' teacher or student today.

Our fear as we conclude this book is that in our emphasis on the inevitable intrication of power and education and in our suggestion that education and social discourse generally face a perhaps unprecedented moment of closure, we may be seen as counselling despair. On the contrary, we think that the near obliteration of alternative ways of construing how we might be governed and how we might perceive the possibilities of our individual and collective lives simply presents us with the necessity of struggle. What the present period requires of the worker in education, as in other fields where intellectual rigour and honesty are under challenge, is a kind of ingenious and supple insubordination, the evasion, the creative deformation and, occasionally, explicit refusal of the more bovine or pernicious of the diktats of an authority that has ceased to think in terms that are in any way related to the task of making women and men free through the pursuit of knowledge. This may seem an outrageous proposal – to deny the will and sometimes the statutory requirements of a democratically elected government. It is in fact not a particularly remarkable proposition. Leaving aside the problems associated with democracy, as it is constituted in its parliamentary form,[39] the argument for non-cooperation – for a refusal to commit to governmental prescription – is neither unusual nor scandalous. Other professions – medicine and law, for example – are bound by professional ethics which may, even in liberal democracies, come into conflict with government policy. When this happens, professional ethics take precedence over bureaucratic stratagem and, if necessary, over statutory legislation. Doctors and lawyers rarely have to come into open conflict with political powers because in both cases the authority of their governing ethic is generally recognised and deferred to by government which treads warily in dealing with these professions for fear of violating an ethos which is held in something close to universal public respect. The problem for the profession of education is that no such clear-cut ethical code exists or is universally recognised; neither government nor the public nor the profession itself is clearly aware of what education's ethical commitments might be. Government thus experiences no impediment to intervention in the realm of education. Education, at least since it became an object of concern to government, has always been more porous to power than other professions, largely because, unlike those professions, it had not developed its own self-invigilating bureaucracy controlling its practices and its formal structures. As a result, its purposes (as we have seen) and its ruling ethic have been, since the institution of national systems of education, open to distortion, perversion and obfuscation by the various factions and interests of government. This was not the case for most of the period covered in this book. Even in the medieval liberal arts university, in a period when thought was ruled by Christian doctrine, the purpose of education was clear. The task, endogenous and beyond question, was to teach the arts of the free man. Throughout the history of education, its aim was to teach men – and sometimes women – how to be free and civil, in the sense of socially literate and responsible human beings. In the Middle Ages, education's responsibility was to teach and to explore how the individuals who make up humanity could be brought to lead the good life that would fulfil God's purposes. In our period, education's task must be to take seriously the claim that we live in a liberal democracy. Thus, at every level and in every corner of the educational field, education's ethical commitments must commit it to forming individuals who are fully conversant with the nature and the history of the polity they inhabit, who are aware of the limitations and contradictions inherent to democracy as it is constituted in societies like ours and who are capable of investigating how they themselves have been formed by that society. In other words, a curriculum and a pedagogy directed towards the formation of subjects equipped with the practical and conceptual knowledge, the know-how and the social and historical awareness needed for them to reflect on their own construction as moral beings and for them to act as morally responsible members of a society. Anything less is domination and an infringement of the valuable idea that government and the social weal are secured by the exercise of freedom. In its efforts to keep democracy honest education should seek to foster in its subjects a self-consciousness that amounts to more than an imposed self-policing; it should seek to develop a self-conscious appreciation, a practical knowledge, of the (inescapable but modifiable) operations of power.

An alert consciousness of the essential ethical commitments of education would offer the teacher and researcher clarity in their roles and some armour for their encounters with the bureaucratic and governmental realms. Such consciousness does not exist widely or with great coherence within the profession and we do not underestimate the scale of the task involved in building such an awareness. However, we see no other possibility for maintaining the idea of the value of intellectual rigour and honesty. The two alternative options are to acquiesce in the necessity of the governmental co-option of education or to accept the truth of what some have argued,[40] that the endeavour of education is fundamentally and irredeemably an exercise of oppressive power and that the technical–capitalist disposition of power that has been formed over the last two centuries has simply been a revealing or unconcealing of the essence of education as domination.

Education is defined more than ever by its manic embrace of change, by hyper-activity and acceleration. Characteristically, as students and as educators, we remain unclear about what we are accelerating into. Afflicted in this way, educational establishments and research institutions advance towards their own limits 'only with their back to it'.[41] The challenge is to turn around, and look into the empty space, the void into which we are drawn. A critical study of education forces us to confront what we are being made to do.

Further Readings

Readers will probably make up their own minds about dipping further into the texts we reference, but we highlight below some of the texts that capture key ideas about philosophy and education.

On philosophy

Carr, W. (2004) 'Philosophy and education', *Journal of Philosophy of Education*, 38 (1): 55–73.

A damning critique of the philosophy of education from one of its most eminent representatives, arguing that its marginalisation is the inevitable consequence of a longstanding division between education and philosophy.

Hadot, P. (2002 [1995]) *What is Ancient Philosophy?* Cambridge, MA: Harvard University Press.

An account of ancient philosophy and the philosophical schools of antiquity. This can be read alongside Hadot's (1995 [1987]) *Philosophy as a Way of Life* which reconstructs our idea of ancient philosophy, arguing that it must be understood in its own terms, that is, as a practice designed to cultivate a way of life.

Nietzsche, F. (1998 [1886]) *Beyond Good and Evil*. Oxford: Oxford University Press.

To understand Nietzsche's critique of philosophy as a symptom of Greek exhaustion it is necessary to return to his first book *The Birth of Tragedy* (Nietzsche, 1993 [1872]). However, *The Birth of Tragedy* is a challenging text and benefits from reading alongside Nietzsche's later work. On the topics of philosophy and scholarship, and their necessary limitations, both 'The prejudices of philosophers' and 'We scholars' in *Beyond Good and Evil* are worth looking at. Nietzsche's style is refreshingly unorthodox, and still has the capacity to upset scholarly and philosophical conventions. His ideas are often enormously compressed, and so his work demands close and careful reading in order to appreciate the wit and complexity of his ideas.

On pre-modern education

Brown, P. (1992) *Power and Persuasion in Late Antiquity: Towards a Christian Empire*. Madison, WI: University of Wisconsin Press.

This short book based on a series of lectures offers an accessible introduction to the role of *paideia* in late antiquity. It explores how members of the educated elite used this common culture of refinement to negotiate imperial power.

MacIntyre, A. (1990) *Three Rival Versions of Moral Enquiry*. London: Duckworth.

For a more detailed development of MacIntyre's argument concerning the virtues of medieval scholasticism, see the relevant chapters in this book, which also includes a careful critique of Enlightenment and Nietzschean thought. This can be read in conjunction with MacIntyre's earlier book, *After Virtue* (1981), which forms part of a controversial and ground-breaking re-evaluation of contemporary moral philosophy in which the author examines pre-modern moral systems, most notably of the Middle Ages, arguing that the fragmentation, incoherence and irrationality of modern moral discourse can only be overcome by an effort, similar to that undertaken during the Dark Ages, to construct forms of community that will ensure the survival of civility and the intellectual and moral life.

Carr, W. (1997) 'Professing education in a postmodern age', *Journal of Philosophy of Education*, 31 (2): 309–327.

Offering a brief account of the medieval university curriculum and its function within society, this paper makes an argument for the revival of a virtue-based approach to education in postmodernity. This paper is also a testimony to the incoherence of contemporary educational practices such as the inaugural address.

Bernstein, B. (1996) 'Thoughts on the trivium and quadrivium: The divorce of knowledge from the knower', in B. Bernstein, *Pedagogy, Symbolic Control, and Identity: Theory, Research, Critique*. London: Taylor Francis. pp. 81–88.

Here Bernstein offers a brief account of how the medieval curriculum functioned and an argument as to why modern education's lack of a moral dimension is a problem.

On humanism

Davies, T. (1997) *Humanism*. London: Routledge.

This book offers an account of the history of humanism, adopting a generally critical perspective, but one which acknowledges humanism's achievements. In Davies' view, we can do better – humanism isn't the end-point of moral thought.

Grafton, A. and Jardine, L. (1986) *From Humanism to the Humanities: Education and the Liberal Arts in Fifteenth and Sixteenth-Century Europe*. London: Duckworth.

This traces the emergence of the modern Humanities curriculum from Renaissance humanism. It is unusual in that, although it is written by humanist scholars, it laments the fact that their discipline, its teaching, produces graduates who, in the main, take up occupations whose ethos runs counter to humanist values.

Kristeller, P.O. (1988) 'Humanism' in C.B. Schmitt and Q. Skinner (eds), *The Cambridge History of Renaissance Philosophy*. Cambridge: Cambridge University Press.

This essay offers a highly readable account of the 'meaning', origins and development of humanist thought during the Renaissance period. The author ends the piece by suggesting that if modern philosophy were to pay more attention to the humanities we might arrive at 'a more complete and more balanced understanding of our world and experience'.

On modernity, critique and reason

Toulmin, S. (1992) *Cosmopolis: The Hidden Agenda of Modernity*. Chicago: University of Chicago Press.

A short history of modernity, which traces what the author sees as the mistaken goal of a rationally ordered society back to the seventeenth century, and explores the continuing consequences of this agenda more than three centuries later.

Horkheimer, M. (2013 [1947]) *Eclipse of Reason*. London: Bloomsbury.

A survey of the gradual ascendancy of reason in Western philosophy and its eventual application to all spheres of life. This brought about not only the transformation of society, but also the transformation of reason itself, where the latter was reduced to a form of instrumental reason, a type of calculative activity that reduces thought to the needs of the moment, and makes critique impossible. To be read alongside *The Dialectic of Enlightenment* (Horkheimer and Adorno, 1977 [1944]).

Borrelli, M. (2004) 'The utopianism of critique: The tension between education conceived as a utopian concept and as one grounded in empirical reality', *Journal of Philosophy of Education*, 38 (3): 441–454.

A vigorous argument for radical critique and a clear statement of the author's views as to the deficiencies of 'dogmatically' empirical research.

Connerton, P. (1980) *The Tragedy of Enlightenment: An Essay on the Frankfurt School*. Cambridge: Cambridge University Press.

This short book traces across several decades the history of Frankfurt School critical theory. It also contains in its introduction an informative account of the history of the concept of critique.

Modern mass schooling

Foucault, M. (1991 [1975]) *Discipline and Punish*. London: Penguin.

This book has become somewhat canonical in educational theory, though its implications are rarely pursued to their fullest, most radical extent. Its claim is that modern subjectivities were and are fabricated across a range of institutional sites including schools, where our very sense of self is a product of those institutions that form us. There is no 'view from the outside' that we might adopt in order to critique the operations of these institutions, since the production of modern subjectivity also involves the production of those intellectual tools by which we understand ourselves. *Discipline and Punish* surveys a range of disciplinary institutions and although Foucault's analysis has been used to critique specific educational practices, its implications for educational practice more generally are very unsettling. It invites us to consider the entire educational endeavour as being historically contingent and without any essential base.

Hunter, I. (1994) *Rethinking the School: Subjectivity, Bureaucracy, Criticism*. New York: St Martin's Press.

A careful examination of the genealogy, or history, of modern schooling, this book also offers a diagnosis of the role of critique in educational establishments. It has been largely ignored within education, almost certainly because Hunter's argument is difficult to accommodate within prevailing orthodoxies. Hunter claims that educators and critics misunderstand education when they judge it and find it wanting according to some vision of what education might become. Hunter argues that in so doing they misunderstand their role as educators, which is to function as ethical exemplars in the formation of a citizenry. Educators and educational critics over-reach themselves when they use their finer ethical sensibilities to judge the system as a whole. Modern educational institutions, Hunter argues, owe their existence to bureaucrats, not idealists. Educators and idealists should know their place.

Universities and the postmodern condition

Wellmon, C. (2015) *Organizing Enlightenment: Information Overload and the Invention of the Modern Research University*. Baltimore: Johns Hopkins University Press.

A survey of the origins of the modern research university and its developing ethos of specialist research, self-discipline and diligent enquiry. Wellmon's argument is that the research university responded to the perceived fragmentation of knowledge (following eighteenth century Enlightenment), by establishing itself as the ultimate giver of epistemic authority.

Lyotard, J-F. (1986 [1979]) *The Postmodern Condition: A Report on Knowledge.* Manchester: Manchester University Press.

A diagnosis of the plight of the contemporary university, and a book that for some announced the end of modernity and the onset of a postmodern worldview. Postmodernism is marked by incredulity towards the grand narratives of modernity, including those of progress, enlightenment and universal justice, and presumably by extension, incredulity to the realisation of those ideals through education.

Notes

Chapter 2: Philosophical Schools

1 Paul Hirst, 'Liberal education and the nature of knowledge', in R.D. Archambault (ed.), *Philosophical Analysis and Education* (London, Routledge and Kegan Paul, 1965); Paul Hirst, *Knowledge and the Curriculum* (London, Routledge and Kegan Paul, 1974); R.S. Peters, *Ethics and Education* (London, George Allen & Unwin, 1966); R.S. Peters, *The Philosophy of Education* (Oxford, Oxford University Press, 1973).

2 Wilfred Carr, 'Introduction: What is the philosophy of education?', in W. Carr (ed.), *The RoutledgeFalmer Reader in Philosophy of Education* (London, Routledge, 2005), p. 2. See also: Wilfred Carr, 'Philosophy and education', *Journal of Philosophy of Education*, 38,1 (2004).

3 Carr, 'Introduction: What is the philosophy of education?', p. 3.

4 Michèle Le Doeuff, *Hipparchia's Choice* (New York, Columbia University Press, 2007 [1989]).

5 Alasdair MacIntyre, 'The relationship of philosophy to its past', in R. Rorty, J.B. Schneewind and Q. Skinner (eds), *Philosophy in History: Essays in the Historiography of Philosophy* (Cambridge, Cambridge University Press, 1984), p. 32.

6 Richard Rorty, 'The historiography of philosophy: Four genres', in R. Rorty, J.B. Schneewind and Q. Skinner (eds), *Philosophy in History: Essays on the Historiography of Philosophy* (Cambridge, Cambridge University Press, 1984).

7 Martin Heidegger, *Nietzsche: Volume IV, Nihilism* (New York, HarperCollins, 1991 [1961]), p. 17.

8 Rorty, 'The historiography of philosophy: Four genres', p. 61.

9 Charles Taylor, 'Philosophy and its history', in R. Rorty, B. Schneewind and Q. Skinner (eds), *Philosophy in History: Essays on the Historiography of Philosophy* (Cambridge, Cambridge University Press, 1984), p. 20.

10 Pierre Hadot, *Philosophy as a Way of Life* (Oxford, Blackwell, 1987 [1995]), p. 53.

11 Ibid., pp. 56–57.

12 Alfred North Whitehead, *Process and Reality* (New York, Free Press, 1979), p. 39.

13 Pierre Hadot, *What is Ancient Philosophy?* (Cambridge, MA, Harvard, 2004 [1995]), p. 78.

14 Ibid., p. 117.

15 Hadot, *Philosophy as a Way of Life*, p. 60.

16 Ibid., p. 61.

17 Ibid., p. 62.

18 Ibid., p. 63.

19 MacIntyre, 'The relationship of philosophy to its past', p. 32.

Chapter 3: Ancient 'Solutions'

1   This chapter draws in places from: Ansgar Allen, *The Cynical Educator* (London, Mayfly, 2017).

2   Peter Brown, *Power and Persuasion in Late Antiquity* (Madison, University of Wisconsin Press, 1992), p. 39.

3   Ibid., p. 42.

4   Ibid., p. 40.

5   Ibid., p. 48.

6   Ibid., p. 42.

7   Ibid., p. 43.

8   Ibid., p. 7.

9   Ibid., p. 4.

10 See ibid., pp. 30–31.

11 Ibid., p. 50.

12 Ibid., p. 52.

13 Ibid., p. 56.

14 Wilfred Carr and Stephen Kemmis, *Becoming Critical: Education, Knowledge and Action Research* (Deakin: Deakin University Press, 1986), p. 33.

15 Wilfred Carr, 'Educational research as a practical science', *International Journal of Research & Method in Education*, 30, 3 (2007), p. 276.

16 Wilfred Carr, 'Philosophy, methodology and action research', *Journal of Philosophy of Education*, 40, 4 (2006), p. 426.

17 Ibid., p. 427.

18 Carr and Kemmis, *Becoming Critical*, p. 33.

19 Ibid., p. 34.

20 Charles W. Harvey, 'Making hollow men', *Educational Theory*, 60, 2 (2010), p. 199.

21 Carr and Kemmis, *Becoming Critical*.

22 Ibid., p. 18.

23 Ibid., p. 14.

24 Ibid., p. 16.

25 Wilfred Carr, 'Education without theory', *British Journal of Educational Studies*, 54, 2 (2006).

26 Wilfred Carr, 'The gap between theory and practice', *Journal of Further and Higher Education*, 4, 1 (1980), pp. 60–61.

27 Carr, 'Philosophy, methodology and action research'.

28 Carr and Kemmis, *Becoming Critical*, p. 39.

29 See in particular Alasdair MacIntyre, *After Virtue: A Study in Moral Theory* (London, Duckworth, 1981).

30 'And if the tradition of the virtues was able to survive the horrors of the last dark ages, we are not entirely without grounds for hope. This time however the barbarians are not waiting beyond the frontiers: they have already been governing us for some time. And it is our lack of consciousness of this that constitutes part of our predicament. We are waiting not for Godot, but for another – doubtless very different – St. Benedict' (ibid., p. 263). We would note, however, that what was faced in the interregnum between

Rome and Christendom was disorder, and what we face now is a complex, intricately structured imperium.

31 Friedrich Nietzsche, *The Birth of Tragedy* (London, Penguin, 2003 [1872]).
32 Ibid., §4.
33 Ibid., §7.

Chapter 4: Education and God

1 Hugh of St Victor cited in Brian Fitzgerald, *Medieval Theories of Education: Hugh of St Victor and John of Salisbury* in *Oxford Review of Education*, 36, 5 (2010), p. 576.
2 Basil Bernstein, 'Thoughts on the trivium and quadrivium: the divorce of knowledge from the knower', in *Pedagogy, Symbolic Control, and Identity: Theory, Research, Critique* (London, Taylor Francis, 1996).
3 Hastings Rashdall, *The Universities of Europe in the Middle Ages: Volume I* (Oxford, Clarendon Press, 1895), pp. 4–5.
4 Wilfred Carr, 'Professing education in a postmodern age', *Journal of Philosophy of Education*, 31, 2 (1997), p. 318.
5 Alasdair MacIntyre, *Three Rival Versions of Moral Enquiry* (London, Duckworth, 1990), p. 64.
6 Ibid., p. 62.
7 Ibid.
8 Ibid., p. 181.
9 Hadot, *Philosophy as a Way of Life*, p. 107.

Chapter 5: Education and Humanism

1 See Nicholas Mann, 'The origins of humanism', in J. Kraye (ed.), *The Cambridge Companion to Renaissance Humanism* (Cambridge, Cambridge University Press, 1996); Paul Oskar Kristeller, 'Humanism', in C.B. Schmitt and Q. Skinner (eds), *The Cambridge History of Renaissance Philosophy* (Cambridge, Cambridge University Press, 1988).
2 Cesare Vasoli, 'The Renaissance concept of philosophy', in C.B. Schmitt and Q. Skinner (eds), *The Cambridge History of Renaissance Philosophy* (Cambridge, Cambridge University Press, 1988).
3 Arabic scholars had maintained an unbroken contact with the texts of the ancient Greeks and the West's reacquaintance with them arrived via the Muslim world.
4 Vasoli, 'The Renaissance concept of philosophy', p. 60.
5 Kristeller, 'Humanism', p. 115.
6 Quentin Skinner, 'Political philosophy', in C.B. Schmitt and Q. Skinner (eds), *The Cambridge History of Renaissance Philosophy* (Cambridge, Cambridge University Press, 1988).
7 Kristeller, 'Humanism'.
8 Anthony Grafton and Lisa Jardine, *From Humanism to the Humanities: Education and the Liberal Arts in Fifteenth and Sixteenth-Century Europe* (London, Duckworth, 1986).

9 Vasoli, 'The Renaissance concept of philosophy', p. 59.

10 Thomas Gaisford cited in Anthony Grafton, 'The new science and the traditions of humanism', in J. Kraye (ed.), *The Cambridge Companion to Renaissance Humanism* (Cambridge, Cambridge University Press, 1996), p. 205.

11 Antonino Poppi, 'Fate, fortune, providence and human freedom', in C.B. Schmidt and Q. Skinner (eds), *The Cambridge History of Renaissance Philosophy* (Cambridge, Cambridge University Press, 1988), p. 645.

12 Vasoli, 'The Renaissance concept of philosophy', p. 61.

13 Kristeller, 'Humanism', p. 126.

14 Quoted in Conor McCarthy, 'Aristotle's poetics and the Name of the Rose', in M. Brown and S.H. Harrison (eds), *The Medieval World and the Modern Mind* (Dublin, Four Courts Press, 2000), p. 55.

15 Michel Foucault, *On the Government of the Living: Lectures at the Collège de France 1979-1980* (Basingstoke, Palgrave Macmillan, 2014 [1980]).

16 Romanticism was a movement in the arts and philosophy which had its roots in the eighteenth century's Enlightenment valorisation of the individual and in a revulsion against the perceived inhumanity of scientific and technological rationality. It opposed the creative spirit of the individual self to the unfeeling abstractions of science's objective gaze. It celebrated the human individual's capacity for originality in thought and action – a corollary of this commitment was a valuing of the true and authentic voice of the self; hence the emphasis amongst some Romantic thinkers on sincerity of expression as the undisguised outflow of an essential human spirit.

17 MacIntyre, *After Virtue: A Study in Moral Theory*, pp. 22–35.

18 Brian Vickers, 'Rhetoric and poetics', in C.B. Schmidt and Q. Skinner (eds), *The Cambridge History of Renaissance Philosophy* (Cambridge, Cambridge University Press, 1988), pp. 715–745.

19 Peter Mack, 'Humanist rhetoric and dialectic', in J. Kraye (ed.), *The Cambridge Companion to Renaissance Humanism* (Cambridge, Cambridge University Press, 1996), pp. 82–89.

20 Kristeller, 'Humanism', p. 114.

21 Ernst Cassirer, *An Essay on Man* (New Haven, Yale University Press, 1944), pp. 215–217.

22 Ibid.

23 Michel Foucault, *The Archaeology of Knowledge* (London, Tavistock, 1972), p. 12.

24 Michel Foucault, *The Order of Things: An Archaeology of the Human Sciences* (London, Tavistock, 1966 [1985]), p. 342.

25 Ernst Cassirer, *The Logic of the Humanities* (New Haven, Yale University Press, 1961), pp. 36–37.

26 Tony Davies, *Humanism: The New Critical Idiom* (London, Routledge, 1997), p. 132.

27 Martin Heidegger, 'Letter on Humanism', in *Basic Writings* (London, Routledge, 2007 [1947]).

28 Davies, *Humanism*, p. 131.

29 Erasmus cited in John Parrish, 'Education, Erasmian humanism, and More's Utopia', *Oxford Review of Education*, 36, 5 (2010), p. 593.

30 Erasmus cited in ibid.

31 Grafton and Jardine, *From Humanism to the Humanities*, pp. xii–xiv.

32 Davies, *Humanism*, p. 132.

33 Karl Marx and Friedrich Engels, *The Communist Manifesto* (London, Penguin, 2002 [1848]), p. 224.

Chapter 6: Enlightenment and Modernity: Locke and Descartes

1 Jonathan Israel, *Radical Enlightenment: Philosophy and the Making of Modernity, 1650-1750* (Oxford, Oxford University Press, 2001).

2 Jonathan Swift, *A Tale of a Tub and Other Works* (Oxford, Oxford University Press, 1704 [2008]), p. 110.

3 Ibid., p. 113.

4 Ibid.

5 René Descartes, *Passions of the Soul* (Indianapolis, Hackett, 1989 [1649]), p. 19.

6 René Descartes, *Meditations on First Philosophy* (Cambridge, Cambridge University Press, 1996 [1641]). All quotations that follow are demarcated by the short meditation they correspond to.

7 Debate on this theme may be traced through Wilfrid Sellars, 'Philosophy and the scientific image of man', in *Science, Perception and Reality* (London, Routledge & Kegan Paul, 1963); to Paul M. Churchland, 'Eliminative materialism and the propositional attitudes', *The Journal of Philosophy*, 78, 2 (1981). This provoked a wide range of responses, including the highly critical (of Churchland) Jerry Fodor, *In Critical Condition: Polemical Essays on Cognitive Science and the Philosophy of Mind* (Cambridge, MA, MIT Press, 2000).

8 John Locke, *An Essay Concerning Human Understanding* (London, J.M. Dent, 1993 [1690]), p. 17.

9 Ibid., p. 45.

10 Ibid., p. 46.

11 Ibid., p. 58.

12 Ibid., p. 91.

13 Ibid., p. 58.

14 Ibid., p. 91.

15 Ibid., p. 185.

16 Ibid., p. 186.

17 Ibid., p. 356.

18 Ibid., p. 180.

19 Ibid., p. 189.

20 Ibid., p. 186.

21 Crawford Brough Macpherson, *The Political Theory of Possessive Individualism: Hobbes to Locke* (Oxford, Clarendon Press, 1962).

22 Locke, *An Essay Concerning Human Understanding*, p. 380.

23 Ibid., p. 279.

24 John Locke, *Some Thoughts Concerning Education* (Mineola, New York, Dover Publications, 2007 [1693]), §190.

25 Ibid., §44.

26 Ibid., §102.
27 Ibid.
28 Ibid., §118.
29 Ibid., §193.
30 Ibid., p. 177.
31 Ibid., §186.
32 Ibid., §190.
33 Locke, *An Essay Concerning Human Understanding*, p. 7.

Chapter 7: Enlightenment and Modernity: Hume and Kant

1 David Hume, *A Treatise of Human Nature: Being an Attempt to Introduce the Experimental Method of Reasoning into Moral Subjects* (London, Penguin, 1969 [1740]), Introduction, p. 45.
2 Ibid., Introduction, p. 44.
3 Ibid.
4 Ibid., 2.1.12.
5 Ibid., 1.1.1.
6 The term 'unknown causes' does not connote spiritual, supernatural or magical powers beyond human ken, but simply indicates that it is a futile endeavour to attempt to trace causes back further than the evidence supplied by sensory impressions. The term 'originary' acts as a sort of admonition not to waste time on such vain activity.
7 Hume, *A Treatise of Human Nature*, 1.1.2.
8 Ibid., 1.1.3.
9 Ibid., 1.1.4.
10 Ibid., 1.3.2.
11 Ibid., 1.3.4.
12 Ibid., 1.3.14.
13 Ibid., 1.3.14.
14 Ibid., 1.3.4.
15 Ibid., 1.2.6.
16 Ibid., 1.3.14.
17 Ibid., 1.4.2.
18 Ibid., 1.3.15.
19 David Hume, *An Enquiry Concerning Human Understanding* (Oxford, Oxford University Press, 2007 [1748]), 5.22.
20 Hume, *A Treatise of Human Nature*, 2.3.3.
21 Ibid., 1.4.6.
22 Ibid.
23 Ibid.
24 Immanuel Kant, *Critique of Pure Reason* (London, J.M. Dent, 1993 [1781]), p. 14, Bxiii.
25 Ibid., pp. 3-4, Avii-Aix.
26 Ibid., p. 23, Bxxxiii.
27 Ibid., p. 33, A2/B6.

28 Ibid., pp. 48–49, A19/B33. Kant later defines the understanding as 'the faculty of judg-
    ing' (ibid., p. 79).
29 Ibid., p. 50, A23/B37.
30 See ibid., p. 54, A29/B45.
31 Meaning 'incontestably true by virtue of demonstration' – in current usage more com-
    monly *apodictic.*
32 Kant, *Critique of Pure Reason*, pp. 54–55, A29/B45–A31/B46.
33 Ibid., p. 84, A77/B102.
34 Ibid., A79/B104.
35 Ibid., p. 85, A79/B104.
36 There is no space here to offer more than a general account of the categories and their
    functions. Kant's elaboration of the categories, their functioning and sphere of opera-
    tion, is contained in the *Analytic of Concepts* (ibid., pp. 91–138, A84-A129).
37 Ibid., p. 61, A41/B59.
38 Ibid., p. 16, Bxvii.
39 Ibid., p. 21, Bxxix.
40 Ibid., p. 101, B135.
41 Immanuel Kant, 'The metaphysics of morals', in M.J. Gregor (ed.), *Practical Philosophy*
    (Cambridge, Cambridge University Press, 1996), p. 16.
42 Kant, *Critique of Pure Reason*, p. 116, B163.
43 Ibid, p. 136, A125.
44 Ibid, p. 137, A127.
45 Ibid, p. 13, Bxi.
46 See ibid., pp. 376–394, A351/B559–A366/B594. The comments that follow are based in
    the main on a reading of ibid., pp. 376–379. References to other pages in the longer sec-
    tion indicated are referenced separately.
47 Ibid., p. 385, A548/B576.
48 Ibid., p. 383, A545/B573.
49 Ibid., p. 384, A548/B576.
50 Ibid., B547/A575.
51 Ibid., p. 517, A802/B830.
52 See ibid., p. 516, A800/B828.
53 Immanuel Kant, *Grounding for the Metaphysics of Morals* (Indianapolis, Hackett Publishing
    Company Inc., 1983).
54 Immanuel Kant, *Critique of Practical Reason* (Indianapolis, The Bobs-Merrill Company
    Inc., 1956).
55 Kant, *Critique of Pure Reason*, p. 519, A806/B834.
56 Ibid., p. 520, A808/B836.
57 Ibid., p. 524, A816/B844.
58 For a useful discussion see Chad Wellmon, *Organizing Enlightenment: Information Overload
    and the Invention of the Modern Research University* (Baltimore, John Hopkins University
    Press, 2015), pp. 123–150.
59 Kant, *Critique of Pure Reason*, p. 32, Bxliii.
60 Ibid.
61 Ibid., p. 30, Bxxxviii.
62 Ibid., p. 525, A818/B846.

63 Ibid., p. 523, A814/B842.

64 Ibid., p. 15, Bxv.

65 Ray Brassier, *Nihil Unbound: Enlightenment and Extinction* (Basingstoke, Palgrave MacMillan, 2007), p. xi. In full: 'the disenchantment of the world understood as a consequence of the process whereby the Enlightenment shattered the "great chain of being" and defaced the "book of the world" is a necessary consequence of the coruscating potency of reason, and hence an invigorating vector of intellectual discovery, rather than a calamitous diminishment ... Philosophers would do well to desist from issuing any further injunctions about the need to re-establish the meaningfulness of existence, the purposefulness of life, or mend the shattered concord between man and nature. Philosophy should be more than a sop to the pathetic twinge of human self-esteem. Nihilism is not an existential quandary but a speculative opportunity. Thinking has interests that do not coincide with those of the living'.

Chapter 8: Modernity and its Problems

1 Kant, *Critique of Pure Reason*, p. 4, Aix

2 Paul Connerton, *The Tragedy of Enlightenment* (Cambridge, Cambridge University Press, 1980), pp. 17-18.

3 Francis Bacon, 'New Atlantis', in S. Bruce (ed.), *Three Early Modern Utopias: Utopia, New Atlantis and The Isle of Pines* (Oxford, Oxford University Press, 1999 [1627]), p. 177.

4 There is disagreement as to whether modernity has or has not ended. Some insist that we still inhabit modernity (as advanced, high or late modernity), while others herald the recent end of the modern era and its passing over into postmodernity.

5 Stuart Hall, 'The problem of ideology: Marxism without guarantees', in D. Morley and K.-H.Chen (eds), *Stuart Hall: Critical Dialogues in Cultural Studies* (London, Routledge, 1996), p. 26.

6 Stephen Toulmin, *Cosmopolis: The Hidden Agenda of Modernity* (Chicago, University of Chicago Press, 1992).

7 Ibid., pp. 43–44.

8 Ibid., p. 41.

9 Ibid., p. 69.

10 Ibid., p. 194.

11 MacIntyre's work has been influential on our thinking, particularly MacIntyre, *After Virtue: A Study in Moral Theory*.

12 Jean-François Lyotard, *The Postmodern Condition: A Report on Knowledge* (Manchester, Manchester University Press, 2005 [1979]).

13 Sigmund Freud, *Studies in Hysteria* (London, Penguin, 2004 [1895]), p. 306.

14 Friedrich Nietzsche, *The Gay Science: With a Prelude in Rhymes and an Appendix of Songs* (New York, Vintage, 1974 [1882]), §125.

15 Ibid.

16 Brassier, *Nihil Unbound*.

17 This translation of *On Truth and Lies in a Nonmoral Sense* is available here at www2.fiu.edu/~harveyb/HI-NietzEssay.htm. A slightly different translation appears in Walter Kaufman, *The Portable Nietzsche* (London, Penguin, 1976).

18 Mark A. Wrathall, *Heidegger and Unconcealment: Truth, Language and History* (Cambridge, Cambridge University Press, 2011), pp. 196–198.

19 Martin Heidegger, 'The Word of Nietzsche: "God is Dead"', in *The Question Concerning Technology and Other Essays* (New York, Garland Publishing Inc., 1977), p. 61.

20 Ibid.

21 Ibid., p. 62.

22 Ibid., pp. 62–63.

23 Ibid., pp. 63–64.

24 Martin Heidegger, 'The question concerning technology', in *Basic Writings* (London, Harper & Row, 2007 [1954]).

25 Ibid., p. 322.

26 Ibid., p. 324.

27 Ibid., p. 325.

28 Ibid., p. 321.

29 Ibid., p. 324.

30 Ibid., p. 332.

31 Ibid., p. 333.

32 Theodor Adorno and Max Horkheimer, *Dialectic of Enlightenment* (London, Verso, 1997 [1944]).

33 Jürgen Habermas, *The Philosophical Discourse of Modernity* (Cambridge, Polity Press, 1985), p. 106.

34 Ibid.

35 Adorno and Horkheimer, *Dialectic of Enlightenment*, p. xi.

36 Ibid., p. xiv.

37 Ibid., p. xvi.

38 Adorno and Horkheimer note that human sacrifice was not a feature of the earliest stage of human history, but appears to be a practice of what we would call the neolithic period when humans had begun to settle into less nomadic social patterns and had greater investment in securing the support of the gods, for example to ensure the reliable continuation of the cycle of the seasonal growth of crops.

39 Adorno and Horkheimer, *Dialectic of Enlightenment*, p. 49.

40 Ibid.

41 Ibid., p. 50.

42 Ibid., p. 59.

43 Ibid., p. 51.

44 Ibid., p. 55.

45 Ibid., p. 57.

46 Ibid., pp. 54–55.

47 Ibid., p. 70.

48 See ibid., p. 83.

49 Ibid.

50 Ibid., p. 26.

51 Ibid., p. 27.

52 Adorno and Horkheimer offer this comment on the movement of the Enlightenment as a liberatory endeavour aimed (very effectively) at ending oppression and the stifling of thought to a system that draws its defences around it, ending up supporting an

enterprise of domination: 'The philosophy that put the fear of death into infamy in the eighteenth century, despite all the book-burnings and piles of corpses, chose to serve that very infamy under Napoleon' (ibid., p. xii).

53 Ibid., p. 16.
54 Ibid., p. 31.
55 Bacon cited ibid., p. 5.
56 Ibid., p. 85.
57 Ibid., p. 15.
58 Ibid., p. 84.
59 Ibid.
60 Ibid., p. 85.
61 Ibid., p. 54.
62 Ibid., pp. 83–84.
63 David Held, *Introduction to Critical Theory: Horkheimer to Habermas* (Cambridge, Polity, 1990), p. 94.
64 Adorno and Horkheimer, *Dialectic of Enlightenment*, p. 55.
65 Habermas, *The Philosophical Discourse of Modernity*.
66 Theodor Adorno, Hans Albert, Ralf Dahrendorf, Jürgen Habermas, Harald Pilot and Karl Popper, *The Positivist Dispute in German Sociology* (London, Heinemann, 1976).

Chapter 9: Modernity and the Figure of 'Man'

1 Modern counterparts, such as German idealism, would attempt to reproduce this kind of cosmic thinking.
2 Max Horkheimer, *Eclipse of Reason* (London, Bloomsbury, 2013 [1947]), p. 2.
3 Ibid.
4 Ibid., p. 11.
5 Ibid.
6 Ibid.
7 Slavoj Žižek, *Trouble in Paradise: From the End of History to the End of Capitalism* (London, Penguin, 2015), p. 8.
8 Ibid.
9 Ibid., p. 249.
10 Jacques Derrida, *Of Grammatology* (Baltimore, Johns Hopkins University Press, 1997 [1067]), p. 49.
11 Adorno and Horkheimer, *Dialectic of Enlightenment*, p. xvi.
12 Max Horkheimer and Theodor Adorno, *Dialectic of Enlightenment: Philosophical Fragments* (Stanford, Stanford University Press, 2002 [1947]), p. 6.
13 Ibid.
14 Another key difference between Foucault, and Horkheimer and Adorno, relates to their respective accounts of reason. Foucault similarly believes that the modern period has seen a process of 'rationalisation' in thought and science that has constrained and possibly obfuscated 'social relations, state organisations, economic practices, and

perhaps even the behaviour of individuals'. Foucault sees 'something in rationalisation, and perhaps even in reason itself" which has led to 'an excess of power', to 'a massive and growing and never really contested implementation of a vast scientific and technical system' (see Michel Foucault, 'What is critique?', in J. Schmidt (ed.), *What is Enlightenment? Eighteenth-Century Answers and Twentieth-Century Questions* (Berkeley, University of California Press, 1996 [1978]), pp. 390–391). But Foucault is cautious when speaking of reason, and does not give it the kind of global exposure and critique that Horkheimer and Adorno do in viewing instrumental reason as if it were a near monolithic force. Rather, Foucault tended to examine more local manifestations of reason, and their on-going relationships to local systems of power and the production of knowledge. Here Foucault's understanding of the processes by which knowledge is produced is thoroughly agonistic, where the human impulse to freedom and knowledge is always, inescapably, caught up in struggle, a struggle that never yields a final victory over the malign effects of power, never achieves a state where reason may flourish free of the distortions of power, and which can only ever effect an adjustment in relations of power. He is perhaps far more conscious of the sinuous intractability of power, and by implication, of the difficulty of escaping the institutions and forms of understanding established in modernity.

15 Foucault, *The Order of Things*, p. 318.
16 Ibid., p. 26.
17 Ibid., p. 27.
18 Ibid., p. 33–34.
19 Ibid., pp. 20–21.
20 Ibid., p. 43.
21 Ibid., p. 239.
22 Ibid., p. xxiv.
23 Gary Gutting, *Michel Foucault's Archaeology of Scientific Reason* (Cambridge, Cambridge University Press, 1989), p. 182.
24 Foucault, *The Order of Things*, p. 313.
25 Foucault, *The Order of Things*, p. 313.
26 Gutting, *Michel Foucault'sAarchaeology of Scientific Reason*, p. 183.
27 Foucault, *The Order of Things*, p. 346.
28 Gutting, *Michel Foucault's Archaeology of Scientific Reason*, p. 183.
29 Foucault, *The Order of Things*, p. 373.
30 Ibid.
31 Ibid., p. 374.
32 Ibid., p. 314.
33 Ibid., p. xxiv.
34 Ibid., p. 387.
35 And here, as before, it is worth retaining 'man' in this formulation, rather than replace it with the genderless 'human', since the death of Man might be welcome in a way that the death of the human would not be.
36 Foucault, *The Order of Things*, p. 312.
37 Ibid., p. 322.

Chapter 10: Critique, Emancipation and Education

1 'Action' here includes social and political interventions – for example, engagement in solidaristic activism that throws into relief intellectual dissent from institutional values – and the public expression of dissent in the media.

2 InvisibleCommittee, *The Coming Insurrection* (Los Angeles, Semiotexte, 2009).

3 The following account of the origins and historical development of the concept of critique is indebted to Connerton, *The Tragedy of Enlightenment*, pp. 16–26.

4 Ibid., p. 17.

5 Kant., *Critique of Pure Reason*, p. 4, Aix

6 Connerton, *The Tragedy of Enlightenment*, p. 21.

7 Immanuel Kant, 'An answer to the question: What is enlightenment?', in J. Schmidt (ed.), *What is Enlightenment: Eighteenth-Century Answers and Twentieth-Century Questions* (Berkeley, University of California Press, 1996 [1784]), p. 59.

8 Ibid.

9 Ibid., pp. 59–60.

10 Ian Hunter, *Rethinking the School: Subjectivity, Bureaucracy, Criticism* (New York, St Martin's Press, 1994), p. 155.

11 Ibid.

12 Fredric Jameson, 'How not to historicise theory', *Critical Inquiry*, 34, 3 (2008).

13 Kant, *What is Enlightenment?*, p. 62.

14 Horkheimer and Adorno, *Dialectic of Enlightenment: Philosophical Fragments*, pp. 2–3.

15 Kant, *What is Enlightenment?*, p. 59.

16 Friedrich Nietzsche, *On the Genealogy of Morals* (Oxford, Oxford University Press, 1996 [1887]).

17 Ibid., p. 29.

18 Ibid., p. 22.

19 Something that is at one and the same time remedy, poison and scapegoat.

20 Bruno Latour, 'Matters of fact, matters of concern', *Critical Inquiry*, 30, 2 (2004), pp. 238-239.

21 This is a theme explored throughout Deleuze's work. It can be encountered in the book Deleuze wrote with Felix Guattari: Gilles Deleuze and Felix Guattari, *Anti-Oedipus: Capitalism and Schizophrenia* (London, Continuum, 2004 [1972]).

22 This is Freud's formulation of the mechanism of psychological organisation that is necessary for entry into the social-symbolic order, into awareness of other minds and participation in a world beyond oneself. The young child experiences sexual desire for the parent of the opposite sex but out of anxiety for the consequences of this desire represses or sublimates it through identification with the parent of the same sex. Freud saw this as the fundamental operation for entry into the social world. Jacques Lacan developed this idea in his theory of the symbolic order. Deleuze saw the Oedipus complex and its social function as a reality but also as a bourgeois restriction of human creativity and desiring.

23 Foucault, 'What is critique?', p. 383.

24 Ibid., p. 386.

25 Ibid., p. 396.

26 Ibid., p. 397.

27 Adorno and Horkheimer, *Dialectic of Enlightenment*, p. xiii.

28 Critical pedagogy has been a particularly active field of research and practice in Australia under the influence of Michael Halliday's systemic functional grammar.

29 Paulo Freire, *Pedagogy of the Oppressed* (London, Penguin, 1996).

30 Hunter has a typically sparkling passage on this theme in Hunter, *Rethinking the School*, pp. 18–27.

31 MacIntyre, *After Virtue: A Study in Moral Theory*.

32 Alasdair MacIntyre, 'The idea of an educated public', in G. Haydon (ed.), *Education and Values: The Richard Peters Lectures* (London, Institute of Education, 1987), p. 28.

33 Ibid., p. 16.

34 James Donald, *Sentimental Education: Schooling, Popular Culture and the Regulation of Liberty* (London, Verso, 1992), pp. 141–142.

35 MacIntyre, 'The idea of an educated public', p. 17.

36 MacIntyre, *Three Rival Versions of Moral Enquiry*, p 229.

37 Hunter, *Rethinking the School*, p. 1.

38 MacIntyre, 'The idea of an educated public', p. 25.

39 Michele Borrelli, 'The utopianism of critique: The tension between education conceived as a utopian concept and as one grounded in empirical reality', *Journal of Philosophy of Education*, 38, 3 (2004), p. 449.

Chapter 11: Education and Government

1 Graham Burchell, Colin Gordon and Peter Miller (eds), *The Foucault Effect: Studies in Governmentality* (London, Harvester Wheatsheaf, 1991).

2 Hunter, *Rethinking the School*.

3 Reinhart Koselleck, *Critique and Crisis: Enlightenment and the Pathogenesis of Modern Society* (Cambridge, MA, MIT Press, 1988 [1959]).

4 Ibid., p. 24.

5 Ibid., p. 29.

6 Ibid., p. 31.

7 Hunter, *Rethinking the School*., p. 40.

8 Koselleck, *Critique and Crisis*, p. 11.

9 Ibid., p. 39.

10 Hunter, *Rethinking the School*, p. 41.

11 Koselleck, *Critique and Crisis*, p. 56.

12 Ibid., p. 54.

13 Ibid., p. 56.

14 Ibid., p. 2.

15 Ibid., p. 5.

16 Ibid., p. 3.

17 Michel Foucault, 'Governmentality', in Burchell et al., *The Foucault Effect*.

18 Koselleck, *Critique and Crisis*, p. 11.

19 Michel Foucault, *The Birth of Biopolitics: Lectures at the Collège de France 1978–1979* (Basingstoke, Palgrave Macmillan, 2008 [1979]).

20 Hunter, *Rethinking the School*, p. 6.

21 Samuel Coleridge cited in Ben Knights, *The Idea of the Clerisy in the Nineteenth Century* (Cambridge, Cambridge University Press, 1978), p. 3.
22 Samuel Coleridge cited in ibid.
23 Ibid., p. 5.
24 Ibid., p. 7.
25 Ibid., p. 6.
26 Ibid., pp. 4–5.
27 Reinhart Koselleck, 'On the anthropological and semantic structure of *Bildung*', in R. Koselleck and T.S. Presner, *The Practice of Conceptual History: Timing History, Spacing Concepts* (Stanford, Stanford University Press, 2002), p. 177.
28 Johann Gottfried Herder cited in ibid.
29 Wilhelm von Humboldt cited in ibid.
30 Moses Mendelssohn cited in ibid., p. 178.
31 Koselleck, *Critique and Crisis*.
32 A. Schmidt, 'Self-cultivation (Bildung) and sociability between mankind and the nation: Fichte and Schleiermacher on higher education', in C. Brooke and E. Frazer (eds), *Ideas of Education: Philosophy and Politics from Plato to Dewey* (London, Routledge, 2013).
33 Johann Gottlieb Fichte cited in ibid., p. 167.
34 Ibid., p. 166.
35 Ibid., p. 169.
36 Fichte cited in Wellmon, *Organizing Enlightenment*, p. 189. We return to this high-minded conception of the modern university in the following chapter.
37 Knights, *The Idea of the Clerisy in the Nineteenth Century*, p. 13.
38 Ibid.
39 Davies Giddy cited in Donald, *Sentimental Education*, p. 20.
40 Patrick Colquhoun cited in ibid., p. 21.
41 Michel Foucault, *Discipline and Punish: The Birth of The Prison* (London, Penguin, 1975 [1991]).
42 Ansgar Allen, 'The examined life: On the formation of souls and schooling', *American Educational Research Journal*, 50, 2 (2013); Ansgar Allen, *Benign Violence: Education in and Beyond the Age of Reason* (Basingstoke, Palgrave Macmillan, 2014).
43 On pastoral power see Michel Foucault, '"Omnes et singulatim": Toward a critique of political reason', in J.D. Faubion (ed.), *Essential Works of Foucault 1954-1984. Volume 3* (London, Penguin, 2002 [1979]).
44 Ian Hunter, *Culture and Government: The Emergence of Literary Education* (London, Macmillan, 1988); Hunter, *Rethinking the School*; Ian Hunter, 'Culture, education, and English: Building "the principal scene of the real life of children"', *Economy and Society*, 16, 4 (1987); Donald, *Sentimental Education*. For an overview of Hunter, see Roy Goddard, 'Towards an engagement with the ideas of Ian Hunter: An argument for an overdue encounter', *Changing English: Studies in Culture and Education*, 16, 2 (2009).
45 Hunter, *Rethinking the School*, p. 155.
46 Ibid.
47 Ibid., p. 157.
48 Sir James Kay-Shuttleworth, *Four Periods of Public Education as Reviewed in 1832-1839-1846-1862* (Brighton, Harvester, 1862 [1973]), pp. 295–296.
49 David Stow, *The Training System, Moral Training School, and Normal Seminary*, 10th edn (London, Longman, Brown, Green and Longmans, 1854), p. 153.

50 Ibid., p. 156.

51 Hunter, *Culture and Government*, p. 77.

52 Stow, *The Training System*, p. 156.

53 Hunter, *Culture and Government*, p. 34.

54 Ibid., p. 41.

55 Hunter, 'Culture, education, and English', p. 573.

56 Hunter, *Rethinking the School*, p. 1.

Chapter 12: Confined to the Present

1 Kevin Flint and Nick Peim, *Rethinking the Education Improvement Agenda: A Critical Philosophical Approach* (London, Continuum, 2012).

2 John Dewey, *Democracy and Education* (Carbondale, Southern Illinois University Press, 2008 [1916]).

3 Thomas Fallace, 'The savage origins of child-centered pedagogy, 1871–1913', *American Educational Research Journal*, 52, 1 (2015).

4 Ibid.

5 Cited in Eliyahu Rosenow, 'The teacher as prophet of the true God: Dewey's religious faith and its problems', *Journal of Philosophy of Education*, 31, 3 (1997), p. 427.

6 Ibid.

7 Nel Noddings, *Philosophy of Education*, 3rd edn (Boulder, Westview Press, 2012), p. 24.

8 Progressive, child-centred teaching came under attack in the 1970s in the Black Papers published by right-wing critics, triggering an official, government-led lurch towards 'traditional' education and neoliberal objectives. Interestingly, it was a Labour Prime Minister, James Callaghan, with his 1976 Ruskin Speech, who called for such a re-orientation. Of interest also was the fact that child-centred teaching had earlier been thoroughly critiqued from a Marxist perspective (in R. Sharpe, A. Green and J. Lewis, *Education and Social Control: A study in progressive primary education* [London, Routledge, 1975]) which contended that teachers had only a hazy grasp of the (in the writers' view, insubstantial) theoretical justifications for such teaching and learning.

9 Horkheimer, *Eclipse of Reason*, pp. 33–34.

10 Ibid., p. 28.

11 Ibid., p. 33.

12 Ibid., p. 29.

13 Ibid., p. 31.

14 Wellmon, *Organizing Enlightenment*.

15 Ibid., p. 50.

16 Ibid., p. 52.

17 Ibid., p. 62.

18 Ibid., p. 44.

19 Ibid.

20 Ibid., p. 27.

21 Ibid., p. 99.

22 Lyotard, *Postmodern Condition*, p. xxiv.

23 Ibid., p. 51.

24 Ibid., p. 50.

25 Ibid., p. 48.
26 Ibid.
27 Ibid.
28 Ibid., p. 52.
29 Ibid., p. 53.
30 Maarten Simons and Jan Masschelein, 'The public and its university: Beyond learning for civic employability?', *European Educational Research Journal*, 8, 2 (2009), p. 209.
31 Michel Serres, *Thumbelina: The Culture and Technology of Millennials* (London, Rowman and Littlefield, 2015).
32 Simons and Masschelein, 'The public and its university', p. 205.
33 Ibid., p. 213.

Chapter 13: Epilogue

1 Michael Oakeshott, 'The idea of a university', *Academic Questions*, 17, 1 (2003 [1950]), p. 28.
2 Ibid.
3 Ibid., p. 30.
4 Ibid., p. 28.
5 Ibid,. p. 30.
6 Ibid.
7 Ibid.
8 Ibid., p. 29.
9 Ibid., p. 30.
10 Ibid., p. 26.
11 Ibid., p. 25.
12 Ibid., p. 29.
13 Ibid., p. 25.
14 Ibid., p. 30.
15 Ibid., p. 27.
16 W.H.G. Armytage, 'The role of an education department in a modern university', in P. Gordon (ed.), *The Study of Education: A Collection of Inaugural Lectures. Volume I: Early and Modern* (London, Woburn Press, 1980 [1954]).
17 Ibid., p. 163.
18 J.M. Morgan's 1933 *Address to the Proprietors of the University of London* cited in ibid., pp. 167–168.
19 J.M. Morgan cited in ibid., p. 168.
20 Two chairs in education were established in 1876, with S.S. Laurie delivering an inaugural lecture in Edinburgh on 31 March 1876 and J.M.D. Meiklejohn delivering his a day later at St. Andrews. The latter address is printed in Peter Gordon's collection of 'Early and Modern' inaugural lectures. Here Professor Meiklejohn makes a case for a reform of schooling and teacher education based on a better understanding of educational processes. This lacks the ambition of Morgan's early nineteenth century proposal, cited with approval in Armytage's inaugural address, which was to mediate the specialisms and ensure that the pursuit of knowledge retains its unity of purpose. Indeed,

Meiklejohn comments on the title of his chair ('founded for the teaching of the Theory, History and Practice of Education'), arguing that 'it is impossible for one man to occupy more than a small portion of the field'. Though he is 'bound to survey the whole of it,' he must also 'invite and urge others to co-operate with him in the cultivation of the whole'. He must pursue his developing specialism, then, alongside other like-minded scholars, and so come to embody the modern research ethos of disciplinary enquiry (J.M.D. Meiklejohn, 'Inaugural address', in Gordon, *The Study of Education*, p. 4).

21 J.P. Tuck, 'Review of *The Study of Education: A Collection of Inaugural Lectures*', *British Journal of Educational Studies*, 29, 3 (1981), p. 271.

22 Armytage, 'The role of an education department in a modern university', p. 175.

23 Ibid., p. 176.

24 Ibid., p. 178.

25 Ibid., p. 175.

26 Gary McCulloch, 'Obituary: Professor Harry Armytage', *History of Education*, 28, 2 (1999), p. 221.

27 Carr, 'Professing education in a postmodern age', p. 315.

28 Ibid., p. 309.

29 William Clark, *Academic Charisma and the Origins of the Research University* (Chicago, University of Chicago Press, 2006), p. 72.

30 Carr, 'Professing education in a postmodern age', p. 315.

31 Ibid., p. 316.

32 Samuel Coleridge cited in Knights, *The Idea of the Clerisy in the Nineteenth Century*, p. 3.

33 Jean-François Lyotard, 'Endurance and the profession', *Yale French Studies*, 63 (1982 [1978]), p. 73.

34 And here it is worth noting that although the profession is perturbed by its performativities it also sustains itself through if not desires them; see Matthew Clarke, 'Terror/ enjoyment: Performativity, resistance and the teacher's psyche', *London Review of Education*, 11, 3 (2013).

35 Harvey, 'Making hollow men', p. 198.

36 Ibid.

37 Samuel Beckett, *Molloy* (London, Faber and Faber, 2009 [1951]), p. 81.

38 James Joyce, *A Portrait of the Artist as a Young Man* (London, Penguin, 2000 [1915]), p. 269.

39 See, for example, Barry Hindess, *Discourses of Power: From Hobbes to Foucault* (Oxford, Blackwell, 1996).

40 Nick Peim, 'The Big Other: An offer you can't refuse – or accept, in some cases. Education as onto-theological principle (empire): An anti-manifesto', *Other Education: The Journal of Educational Alternatives*, 1, 1 (2012); Nick Peim, 'Education, schooling, Derrida's Marx and democracy: Some fundamental questions', *Studies in Philosophy and Education* 32, 2 (2013).

41 Foucault, *The Order of Things*, p. 374.

Index